Power Collecting

Power Collecting

Automation for Effective Asset Management

Frederick A. Piumelli
David A. Schmidt

John Wiley & Sons, Inc.

New York • Chichester • Weinheim • Brisbane • Singapore • Toronto

Library of Congress Cataloging-in-Publication Data:
Piumelli, Frederick A.
    Power collecting : automation for effective asset management / Frederick A. Piumelli, David A. Schmidt.
        p.   cm.
    Includes bibliographical references and index.
    ISBN 0-471-18043-2 (cloth)
    1. Collecting of accounts—Data processing.   I. Schmidt, David A., 1953 Apr. 22–   II. Title.
    HG3752.5.P58   1998
    658.8'8—DC21   97-34854
                                                                         CIP
                                                                         r98

Printed in the United States of America.

10   9   8   7   6   5   4   3   2   1

*This book is dedicated to
Dianna and Sue, their commitment
and support made this work possible.*

Contents

Contents

Contents

Contents

Contents

Preface

This book has been written to illustrate the powerful dynamics that an automated collection process can bring to a business. The contribution of collections to corporate liquidity are far reaching and cannot be downplayed. Still, many companies that have automated and streamlined large segments of their operations have failed to address the inefficiencies inherent in their current collection practices. In large part, that is because there have been few guideposts marking the pathway to an automated collection environment. The companies that have automated collections have had to cut their own path. That is no longer the case. The route is now clear, and our hope is that this text will help illuminate the way.

Automation, however, is not the whole story. Automation is merely an adjunct to the collection process, a process that over the years has developed some serious impediments to improvement. Without first devising a better way to collect, automation is handicapped. Power collecting requires the development of more efficient practices that can then be automated. It is the synergy created between a re-engineered collection process and technology that delivers the most dramatic improvements. A vision of how a re-engineered collection process will function is therefore also central to this book.

To accomplish this, the book has been broken down into three parts. The first addresses the issue of why collections needs to be fixed. Current collection practices are examined in detail. The road that has brought collections to this juncture is also reviewed, as are the inherent problems faced by the traditional collection function. Pivotal to this is corporate America's common reliance on manual collection processes tied to computerized accounts receivable systems. Having documented the limitations and inadequacies of such an environment, the benefits of re-engineering collections is set forth.

The second section addresses the actual task of automating collections. It provides solutions to the difficulties confronting manual collection practices and lays out the objectives of a re-engineered, automated collection process. In so doing, it also points out automation pitfalls that can severely impede results. The dynamics of an automated collection process are discussed in detail, in particular the use of collection strategies to optimize collector resources and cash flow.

The last section investigates the actual use and application of an automated collection process. It looks at account monitoring, deductions, cash applications, third-party collections, and using the Internet. These are the hands-on activities with which collectors interface daily. Furthermore, within these areas additional productivity can be, and in fact is being, realized.

Whether you are a collector, credit manager or analyst, controller, treasurer, CFO, IS developer, change management specialist, or business owner, we trust this book will serve you well as a road map to dramatically improved collections. Every situation is different, and there is no exact answer to every company's particular circumstances. Even so, we are confident the principles and examples laid forth in this text will lead you toward a much more efficient and productive collection function. Good luck on your journey, and may the cash be with you!

Frederic A. Piumelli
David A. Schmidt

May 1998

Acknowledgments

The concepts that form the foundation for this book have evolved over the years. That foundation is all the stronger because of the many credit and collection professionals who have contributed their insights and experience. Some are credit managers who have built their reputation on the tough job of cleaning up one collection department after another, a task made easier with automation. We could not have gotten to this point without the cooperation of these visionaries who shared our belief that there had to be a better way.

In particular, writing this book has been greatly augmented by the collectors who were willing to talk about the process of automating collections and share their experiences working with automated collection systems. They are representative of the many hundreds of people who GETPAID has already assisted in automating their collection process. They are pioneers in the true sense of the word. Contrary to popular opinion, they have committed themselves to doing what others have said was impossible. Despite the fact that their corporation's numbers were the best in the industry, they believed they could do better. Despite the irrepressible demands created by fast-growing companies, they believed liquidity could be improved. Despite downsizing and limits on their resources, they believed the bottom line could be increased. The collective knowledge accumulated through all these automation initiatives would undoubtedly fill many more volumes. It is not possible to name everybody who contributed to this project, but that in no way diminishes our gratitude.

Nonetheless, we would like to thank the following people who have helped us illustrate the dynamic improvements achieved by automating collections. In particular, we appreciate Sue Delloiacono, Credit and Customer Support Services Manager at Dialogic Corporation, taking the time to review a six-year, evolutionary time span in Dialogic's collection function. The same goes for Scott Wade, Credit Manager with Dunlop Slazenger, who was also an early adapter of automated collection technology and remains ever willing to share his extensive experience.

Several other people also talked with us at length. They are Ross Fisher, who was Division Credit Manager at Nalco Chemical Company and is now involved in the area of change management; Sue Izzi, Director of Credit, Liener Health Products; and Robert Schultz, Vice President of Corporate Credit and Customer Finance, Sony Entertainment. They each shared unique insights into the automation process that we found invaluable.

Another company that has illustrated the potential that can be realized from automating collections is Dell Computer. Their story begins with Michael Dell's and CFO Tom Meredith's vision regarding the importance of liquidity and their commitment to an automated collection process. Right from the start, which included an inspiring kick-off meeting for Dell's collectors, they demonstrated how to automate the right way. The end result has been a 10 percent yearly reduction in DSO for four years running. We appreciate Tom Meyer, Dell's Financial Services Manager, for graciously sharing with us the details of his company's continual quest for improvement in the cash collections cycle.

Acknowledgments

We also talked with a number of other people about specific situations and aspects of the collection process. Much thanks to Dan Beal, Director of Credit, Pillsbury; Evan Bosinoff, Senior Sales Representative, GWA Information Systems; Peggy Miller, Director of Credit and Collections, Ortho-Clinical Diagnostics, a Johnson & Johnson Company. In addition, Mike Durant, Director of Research, Credit Research Foundation, graciously provided us with historical collection statistics.

One other group of people also deserve a great deal of credit. They are GETPAID Software's employees. Few people realize what drives their commitment to help people automate collections. Their passion for this work is driven by their individual commitment to the possibility of integrity. The way they see it, past due invoices evidence the breaking of an agreement, an act that diminishes the integrity of the relationship with the customer who has failed to pay according to terms. By helping customers keep their agreements, collectors create integrity every day. GETPAID's employees' commitment to enabling collectors to create integrity is central to the creation and implementation of automated collection systems that make a difference for everybody they touch.

Lastly, we dare not leave out Sheck Cho, our editor at John Wiley & Sons, who has been both patient and encouraging. Thank you for sticking with us throughout this project.

Part One

Imperatives for Automating Collections

1

Unable to See the Forest for the Trees

Even credit veterans can get lost in the woods. The daily demands of credit and collections can be overwhelming, especially when the unexpected hits. Often, it takes very little to knock a smooth-running credit and collection operation off track. Then, what was once an organized, methodical collection machine becomes a seemingly endless fire drill. By the time one brush fire is brought under control, two or three or four more have ignited. It doesn't take long for a credit staff to get scattered throughout the forest, racing from one conflagration to the next, unable to see the forest for the trees.

Tracking down proofs of delivery, copying and faxing invoices, contacting other departments within the company to answer customer claims, responding to requests for credit references, and releasing orders on credit hold, though necessary activities, are all tasks that distract collectors from their prime objective. These distractions are just a small sample of the many activities that, taken together, serve to greatly reduce the number of collection calls being made.

A major reason this happens so easily is the scarcity of

comprehensive management tools available to commercial credit and collection professionals. While many task-oriented products and services have been developed over the last three decades, very few integrated systems have been produced, and most of those have been developed "in-house" and therefore never made available to the marketplace. As a result, most credit and collection systems consist of a patchwork of products, services, and procedures.

For example, though billing was one of the first activities to be computerized, and despite ongoing advances in technology, most companies still store invoices in paper files. When a customer requests an invoice copy, the collector must go to the file, find the invoice, copy it and mail it or take it to a fax machine, wait for it to go through, then refile the invoice—a very time-consuming task that easily lends itself to automation.

Unfortunately, the sum of many independently automated tasks is often less than the whole. Much of today's technology has served only to make credit and collection systems more susceptible to failure due to corresponding increases in complexity. This is because tasks have been automated independently rather than as part of an integrated process or system. The benefits of computerization are squandered when automated tasks require manual feeding. Automating one task can make that particular operation much more efficient, but if the rest of the process is manual, overall productivity gains may be negligible. A complicated, labor-intensive infrastructure must be avoided when designing efficient collection systems.

Here is an example: Many accounts receivable systems generate a list of customers that have balances greater than some amount, say $5,000, and over 60 days past due. These are obvious candidates for collection activities. The list is a good tool to start with, but after a few days it becomes obsolete and its continued use counterproductive. During this short time span, some invoices have been paid while others that were just under 60 days are now over that benchmark. Print the list again and the differences can easily be seen. Another problem is that the second list will contain transactions that have already been identified as problems and are currently being addressed by another department in the company.

The solution to the dilemmas caused by piecemeal automation is a complete overhaul of credit and collection processes and systems. Automation by itself is not the answer, because merely automating the present way of doing things serves only to further institutionalize the inefficiencies in manual processes. Instead, processes need to be redesigned from the ground up. Only then can automation be used effectively to bring about significant and lasting improvements in credit and collection performance.

Champy and Hammer called this re-engineering. The short definition for that is "starting over."[1] In the context of a company, they go on to say that re-engineering means "tossing aside old systems and starting over. It involves going back to the beginning and inventing a better way of doing work."[2] Their formal definition states, "Reengineering is the fundamental and radical redesign of business processes to achieve dramatic improvements in critical contemporary measures of performance, such as cost, quality, service and speed."[3] Redesigning and automating the collection process requires no less than this.

Before overhauling the collection process, the methodology that, combined with the proper automation, can yield radical improvements must be distinguished. One needs to be able to not only retrace one's footsteps, but also see where he or she is going. However, linear vision, the ability to see the path ahead and behind, isn't enough. One needs to see the forest for the trees. With introspection one can understand why a particular path and not some other was chosen. (See Exhibit 1.1.)

Exhibit 1.1   **Allegory of the Lumberjack**

The story has been told before of the lumberjack who finds himself working harder and harder to keep up his production quota. At one time, he could down a dozen trees in a day, but he now finds himself struggling to fell only seven or eight. He tries working longer hours, but that is effective for only so long before his work time cuts into the remaining hours for sustenance and sleep. Working at a frantic pace helps for a while, but after a few days he is exhausted, and his productivity slips even further.

One day, a young boy was walking through the forest when he came across the lumberjack struggling to fell a mammoth tree. "What's the matter, mister?" he asked. The lumberjack winced at the young boy's naivete. "You're obviously too young to understand what hard work it is to cut down trees," the lumberjack replied. "It used to be that a dozen trees were not too many for me to fell in a day, but this job is wearing me down."

The boy watched the lumberjack sweat and groan. Chips of wood flew in every direction with each blow of the axe. Eventually, a puzzled expression spread over the boy's face, and he asked the lumberjack, "Why don't you sharpen your axe?"

Of course, sharpening his axe will help the lumberjack re-attain his previous level of productivity. In fact, by eating well, getting enough sleep, exercising to further develop his strength, and working on his axe-swinging technique, he might even achieve some incremental gains in productivity for a time. But, eventually, his axe will get dull again, or he'll get a cold or have an accident, and productivity will suffer.

CREDIT MANAGEMENT IS NOT THAT DIFFERENT FROM FOREST MANAGEMENT

Many credit operations face this situation. A little training, some new software, and other incremental system improvements add up to only marginal productivity gains. Nothing has been done to correct the underlying weaknesses of the system. Everything out of the ordinary exerts a disproportionate strain on the system, so faced with staff reductions, mergers and acquisitions, or other changes to the company's fundamental business processes, the credit and collection staff's productivity is severely affected.

This is the situation Sue experienced when she took over the credit and collection function at Dialogic, a computer telephony company located in North Jersey. It was 1991, and she was the entire credit and collection department for a company doing roughly $40 million in sales. During the next year, little changed except that sales reached $65 million, forcing Sue to hire Tim, an experienced collector, to help out. As the workload increased, Sue supplemented her human resources, but it was not enough to keep up.

At this point in time, Sue and Tim found themselves essentially managing two parallel credit operations. Sue had her accounts and Tim had his, and neither really knew much about each other's customers. Orders were processed manually throughout the day. Sue recalls constantly doing laps around the building between sales, order processing, and her own office. "Whenever I got back to my office, there was a new pile of orders waiting to be processed, so I would simply start out on another circuit," she says. Trying to keep up, they both began working ever longer hours. If either was absent, the other person was overwhelmed trying to hold everything together. In fact, when Dialogic began expanding its international operations, Sue had to take a business trip to Europe, leaving Tim on his own for a week. He was forced to spend almost all of his time processing orders and neglecting the rest of his duties.

Around the time Tim was brought on staff, Sue became involved in Dialogic's total quality management (TQM) initiative. For Sue, the experience was similar to someone's suggesting that she sharpen her axe. As a result of the TQM program, she was able to see her credit and collection department physically moved into the sales area. That cut down on much of the time wasted running around the building. In addition, the credit department was given access to the sales department's contact management software and database. Before, credit and collections was seldom aware of what sales had arranged with customers. The software also made it easier for them to communicate with sales and automated their own record keeping. Sue and Tim were now processing orders faster than ever, but these incremental improvements were still not enough. Sales for 1993 passed $95 million, forcing Sue to hire a third collector before the end of that year.

Despite the improvements, Sue was still dealing with huge inefficiencies. For one, they were working with multiple software systems, looking up and recording notes in the contact manager, and then switching back and forth to the accounts receivable system for billing details. Sue says they would "write down what the customer was saying, and later type it into the contact manager. I mean it was ridiculous. I literally was in the office from eight o'clock in the morning until midnight. Five days a week. No vacation. No time off. Don't get sick, and don't have an emergency at home." The incremental improvements proved to be no more than a temporary patch. "We were running out of gas real quick," Sue says.

In May 1993, Sue attended the National Association of Credit Management (NACM) Annual Credit Congress in Seattle. While there, she agreed to go with a friend to an after-hours software demonstration and reception. She agreed to go, not to evaluate the software her friend was interested in, but for the refreshments. Ironically, Sue's friend left early, but she stayed to learn more about what GETPAID Software could do for her collections. "I never even thought collection software would be an option for me," Sue recalls. "I would, of course, have loved to automate collections but was completely unaware of what could be done. So when I saw the system demo, I just knew immediately that I had to have it." For Sue, the idea of a software-driven automation solution was entirely out of the box. The experience was similar to the old lumberjack in Exhibit 1.1 seeing a chain saw demonstrated for the first time. While it was impossible to catch up using the old way and the old tools, here was a new system that would get the job done like never before.

Of course, Sue still had to convince management to employ this new technology. Despite the incremental improvements, the collection system was still running at capacity, the company was still growing rapidly, and any breakdown in the collection system would severely impact the company. Even though Dialogic is an innovative, high-tech company, its financial management nevertheless remained reluctant to change the status quo. After eight long months, Sue still had not convinced management that the old system was inadequate. "In the end, during an emotional meeting, I pointed out to the CFO (chief financial officer) that we were spending more on pizza in a month than the $5,000 it would cost to try the software," Sue says. "I had to almost have a nervous breakdown before they said 'let's give it a try.'" Losing Sue would have been a catastrophe, because she really was the system. Her knowledge of how things were done at Dialogic held all the random pieces of the system together. "It was all up here, all the little nuances, in my head," Sue says. By getting management to agree to give the collection software a try, Sue could finally see the forest for the trees.

Despite having limited internal programming support, the

collection software did not take long to install, nor did it take long to see improvements. "We saw an immediate improvement," recalls Sue. "Roughly $1 million extra was collected the first month, dropping our DSO (days sales outstanding) by over ten percent." Maybe even more important was the fact that credit and collections began running smoothly. Crisis management was no longer the norm.

Nearly four years after automating collections, Dialogic's sales have grown to over $250 million. In spite of this, Sue only has three collectors handling domestic accounts and one person handling international customers part time. "Without collection software, we would have to double the staff," she says. Her job has become much saner, even though her responsibilities have expanded. "Automation proved very effective at identifying customer service problems," Sue says. "We took that information and went to the other departments and insisted they fix their systems." Her success in this area is part of the reason that besides holding the title of credit manager and reporting to the CFO, Sue is now also the customer support services manager reporting to the vice-president of sales for North and South America. She says, "Now we don't have any lingering problems, just fixes. As soon as a problem turns up with a collector, it is being researched by a customer service rep. We handle the problem right away because there is nowhere else to go with it."

This added responsibility keeps her out of the flow of the daily collection routine, but she is able to manage it more effectively since the process has been automated. Sue says, "I like looking at the performance of the individual collector. I had no visibility of that before. You could not put a performance improvement plan in place for an employee. You could not show him or her how to get things done better. You could not manage your employee. You were just hoping at the end of the day that you were breaking even."

With the automated system, "it is very easy to train new members," Sue says. "They can see the account's history and immediately understand the essence or character of each customer. You cannot even begin to train somebody on that. That type of customer knowledge takes a year to develop for a collector working with a manual system. You know that when new collectors come in, they are going to hit the ground running." The customer intelligence is now in the system rather than just with the collector.

All of this is a far cry from frantically trying to chop more wood. Instead, Sue and her staff are able to work the system to get the most out of their accounts receivable portfolio. "I like the idea that I am so completely in control," says Sue. "I have all the details to immediately deal with any customer situation that arises. The collectors feel the same way and enjoy a sense of accomplishment by being on top of their work, rather than being overloaded and constantly frustrated."

AUTOMATION TO THE RESCUE

Any number of events can dramatically illustrate the weaknesses of a company's collection system. As a result of downsizing, Dunlop Slazenger, a sporting goods company located in Greenville, South Carolina, lost nearly 50 percent of its credit staff. Its 16-person department was reduced to nine positions as part of a massive company-wide reorganization. Being in a seasonal business made the impact of the staff reduction more acute. Keeping up with collections during the peak seasons was impossible with Dunlop's existing systems. To make matters worse, its parent company had mandated aggressive goals in terms of accounts receivable performance.

Like the lumberjack in the parable, Dunlop initially thought the solution was to work harder to compensate for the staff reduction. It was able to maintain its accounts receivable balances at levels consistent with other companies in the sporting goods industry. However, the stress was having an impact on the collection staff's performance. With every collector working at his or her maximum capacity, the loss of just one person would surely have caused overdue accounts receivable to go through the ceiling. Adding staff was not an option, so Dunlop began looking for an automated solution to its collection dilemma.

One feature Dunlop sought was an automated follow-up (tickler) system. Dunlop's collectors were using calendars and other hand-written notes to remind themselves when it was time to make follow-up calls regarding customer promises or deduction issues. Although their accounts receivable software contained a collection notepad feature, it could not drive the process because it required looking up the account before the follow-up date could be seen. Dunlop's computerized notepad provided no calendar feature or other automation tools. It simply substituted the computer for paper. Not surprisingly, the collectors preferred to keep their notes on their individual printouts of the aged accounts receivable trial balance.

Another priority was the ability to automatically generate faxes and other correspondence. Dunlop's collectors were spending a lot of time making phone calls without necessarily reaching the person they needed to contact. An automated fax capability would enable them to send a fax quickly and easily if they couldn't make contact with a phone call.

While these two features would automate two important tasks, by themselves they would not go very far toward automating the entire collection process. Therefore, Dunlop's main interest was to find a way to implement a process for consistent collections and follow through. It wanted to contact every account at the most appropriate time in the most appropriate way, depending on where the receivable was in the collection process.

Given the manual process for selecting customers for contact, the choice of who to contact each day was at the whim of each collector. The typical pattern was to contact large and old balances first. Small balances were given the least attention. The problem with this approach, especially when a collection department is understaffed, is that current receivables are allowed to get significantly past due before any serious contacts are made. In Dunlop's case, small balances were not even touched until they reached the 60- to 90-day column on the aged receivables trial balance.

Dunlop installed collection software in July 1994 that met all these criteria. That month, it collected $7 million more than anticipated, a 100 percent increase in overdue receivables collected! This was not because the collectors had been doing a poor job before. Prior to automating collections, each of Dunlop's measures of collection performance matched the industry norms. This breakthrough in performance also could not be explained by incremental gains in productivity. Clearly, automation combined with a radical redesign of the collection process had raised the capacity of Dunlop's collectors many times over.

That Dunlop's collectors were operating at a higher level is evidenced by the incremental gains that began to accrue after they got used to the new system. During 1995, which was a tough year for sporting goods manufacturers, Dunlop's collection staff reduced DSO[4] an additional 10 days and cut bad debt write-offs in half. Process improvement had greatly increased their capacity to collect receivables. Automating the process gave them the tools to continue to increase productivity beyond the new standard they had established from the start.

One reason Dunlop has been able to continue improving its collection performance is the intelligence gained by working the automatic system. On the one hand, the system collects information that can be analyzed later every time a problem is encountered. On the other hand, Dunlop has been able to fine-tune and individualize the particular collection strategies assigned to each segment of its customer portfolio. The ability to collect data and then turn it into information that can be used to further improve practices can produce very significant results.

By tracking problems, Dunlop's collectors were able to not only identify the internal company practices that were causing payment problems, but also quantify this data. They were then able to share this intelligence with other departments in order to develop and cost justify system-wide fixes. Without this information, the collectors were seldom able to break down departmental walls. With it, they found it much easier to get the attention of the affected department heads. This information has also opened up communications between the collectors and the customer service department, motivating all involved to both solve and prevent customer problems. Not surprisingly, customer satisfaction also improved.

Customer trends and characteristics are also more readily apparent. Dunlop used this information to select and fine-tune the most appropriate collection process for each segment of its customer portfolio. In effect, the more the system is used, the more effective it becomes. The result is a continual reduction in the number of days it takes for customers to pay their bills until they are paying on a current basis.

At industry credit group meetings, it became increasingly apparent that Dunlop was being paid faster than its competitors. Dunlop's ability to efficiently extract payments from shared customers had become a significant competitive advantage. As a result, several companies in this small, competitive market automated their collection processes. Etonic/Tretorn Puma, faced with a similar downsizing, was the first to follow suit. It was soon followed by Mizuno, who also chose to automate collections to remain competitive.

EVOLUTION OF CREDIT AND COLLECTIONS IN THE INFORMATION AGE

In order to understand why companies need to change the ways in which they manage commercial collections, it is necessary to understand how the current state of affairs came about. After all, a lot has changed already, especially in the last 30 years, and computerization, not surprisingly, is largely responsible for this.

We need to go back to the precomputer era to really appreciate the deficiencies built into collection processes in recent decades. Companies extended credit long before they had computers, and the manual collection systems that predated computerization were quite efficient. By understanding how manual systems worked, one can then see where companies have gone astray and in so doing rediscover the principles that worked so well in the past.

WHEN LEDGER CARDS DROVE THE PROCESS

Through the first half of this century, credit and collection systems and procedures flowed from the information kept on ledger cards. Ledger cards provided a structure for scheduling collections, reviewing new orders, and tracking problems. Because they provided a single repository for all credit and collection information, collections could be pursued in an effective manner. Not surprisingly, keeping up-to-date information on the cards was a very labor-intensive process as was the task of compiling any management reports. After all, these were manual business systems. The bottom line was that the ledger cards worked and, in fact, actually worked quite well. (See Exhibit 1.2.)

A great deal of information was kept on the cards. First and foremost, all invoices, payments, credits, and debits were

Exhibit 1.2 Sample Ledger Card

Customer Name: _____Jone & Smith Distributing_____ Customer # ___2231___

Address: ___1509 Broadway___ City ___NYC___ State ___NY___ Zip ___10002___

Contact: ___Bart Billingham___ Phone: ___PE9-5400___ Credit Rating ~~1A2~~ Limit ~~15,000~~

2A2   20,000

DAS 1/1/56

Reference #	Date	Debit	Credit	Balance	Comments	
				7,523.61	Balance Forward	
115643	8-12-55	273.35		7,796.96	Promised 10/2	Pd 10/5
115922	8-19-55	2,322.19		10,119.15	Promised 10/2	Pd 10/5
✓#3275	9-4-55		7,523.61	2,595.54		
✓#3764	10-5-55		2,545.54	50.00	Disputes Price - #115922	
120520	1-7-56	5,924.50		5,974.50	Promised 2/4	Pd 2/2
CM120520	1-15-56		124.50	5,850.00		
✓#4121	2-8-56		5,800.00	50.00		
122313	2-28-56	3,175.42		3,225.42	L/W 4/27	
CM115922	3-1-56		25.00	3,200.42	Agreed to pay half	
122977	3-21-56	852.45		4,052.87	L/W 4/27	
123632	4-10-56	83.10		4,135.97		

General Comments: _____Pays 1st & 3rd Mondays each month_____ posted on the cards, enabling a running total to be kept of each customer's open balance due. In addition, credit ratings were posted on the ledger cards along with the customer's credit limit. This had an added advantage in that each time either the credit rating or credit limit was changed, the old information was visible so that anyone glancing at the card could quickly identify any trends that required attention.

The ledger cards also provided a place to record customer contact information. Any calls or correspondence were noted so that the next person looking at the ledger card knew the customer's collection status right away. Clerks also wrote notes next to open items. If there was a deduction, one could readily see why it occurred. The same was done for disputed items or invoices that were due to be credited. Everything one needed to know in order to make a collection call was at his or her fingertips.

Of course, keeping these ledger cards up to date required a staff of accounting clerks in addition to the collectors and credit analysts. Posting invoices and payments was a never-ending process. In fact, during times of peak activity, posting might lag billing or receipt of payment by several days. Also, because postings were being done manually, there was a greater likelihood of errors. Corrections required that a time-consuming account reconciliation be completed. Very simply, a large, competent credit department composed of supervisors, collectors, and clerks was essential in order for use of this system of ledger cards to be effective.

In terms of collections, ledger card systems proved very efficient. The key was the fact that all necessary credit and collection information was consolidated on the ledger cards. In addition, cards could be pulled, searched, sorted, and reorganized a multitude of ways to facilitate collection calls.

Follow-up was also handled in a simple, straightforward manner through the use of colored tabs that were clipped to the ledger cards. If a red tab indicated those accounts that should be contacted on the tenth day of the month, the clerks would pull those files on the morning of the tenth and give them to the collectors. As calls were made, the ledger cards would be refiled with the appropriate colored tab indicating the next follow-up date. The clerks would also change the tabs as promised payments were received. Thus, by working the system, credit departments were able to maintain solid control over their collection process.

The biggest drawback to this system was that management reports were not readily available. Balance and aging information would typically be tallied at the close of each month, but there was little else that was worth the effort required to produce a comprehensive receivables report. Generating any type of report required a credit clerk, or several clerks, to add totals from the ledger cards—another time-consuming, labor-intensive activity.

HOW COMPUTERIZATION FRAGMENTED THE PROCESS

The advent of the corporate computer brought the promise of automation from the start. Labor-intensive transaction processing was an early target for computerization. Not surprisingly, accounting departments became early adopters of computer technology. However, comprehensive solutions were few and far between, and most computerization projects were task oriented.

Billing and cash applications naturally availed themselves to computerization. Credit clerks were in effect replaced by data-entry operators who were not part of the credit department. In so doing, companies saved time because they were now able to update receivables much quicker than when it was done manually, and they saved money because they needed fewer data-entry clerks.

Another advantage of computerizing receivables was the ability to generate receivables reports on demand. Most significant was the advent of the aged accounts receivable trial balance. Because there was no longer a need for ledger cards, the accounts receivable trial balance became the focal point for all collection activities. Whereas the ledger cards provided a single data source for all the relevant information about each individual customer, the accounts receivable trial balance provided a snapshot of all open items for the entire customer base. The problem is that companies collect from each customer individually, not from the entire customer base. Thus, computerization inadvertently dealt a serious blow to what had been an effective collection process.

With nowhere else to record collection details in the absence of ledger cards, collectors were left to their own devices. Call logs were often used. However, these were kept either in the customer's credit file, attached to the inside front cover, or in a loose-leaf binder. The problem with using the files was that they had to be constantly retrieved and filed again. Remember, the credit clerks were laid off, so the collectors often had to do this themselves, which took away from the time allotted to collection calls. If each collector used a loose-leaf binder to keep their call logs at their desk, however, this information was not readily available to anyone else reviewing a customer's credit file.

Because maintaining this information was tedious, many collectors simply recorded collection notes right on the accounts receivable trial balance. This provided them with convenient access to consolidated information. The problem with this was that the information wasn't readily available to anyone else in the organization. If one managed to obtain a collector's hard copy aging report, the collector's handwritten hieroglyphics also had to be interpreted.

In addition, contact information was now separate from

the follow-up process. This was true whether the collector was recording notes on an accounts receivable trial balance or on a call log. One option was to set up a separate tickler file for scheduling follow-up calls, but the more common alternative chosen by collectors was to simply make a note on their calendar.

This was not the only problem. The accounts receivable trial balances became obsolete quickly as new billings were posted and payments made. New billings did not cause the collectors much of a problem, unless they also had order-approval responsibilities, in which case credit limits could unknowingly be exceeded since new shipments were not reflected. Payments, however, were a vital data element to the collection process. Therefore, collectors began manually noting payments on their accounts receivable trial balance whenever remittance advice was received. This took additional time away from collections, in what was essentially a return to the manual posting process of the ledger card era. To make matters worse, all this data was posted by the collectors, not credit clerks. This reduced the number of collection calls being made.

Exacerbating the problem was the need to transfer most of these handwritten notes from the old accounts receivable trial balance every time a new report was generated, which was usually once or twice each month. This also meant that some historical information was lost with every new accounts receivable trial balance. If call notes were not also being recorded in a permanent file, any notes regarding items cleared from the accounts receivable trial balance were not transferred to the new report. This practice had serious ramifications when the occasion arose that an account had to be taken to court, because it further reduced the efficiency of the collection process in terms of identifying and resolving recurring problems.

Not surprisingly, some of the best collectors were not the people with the best negotiation abilities but those with the best memory of all the details that might occur with an account over a period of time. Collectors thus were the repositories of a tremendous amount of corporate information that was not readily available to anyone else in the corporation.

This lost corporate intelligence caused a further drain on productivity. The ability to identify and quantify recurring problems made it difficult to convince anyone in sales, customer service, manufacturing, or distribution that corporate practices were contributing to slower payments. The most significant impact was the hidden costs associated with resolving these same issues on a customer-by-customer, transaction-by-transaction basis.

Rather than create an efficient, highly automated collection environment, computerization had instead mutated the manual collection process into a disorderly arrangement of disconnected tasks. The gains realized by the accounts receivable department from automating transaction processing were unwittingly offset by the compensating manual tasks that evolved to augment the fragmentation of the data sources used by collectors. Credit activities also suffered similar consequences from computerization. While sources of credit information increased along with electronic delivery options, few automation tools were made available to analyze and warehouse this data. This further muddied the waters for collectors and credit analysts controlling customer credit limits and releasing orders when automated credit hold programs needed to be overridden.

What was once a simple manual system is now a complex of fragmented processes. To effectively integrate computerized receivables with the collection process requires a degree of clerical support in excess of the ledger card based collection process. From the collector's point of view, computerization has been clearly less cost effective than its promise. Despite this reality, the trend, especially over the last two decades, has been to reduce the manpower available to credit and collection departments. In these situations, performance suffers, and credit personnel are increasingly stressed trying to effectively maintain the hybrid systems that evolved from the early years of the information age.

PROMISE OF AUTOMATION DONE RIGHT

Despite the disappointing performance of accounts receivable systems over the last 30 years, there is no reason credit and collections cannot still benefit from computerization. The goal, however, needs to shift from automating the generation of financial data to facilitating business processes.

In the case of collections, computerized operations offer a number of possibilities. The return to a single data source that can drive collection decisions and activities is of prime importance. The automation of the clerical activities that consume so much of a collector's time then becomes possible. In addition, advances in communication technology hold the promise of further improvements in terms of throughput.

Network and Internet technologies are making it much easier to re-integrate the multitude of information sources used by credit and collection departments. Giving collectors a single source for all required customer account information is a time saver in itself, but in so doing there is also the opportunity to create additional intelligence. Credit departments have always enjoyed access to a tremendous amount of corporate information, but until recently there have been no vehicles to logically store, analyze, and disseminate this information. Imaging and other database technologies are making it easier to store and retrieve more information than ever before. Collectors working with such an automated system will "know" much more than before, which will in turn translate into more effective collection calls and better resources for solving the internal causes of delayed payments.

Automating clerical activities is also critical. It is at this juncture that process improvement demands careful thought. Automation must not be used to institutionalize the old way of doing things, but rather to provide ways to do things faster and more accurately. It is the time and quality improvements achieved through automating collections that create significant cash flow improvements. Simplified processes, the elimination of unproductive activities, and fewer hand-offs of information and documents have been proven to yield dividends when implemented in conjunction with a well-designed computerization scheme.

Collections will always be an exercise in communication, so it is not surprising that technological advances in this arena are of great benefit. The rapid adoption of faxes in the 1980s was a boon to collectors, who gained a tool that helped mitigate delays caused by a reliance on the postal service. Still, the use of faxes was primarily a manual activity. Automation coupled with advances in communications will result in even more dramatic improvements in productivity. The Internet, e-mail, fax servers, and electronic data interchange (EDI) are all tools that can be integrated within an automated collection system. Advances in broadband telecommunication technology, just over the horizon, will make these instruments even more powerful.

Automating collections is not about increasing productivity. It is about increasing production capacity. By integrating process improvements, programming computers to automate clerical routines, and adopting advanced communication technologies, a company's collection function can be taken to a new level. The contrast between an automated collection department and one that has been semi-automated is as stark as that between an axe and a chain saw.

Automated collection systems offer a much greater capacity than the fragmented hybrids spawned by today's computerized accounts receivable and the manual collection process. As a result, automated systems generate immediate improvements to a company's production process, customer satisfaction, and cash flow. The benefits do not stop there. Productivity gains continue on top of this higher capacity level as the automated collection system builds intelligence and the collection staff develops new collection muscles they never even knew they had. Direct feedback from customers is quickly disseminated, to the advantage of the enterprise in its entirety. All the while, intelligence is being built to feed other business processes.

SUMMARY

Incremental, rather than comprehensive, computerization schemes have left the practice of credit and collections only marginally better off, if at all, than when ledger cards provided the basis for an efficient credit and collection process. In particular, the computerization of accounts receivable activities without commensurate automation of associated collection tasks created multiple data sources and additional, nonproductive clerical tasks that mitigated any productivity gains achieved as a result of computerization. Nothing short of re-engineering the entire collection process will free collectors to achieve dramatic increases in cash flow.

The benefits from fully automating the collection process are transformational. Rather than spending most of their time gathering information and documenting problems, collectors using an automated collection system are able to devote the bulk of their time to contacting overdue customers. The result of this renewed focus on a collector's core responsibility is, not surprisingly, much improved corporate collections. In effect, automation provides collectors with that scarce commodity— time.

Existing collection systems simply require too much time for each past due account contacted. The primary advantage of a fully automated system over existing systems is the capacity to contact two or three or even four times as many accounts each day. A re-engineered and computerized collection system will also create its own intelligence; hence, not only are many more collection calls being made and customized letters and faxes sent, but these collection activities can be more appropriately targeted to maximize collections. As a result, companies that automate collections realize an immediate substantial increase in cash received, and then as their collection systems build intelligence and are fine-tuned, an ongoing improvement in all measures of collection performance.

ENDNOTES

1. Michael Hammer and James Champy, *Reengineering the Corporation* (New York: Harper Business, 1993), 31.
2. *Id.*
3. *Id.*, p. 32.
4. DSO is a measure of collection effectiveness. In its simplest format, the accounts receivables balance is divided by the average daily value of sales to calculate the number of days of sales in a company's receivables.

2

New Paradigm

Most credit departments have been organized as functional silos. Tasks are assigned to the credit function because they bear
some relationship to credit and collections. Meanwhile, related
tasks or procedures may be put under the control of other departments. The result is a vertical orientation to the duties and
responsibilities given credit departments, despite the fact that
related and necessary activities critical to effective credit and
collections are being performed by other departments.

WHEN CREDIT AND COLLECTIONS IS A DEPARTMENT

In this environment, the credit approval of new customers and
the extension of additional credit to existing customers are distinct and separate tasks that follow the prospecting and enlist-
ment activities of the sales department and the order
fullfillment activities of the customer service department. This
is why credit departments are often the last to know about a
new customer or an order put on "credit hold" by the accounts
receivable system. When a new customer's order is accepted by
sales before the credit department even knows the customer exists, the credit department is often pressured to cut corners in

the credit review process to avoid a confrontation with sales, and also to prevent delivery promises made to the new customer from being broken.

Orders with existing customers cause a similar problem. In this case, there are two negative outcomes that spring from the organization's structure. First is the recurrent pressure to approve the customer orders so that the company's integrity remains intact with regard to shipping commitments. The second is the time lost by the credit department because systematic collection activities are circumvented to handle any open orders. In this case, the proactive collection function is replaced by a reactive response to the pressure created by the new sales and order fulfillment departments. The whole process strains the organization and tends to get worse as the collection function gets further and further behind in proactively contacting customers before they go to credit hold.

Once the collection process begins, the impact caused by other departmental silos becomes apparent. Any errors committed by a company's manufacturing, distribution, or fulfillment functions have a high probability of showing up when it tries to collect from its customers. At this point, all the departmental barriers erected within a company conspire to help the customer pay more slowly. Because collections is in a functional silo, collectors must wait for the shipping department to get proofs of delivery, customer service to investigate a pricing question, quality assurance to arrange for goods to be returned and tested, and so forth.

The consequence is that credit and collections becomes an accumulation of disjointed tasks. A customer's account might come up several times in the course of a day as cash is applied, orders are approved, calls are made for past due balances, and discrepancies are resolved. Only the skill of the individual credit and collection staff members can bring any synergy to these assorted tasks if systems are not integrated. The busier things get, the more chance there is for breakdowns under this scenario, and the more stressful the job is for the credit and collection staff.

Breaking down the functional silos that isolate credit, within the finance or treasury department as well as from other corporate functions, is necessary to effective credit and collections. However, destroying these functional walls requires that some other structure be put in their place. To do that, it is important to understand the effects of credit policy on credit and collection performance. That issue deals with where credit and collections finds its home. It is also necessary to understand credit and collections' relationship to sales, because credit and collections, in many respects, is much more intertwined with that function than with finance.

EFFECTS OF CREDIT POLICY

The traditional role of credit and collections has been to provide security. Credit managers have long been charged with preventing risky sales and preventing customers from stealing accounts receivable. Those outside the finance department have even been known to call credit and collections the "stop sales department." That is to be expected when a department's primary purpose is to provide a check on otherwise unrestrained sales personnel who will sell to anyone and everyone.[1]

This mindset is focused on containing costs, whether due to bad debts or the lost use of uncollected funds. Problems arise, however, because containing costs does not necessarily translate into increased profits. Expending excessive amounts of time and money on credit analysis tasks will reduce subsequent slow payments and bad debts, but these incremental savings may not be justified in terms of profitability. Restrictive credit policies will often miss opportunities to increase sales and profits by refusing to sell to marginal accounts that when properly managed could contribute to the bottom line and expand market share.

In corporations in which credit managers are evaluated on their ability to minimize costs, that ability is constrained only by the political risks resulting from any credit and collection decision.[2] Conflicts with other departments arise only when a credit manager's actions are viewed as too severe. Otherwise, the credit manager is not evaluated on the effects these decisions may have on revenues or on the indirect costs associated with such decisions. Corporations that maintain a traditional credit department structure will invariably measure credit and collection performance on the basis of cost-based targets.

However, when the express goal of credit and collections is to maximize profits, things change. Sales and credit now have the same focus. Decisions are no longer made only on the merits of the individual customer but, rather, on the benefits the customer and others of the same class can bring to the corporation. Accounts receivable is now viewed as a portfolio that must be managed to produce maximum value for the corporation and the shareholders.

One result may be to assume more risk in order to increase sales and profits. This may mean more bad debt losses, but the risk of that, if handled properly, will have already been accounted for in the decision-making process and therefore more than compensated for through increased profits. Maximizing profits also encourages the credit department to focus on ways to complete the sales transaction rather than simply falling back on the old standby, the credit hold. This is not to say that orders may not be held, but rather that the long-term interests of the corporation need to be addressed rather than the one-dimensional goals of minimizing risk and reducing costs. Risk reduction and limiting receivable balances are still worthy activities, but only within the framework of maximizing profits.

CREDIT AND COLLECTIONS' RELATIONSHIP TO SALES

Sharing a common goal, maximizing profits, will transform the relationship between credit and sales. In traditional structures, what was once an adversarial relationship now has at least a chance of becoming complementary. Business strategists have long advocated cooperation between credit and sales. However, cooperation implies different agendas. That peaceful but separate co-existence was possible in yesterday's less competitive, transaction-driven world. Given the time-critical nature of today's just in time (JIT) manufacturing environment that requires close vendor–customer relationships, this dichotomy no longer works. If credit and sales are to forge a truly complementary relationship, their goals must be the same.

When credit joins sales in focusing on maximizing profits and ultimately shareholder value, credit analysts and collectors then become much more interested in developing long-term customer relationships. While there are always exceptions, most salespeople recognize the importance of cultivating their customers. After all, it has been documented that it is easier and less costly to sell more to an existing account than to enlist a new customer. Similar dynamics are at work on the collection side of the equation. By the same token, credit approval decisions will change when long-term customer profitability is considered, and these decisions will ultimately impact the collection process. (See Exhibit 2.1.)

Under these circumstances, it becomes much more important and apparent that sales and credit need to begin communicating early in the customer-acquisition process. The experiences of collectors are extremely useful in helping sales identify the types of customers that will be the best payers. At the same time, sales has an interest in becoming a more active partner in the credit information-gathering process, sharing not only what they know about prospects but their performance ex-

Exhibit 2.1   **How Technology Is Helping Change Credit**

The big payoff from the technology revolution is not so much the ability to crunch numbers. It's the ability to locate information and to use it intelligently. Automated decision systems, credit scoring, data warehousing—these tools are great for fulfilling the classic role of the credit professional: landing the business. They can dramatically accelerate the speed of decision making, lower the cost of sales, and improve cash flow. And they do it by putting the routine credit decisions where they belong—on your sales reps' laptops.

You [credit professionals] can raise approval rates, improve payment performance, and become a hero to your colleagues in the sales department. Yes, you make fewer decisions, but you retain control because you set the decision parameters. And you get more time to focus on the strategic issues, the big-dollar, high-risk situations, the problem accounts, global risks, consulting, and customer relations.

Source: Excerpted from a speech by Terry Taylor, Chairman and CEO of the Dun & Bradstreet Corporation, made at the 101st Credit Congress of the National Association of Credit Management, Salt Lake City, UT, May 12, 1997.

pectations as well. The end result is that sales and credit both end up knowing much more about their customers from the very beginning and are therefore able to take actions that will maximize the relationship.

The interaction between sales and credit will not necessarily stop after the customer has been set up. Information must be exchanged when the volume of orders changes, when there are payment discrepancies, and when there are collection problems. It is an ongoing process throughout the life of the customer relationship. At each of these junctures, it is much easier to reach decisions and take actions acceptable to all parties when sales and credit are focused on maintaining profitable long-term customer relationships than when credit has been charged with minimizing costs and risks as its first priority.

In this environment, handing off rather than solving customer issues is much less of a problem. The most important by-product is increased customer satisfaction. Collectors who are in tune with the sales department's objectives and who have easy access to customer records are much more able to solve problems as they arise, rather than passing the problem along to another department or seeking other assistance. One of the issues here is empowering collectors to solve problems, but just as important is providing the collectors with the necessary tools to do the job on their own. From the customer's point of view, getting a problem solved by the first person he or she talks to is customer service nirvana. Getting referred to another person or department or being told you will be called back with an answer is much less satisfying, though not necessarily as frustrating as the problem that just will not go away.

COLLECTIONS IS A PROCESS

While approving credit is clearly part of the order fulfillment process and collection activities are often driven by the order release process, collections can be considered a process in its own right. On the one hand, an order cannot be shipped until judgment has been passed on the customer's creditworthiness. That decision must come somewhere between the point in time after the order is received and before the finished goods are shipped or services delivered. Collection activities, on the other hand, often follow these events and are not critical to the order fulfillment side of the equation, provided the goods or services requested by the customer are delivered correctly at the agreed price.

This is not to dispute that collections is the last step in the order to cash process of the supplier. After all, the sale is not complete until the check has been received. Also, collectors and customer service representatives are often dealing with the same issues and talking to the same representatives of the customers. However, collectors and customer service representatives are doing very different things and are dependent on different, though overlapping, knowledge bases. Collections requires a distinct set of skills, information, and activities. It is helpful to the customer service representative and the collector to understand what their counterparts are doing. In fact, a good automated collection system will provide the data transfer necessary for the overlapping information to be shared between these two areas.

Another problem arises when collectors are made part of the order fulfillment process. Customer service representatives are naturally inclined to be customer advocates, that is, answering customer questions and fulfilling customer requests. Collectors, however, desire to convince customers to part with their money. In fact, it is no longer their money but the supplier's. After all, the goods have already been delivered or services rendered and the agreed payment date has past.

Because of this, collectors and customer service representatives have been grouped in teams and cross-trained to perform each other's duties. In this environment, there is a strong tendency for customer service issues rather than collections to dominate each team member's time. While this type of arrangement has its advantages, such as a single contact person for the customer, there is a tendency for collections to suffer. There simply cannot be as much of a focus on collections when the employees' focus has been broadened. Collector skills are normally not as high because the collector is now a generalist rather than a specialist.

Because of the problems that arise if collections is made the last step in the order fulfillment process, collections must be justified as a stand-alone process or find another home. Because there are no obvious choices that fit the latter, it is important to examine whether collections can be viewed as its own process.

SUMMARY

Although credit approval is a function of the order fulfillment process, the activities required to collect receivables can be considered a process unto themselves. This enables the redesign or re-engineering of the collection process to be carried on within the credit and collection function without having to involve other departments or functions. At the same time, however, consideration needs to be given to the needs those other functions may have as customers who are served at least in part by the collection process.

For this reason, critical to the redesign and automation of the collection process is an understanding of the effects of credit policy on credit and collections. Different decisions will be reached if the role of credit is to reduce costs rather than to enhance profits. When credit and collections becomes the "stop sales department" in order to limit risk, profit opportunities are mixed and customer relationships become less important. However, when the goal is increased profits, credit and sales are focused on the same objective so that appropriate decisions are not only made but shared.

The relationship of credit to sales also deserves special consideration before one begins redesigning the collection process. Companies that have renamed credit and collections the customer financial services department recognize this. When credit joins sales in an effort to increase profits, long-term customer relationships become paramount. In this environment, credit and collections is focused on the best way to handle transactions to maximize long-term profits. This may mean an occasional increase in bad debt. However, those losses will be more than compensated by the increased profits that will result from this partnership of sales and credit.

ENDNOTES

1. This does not mean that salespeople are bad or acting in the disinterest of the company. Credit checking is just not part of their traditional charter. An alternative method is to realign the objectives of the sales force by paying commissions or bonuses based on customer payments.
2. Frederick C. Scherr, *Making Sound Credit Policy Decisions*. Columbia, MD: National Association of Credit Management, Publications Department, 1996, p. 16. This text does a good job of providing a logical, value-added framework for the credit decision processes.

3

Collection Process

A process can be defined as a series of interrelated activities directed toward a common goal. A business process has been defined "as a collection of activities that takes one or more kinds of input and creates an output that is of value to the customer."[1] In the case of collections, there is an assortment of activities: setting priorities, preparing for contact, contacting the customers, following through on the import of the contacts, and reporting results. There are various inputs that drive these activities: the open invoices, adjustments, and not-yet-posted payments, along with different types of customer information. The result is either a paid or credited bill that allows the customer to continue purchasing goods and to maintain a good credit standing. On this basis, collections fits the model of a business process.

Viewing collections as a process in its own right allows a corporation to identify the factors necessary to a successful collection effort and to then redesign the activities and inputs that support the collection process. After identifying the process involved in collections, the jobs and structures necessary to support that process can be defined. That is where automation comes in, but the manual process must first be defined.

The collection process consists of five steps: prioritization, preparation, contact, follow-up, and reporting. These are illustrated in Exhibit 3.1. They are essentially the same five activities listed above in the comparison of collections to the definition of the business process. Understanding all that is involved with each of these collection steps is a necessary precursor to an effective automation effort.

PRIORITIZATION

The first stage of collections involves setting collection priorities. Determining priorities is fairly straightforward, and once

Exhibit 3.1 **Five Steps in the Collection Process**

A Day in Collections . . .

1. Prioritize

5. Report

2. Prepare

4. Follow-Up

3. Contact

Source: Reprinted with permission from *New Trends in Transforming Receivables into Cash: A White Paper Report on Accounts Receivable Collection Strategies for the 90s.* Copyright © 1996 by GETPAID Software.

parameters are set, only fine-tuning remains. A typical prioritization scheme is outlined in Exhibit 3.2.

These priorities are nothing more than a logical guide to help collectors rationally and systematically work through their past due accounts. Pending orders get top priority because not only does a company want continued sales[2] but also because, as a rule, people who want to buy goods are generally willing to clear up old bills in order to speed up their shipments. Broken promises are followed up next, because communicating clearly to these customers is important to maintaining the integrity of all outbound calling activity. Large dollars are attacked next because of the obvious effect on a company's cash flow. In addition, collectors do not want large dollars to become depreciated old dollars. The next priority is old balances, because these are a company's problem situations that have for whatever reason failed to resolve themselves in the normal course of business. Finally, the large population of not-so-big and not-so-old balances that make up the bulk of the accounts receivable are addressed. Whether a collector can get to all of these accounts is another matter.

Whereas setting the priorities is a relatively easy matter, actually prioritizing the individual accounts in an accounts receivable portfolio for maximum results is entirely something else. It all depends on the tools available to help iden-

Exhibit 3.2 **Sample Collection Priorities**

- Accounts on credit hold with pending orders
- Follow-up on broken promises
- Large past due balances
- Old past due balances
- The remaining past due balances

tify who has orders, large balances, old balances, and so forth. This process may consume a considerable amount of time and effort. Failing to prioritize will cause the collection effort to lack any focus at all. Having too simplistic a prioritization scheme will result in less-than-optimal collection efforts. A prioritization scheme must be well thought out and methodically executed.

PREPARATION

Once it is known who is going to be contacted and in what order, the next stage in the collection process involves gathering together all of the information and resources that will enable collectors to effectively and intelligently ask their customers for payment. There are several sets of information involved here: general customer information, transaction details, notes on items open from prior contacts, and information about the customer's operations and habits.

Most basic is general information about the customer. What is the customer's phone or fax number? Who should be contacted, and if he or she is not available, who else can be of assistance? What time zone is the customer in (so that contact is made during normal working hours)? These may seem like obvious things, but this information is still part of the process, and it is necessary to collect it prior to each and every contact a collector makes.

In addition, collectors need information regarding the transaction in question. What was the assigned invoice number and the customer's purchase order number? How much is owed and when was it due? Essentially, this is the matter collectors are calling about. Obviously, it is important to have the necessary details in hand before any sort of contact is initiated.

Along with this, the collector needs to review any open issues from the last contact. Damaged or lost shipments, quality issues, or any number of disputes may remain unresolved. The collector needs to know the status of these in order to be able to move on to new issues.

There must also be information regarding each customer's characteristics. Collectors can still do their job without this information, but having it in hand will make collecting much easier. Do they pay by invoice or statement? Do they regularly request duplicate documentation for such things as invoices or bills of lading? What was the result of the last conversation with the customer? All these details assist the collector in determining the best way to get the customer to pay. Knowing each customer's policies and tendencies will make collection efforts both more efficient and successful.

MAKING CONTACT

This step is central to an effective collection operation. The time and effort put into making contact with customers is directly related to how much money will be collected. The more contacts made and the better quality the contacts, the faster the accounts receivable will be collected.

Contacts can be made on a number of different levels. From a collector's point of view, it is preferable to personally contact the payment decision maker for the customer. When this is not possible, a secondary contact person must suffice, or another alternative must be pursued such as sending a fax, e-mail, letter, or statement, or leaving a message.

Clearly, some of these alternatives are more effective than others, depending on the situation. A first collection letter, for example, is much more effective than a second or third letter. For this reason, it is important to have as many contact tools as possible available for the collector's use. It is unlikely that a single method of contact will get the job done, so there should also be guidelines indicating a strategy of how and when the different tools are to be used.

Making contact, especially when it involves a phone call, also involves identifying and resolving problems. It is never enough just to ask the customer to pay. The key is to overcome the customer's objections to paying. This requires analytical, interpersonal, and communication skills on the part of the collector. A collection system that provides a collector with a good knowledge base is much more effective in the contact phase than are systems weak in this area.

FOLLOW-UP

Every time a customer is contacted, there are follow-up activities that must be completed. These activities can range from sending invoice copies, providing proofs of delivery, passing along a request by the customer to have the salesperson call, reconciling the account balance, reviewing the pricing of the invoice in question, scheduling the next follow-up date, and so on. Without effective follow-up procedures, a collector's efforts at making contact can be rendered a waste of time.

Follow-up includes any and every activity that is necessary to consummate the collection. Follow-up involves ongoing communications with customers as well as with other functions within the collector's own company. Clerical, analytical, and organizational skills are required for follow-up.

Follow-up is also a critical component of the collection process. It is not simply a task that is done as a result of having contacted the customer. Follow-up procedures send a strong message to the customer. Collectors who are lax in their follow-up find that their customers will take the attitude that it is not essential to pay right away or, even worse, that they are not valued as a customer. Consistent and persistent follow-up procedures, however, set a high standard for customers by sending the message that the collector is serious about collecting the outstanding bill and that he or she is ready to do whatever is necessary to get paid.

The sooner a follow-up activity is completed, the better. The primary reason is to maintain the momentum created from the previous contact. This is served by proving that the follow-up matter is important by giving it immediate attention. The downside of the sequence is the impact on collector productivity. Due to human nature, repetitive outbound calling is more productive and less tiresome than performing a variety of collection activities. When the system is interrupted, the ability to return to the calling process is diminished and overall calling volume decreases. Batching follow-up activities together, especially those that cannot be completed during the actual collection call, is more productive than making a call and then completing the follow-up activities before moving on to the next call. However, this robs the collector of the thrill of the hunt that more complex activities provide. In the best of all worlds, follow-up activities would be completed during the contact process, while the customer is still on the line, or within seconds of the call's termination.

REPORTING

Without feedback, it is impossible to measure the effectiveness of the collection function. The data organized during the reporting phase of the collection process provide information for reallocating collection resources for maximum results. This is an internal collection department use of data, as is collector performance evaluation. Reporting also identifies where customers have fallen through the cracks, enabling the supervisor to redirect collection activities.

By the same token, a number of different functions also

have an interest in reports based on collection activities and results. Sales and customer service have an interest in this information in order to identify problem areas for the purpose of not only solving problems but ferreting out their root causes, and also for better allocating their efforts toward those customers that can contribute sales and profits. Treasury is interested in cash flow projections, while finance wants to know how bad debt is being managed.

Therefore, reporting occurs at both the beginning and the end of the collection process. In order to set collection priorities, the collector must review reports detailing his or her last collection cycle. The review and analysis of this information is a critical component of effective collections. Without an accurate and comprehensive reporting function, your collection efforts will be less than optimal.

With the possible exception of performance appraisals during the reporting process, only two of the five stages of the collection process add value to the collections outcome. That is the process of contacting customers and delivering follow-up materials. Prioritization, preparation, and, for the most part, reporting instead take time away from more productive activities.

IMPROVING THE PROCESS

Unless the collection process is understood, it cannot be made more efficient. Simply automating current practices will not bring about dramatic improvements. Although such automation might provide some incremental improvements, it will mostly serve to further institutionalize the inefficiencies that have become a part of current collection practices.

Automating collections without redesigning the process would be akin to attaching an axe to a motor. While the motor could drive the axe many more times in a day than could the lumberjack (See Exhibit 1.1), it would not necessarily be more efficient. The lumberjack, after all, was skilled in swinging the axe and would change the angle of impact with each blow. Unless the machine was made to do something similar (which would require a much greater amount of complexity, and therefore a greater chance the machinery would break down), the axe would keep hitting the tree at the same point and from the same angle—an inefficient process.

The chain saw, however, revolutionizes the process. The lumberjack does not just become more efficient, his production capacity is increased significantly. Although he is still cutting down trees, his methods have changed. Likewise, if an automated tool for collecting accounts receivable is to be created, it cannot be expected to continue using the same methods that have become part of the automated accounts receivable, manual collection process. This would be repeating the errors made when accounts receivable transactions were first automated without enough forethought given to the effects this would have on credit and collections.

The new tools and new methods must go together. Without the chain saw, methods designed to work with mechanized tools might even be counterproductive. By the same token, swinging the chain saw like an axe is more likely to cut off the collector's limbs than the tree's. If collections are to be automated, the collection process must be simultaneously refined. Automation in support of redesigned processes is the key to breakthroughs in performance.

By starting with the collection cycle, a number of opportunities become obvious. Since much of the cycle is spent on support activities—prioritization, preparation, follow-up, and reporting—it makes sense to eliminate, shorten, or otherwise reduce the time spent doing these things. By the same token, the greater the number of contacts each collector can make, the better the chances of bringing in more money faster. Very simply, collectors want to reduce the time spent on support activities while both increasing the number of contacts that can be made in a set period of time and increasing the time available for making those contacts. (See Exhibit 3.3.)

A major component of these twin goals is a single repository for the information needed by collectors. By using a single integrated database, it is possible to automate first the information-gathering process, then the analytical tasks, and finally, the clerical support functions. The database will in effect drive the whole collection system and at the same time gain added intelligence each time through the collection cycle.

Because there will be more time available for contacting delinquent accounts, the benefits of this will not be simply a more efficient collection system but, rather, a much greater capacity. This is why companies that have automated collections,

Exhibit 3.3   Rationale behind an Automated Collection Process

1. Shorten the time spent on support activities.
2. Increase the time spent contacting delinquent accounts.
3. Increase the effectiveness of each contact.
4. Increase the number of contacts that can be made within a set period of time.
5. Provide immediate follow-up documentation to customers.
6. Rely on a single integrated database.
7. Disseminate information gathered during collections throughout the entire organization.
8. Generate additional feedback.
9. Support improvement in the professional and communication skills of the collection staff.

such as Dunlop Slazenger, are able to realize dramatic improvements in collections right from the start.

In contrast, if capacity is increased by adding more collectors, for example, by hiring some temporary collectors, there will most likely be gradual improvements over a three- or four-month time period. In this scenario, the collection cycle is only marginally shortened, if at all. With automation, the collection cycle is significantly reduced right from the start.

Another benefit is improved feedback. Though less time will be spent on the reporting phase of the collection cycle, more useful information will be readily available. Individual collector performance will be much easier to measure and benchmark. The aging reports currently used do not do a good job of this. Cash forecasting is another area that benefits from a single database. Also, identifying and evaluating different segments of an accounts receivable portfolio becomes an easier task. Furthermore, improved portfolio management will enhance the entire collection process by allowing maximal results to be obtained with limited resources.

SUMMARY

The last component that must be understood before the collection process is redesigned and automated is the actual steps that make up the ongoing collection cycle. They are prioritization, preparation, contact, follow-up, and reporting.

The rationale for improving the collection process naturally follows. Simply stated, by increasing not only the time spent making contact but the efficiency of those contacts, while reducing the time spent on each contact, dramatic improvements in collections can be achieved. This also involves eliminating or automating many of the clerical activities that consume so much time in the other four stages of the collection cycle.

ENDNOTES

1. Frederick C. Scherr, *Making Sound Credit Policy Decisions*. Columbia, MD: National Association of Credit Management Publications Department, 1996, p. 35.
2. This is not to mention the calls from the sales representatives into the collections department if credit holds are not released promptly.

4

Re-engineering Collections

The first step in re-engineering the collections process is to establish aggressive goals. Modest goals will not suffice if you intend to create dramatic improvements, because modest goals could be achieved with mere incremental improvements. Goals need to be set that are impossible under the current reality. This requires an environment in which completely re-inventing the collection process is not just a possibility but a necessity. Goals need to be set so that the team empowered to bring about the changes must admit that there is no way they can succeed given current methods. Until this is done, the reluctance to get rid of existing habits and methods is just too powerful.

These goals must address several issues. First and foremost is the effect on cash flow. Cash flow targets and measures of receivable performance reflect tangible results and are easy to set. The best metric to use is the reduction in overdue receivables. This is a simple, tangible number, and it is by definition part of a condition that should not exist. Receivables should not be overdue, and therefore eliminating 25 percent of these is a modest enough target, yet a significant enough statistic to motivate process change.

Another useful cash flow metric stipulates the percentage of outstanding receivables that will be collected in the upcoming month. If the previous average has been 60 percent of outstanding receivables, setting a goal of 75 percent postautomation requires a 25 percent improvement. Of course, there can be the tendency to skim off the easily collected receivables in the first month, but in a short time total receivables will be reduced, necessitating more attention to the tougher-to-collect debts in order to reach this target in subsequent months. In fact, a combination of reducing both past due and overall receivables will help drive significant process improvement.

Contact goals present another area that can drive change. It is common for the number of collector contacts (left messages excluded) to more than double as a result of automating the collection process. This should be institutionalized as a goal of the change process. Obviously, the more contacts made, the more receivables will be collected. Just by doubling the number of contacts (or in a sense, collector productivity), tremendous performance gains can be realized. This type of target can also be broken down into subsets—primarily, the number of phone calls that connect with a customer's representative and faxes sent. The determining factor here is human resources, because sending too many faxes can create too good a response (if that is possible), requiring more follow-up work than the staff can handle. The point is that being overly ambitious can cause the collection staff to be overwhelmed in unanticipated ways. It is better not to try to be the python that swallows the pig whole but rather to carve it up efficiently. Contact targets backed by sound strategy can do just that.

Another area to consider affects quality. Quality goals can sometimes be elusive targets, especially when not well defined. What can be measured are lapses in quality, and the reduction of those items provides useful metrics. In terms of collections, the problems that most often arise are customer service issues. A goal to cut the average time to resolve deduction issues from 120 days to 60 days will require dramatic improvements in not only the resolution process but also the elimination of the causes of deductions in the first place. Such improvements very positively impact customer satisfaction. Goals that require quicker response times or reduced errors, such as in invoicing, will translate into significant service improvements.

Commensurate with any goals that are set for a re-engineered collection process, there must be a strict adherence to policy by all participants. First, this requires some thought as to just what that policy should be, necessitating an understanding of both the marketplace and corporate requirements. Second, process change requires new ways of doing things, and there is a natural inclination by workers to hold on to the old ways. Collectors are no different, and they can unintentionally sabotage the benefits of automation by hanging on to unnecessary tasks. For a re-engineered process to work, collectors must understand up front that there will be no more aged receivable trial balances or calendars to record notes on, nor any of the many other pet practices that veteran collectors have developed over the years to help them deal with computerized receivables and a manual collection process. Automation will require more conformity than collectors are used to, but they must learn to work the new system properly from the start. Improvisation must not be tolerated. Adherence by everyone to the plan is essential. (See Exhibit 4.1.)

Another important consideration when setting goals is the cost of capital. Even before goals are set, the dollar benefits to be achieved must be identified, and these will in part be determined by the corporate cost structure. Accounts receivable represent a holding account for funds that, once collected, can be put to use in more productive pursuits such as investing in production capacity, research and development, or market share.

Exhibit 4.1 **Aggressive Goals Trigger Impressive Results**

When Dell computer automated its collections system, it did not do anything halfway. Top management was committed to the project, including the attendance of Michael Dell to speak to the troops at the kickoff meeting that launched the project. Training for Dell's 55 collectors was also an important component of the pre-installation process, but the driving factor to Dell's success was its aggressive goals.

In the performance area, Dell's collectors were committed to making three verbal contacts and sending two faxes to every past due account within the first 60 days after implementation of the automated collection system. By adhering to this policy, Dell doubled its days sales outstanding (DSO) goals in the first 6 months of operating with the new system. Depending on the individual business unit, Dell was looking for a 3- to 5-day reduction in DSO, but instead realized a 6- to 10-day improvement, amounting to a nearly 25 percent gain. After 18 months, Dell's DSO had gotten as low as 36 days on primarily net 30 day terms.

The other significant financial gain was in the area of operating costs. With a growth rate that approaches 60 percent annually, the automated collection system enabled Dell to significantly slow the pace of hiring in its collection area. While the DSO improvement produced an immediate cash flow benefit, the holding down of operating costs is a long-term advantage that keeps accruing dividends with each new fiscal period.

In addition, the cost structures that directly support collections can be readily measured, but there are also hidden costs in terms of lost opportunities (i.e., correcting errors rather than calling more past due customers) and the cost of collectors' activities that are not related to collections. Having a handle on all this information beforehand is also necessary when measuring the impact of the re-engineered collection process.

When targets for each of these areas are set, the goals will then drive the process. These goals must be ambitious enough that the chance of meeting them within the old system are clearly impossible. If goals do not drive the process improvement program, it is because they have been selected with an eye toward past collection performance. This must be avoided. Goals must establish standards that require systems to be built that can support the desired parameters. By so doing, the benefits will be realized not just in collection operations but throughout the organization.

ACCELERATING CASH FLOW

Nobody will argue that enhancing cash flow has far-reaching benefits for today's corporation. Cash is king. It has also become a critical measure of an organization, often carrying more weight than profits or shareholder value. Paper profits can turn worthless, and shareholder value can plummet in the face of a liquidity crisis. When a company stops generating positive cash flow, tough times are not far behind. Growth is impacted and investors stay away. When cash is dear, capital improvements are canceled or delayed, hurting future capacity and productivity. The result is a downward spiral that is tough to halt.

A positive cash flow has just the opposite effect. As funds are made available for debt reduction and capital improvements, costs are reduced and profits increased. Growth is less costly to finance when supported by a positive cash flow. A sustainable positive cash flow amplifies these benefits time and time again.

One way to enhance cash flow is to set aggressive goals for days sales outstanding (DSO). Very simply, the lower the DSO, the faster the cash flow. A company is better off if it can turn over its receivables every 40 days rather than every 50 days. Over the course of a year, improvement of that scale means accounts receivable will turn over nearly two more times than before (9 versus 7.2 times). Not only that, but accounts receivable will have been reduced by 20 percent. If the accounts receivable balance was $10 million when the DSO was 50 days, it drops to $8 million when DSO is reduced to 40 days, all else being equal. That is $2 million the company can put in its bank account without having to sell more. Assuming that DSO does not subsequently rise, that money can be invested in the future, ongoing profitability of the organization.

Reducing the DSO from 50 to 40 days is not just some pie in the sky example. In fact, the more the DSO is beyond standard terms, the more agressive a company must be in setting its goals. In fact, if the terms were 30 days and the DSO had been running around 60 days, a goal of 45 days—a 25 percent improvement in cash flow—would not be overly aggressive.

There are other benefits from reducing DSO and the company's investment in accounts receivable. For one thing, the amount of risk in accounts receivable will generally drop. The most obvious risk component that improves is the risk of being paid slowly, because current dollars are likely to be paid before past due dollars. When the dollars in the company's receivable portfolio are reduced, most of those dollars initially come from past due accounts. After all, very few customers will pay before their invoices are due. This means that current receivables, those invoices that are not yet due, become a significantly larger percentage of total receivables.

By the same token, the risk of not being paid drops. The older a receivable is, the greater the chance that it will not be paid. By reducing the number and dollar value of past due invoices, the risk of not being paid is consequently reduced. Exhibit 4.2 illustrates this. It shows very clearly that the longer a receivable stays on the books, the less value it has. The bottom line is that if DSO is reduced, past due balances will be reduced as well as future bad debts.

Exhibit 4.2 **Present Value of Receivables Collected**

Cost of Money	8.0%	10.0%	12.0%
Days Outstanding		Value/$1000	
30	$993.33	$991.67	$990.00
90	$980.00	$975.00	$970.00
180	$960.00	$950.00	$940.00
360	$920.00	$900.00	$880.00

Note: Receivables lose value for two reasons. One factor is that receivables depreciate because there is a cost associated with holding receivables rather than paying off debt (the usual scenario) or investing in future profits. This is shown above. The other factor is the probability of nonpayment due to business failure or unresolvable dispute. The following list summarizes the findings of a U.S. Department of Commerce study.

Amount Overdue	Value of $1 over Time
Three months	$.99
Six months	$.67
One year	$.46
Two years	$.27

Note: With both factors at work, the effect is that a 6-month-old receivable, assuming the cost of money is 10 percent, is worth barely 64 percent of its original value.

This being the case, it makes sense to not only set DSO goals, but to also set receivables aging targets. Current balances in excess of 90 percent are achievable. Looking at it another way, balances over 60 days past due should be limited to no more than one or two percentage points. In this sort of a scenario, it is easy to know where problems are and to deal with them appropriately. That alone will reduce risk over time. It also makes for a more efficient collection function.

MORE EFFICIENT PROCEDURES

The benefits from improving cash flow provide ample justification for re-engineering and automating collections. However, the effects of more efficient procedures can be more dramatic than the gains derived solely from increased cash flow, and can even have a much greater positive impact on an organization. This is possible because of all the marginally productive tasks that are necessary to hold today's hybrid collection systems together. Eliminating this plethora of inefficiencies is what increases collection capacity. It is not just more efficient procedures but rather the ability to do more. (See Exhibit 4.3.)

One idea to keep in mind when re-engineering the collection process is to use as few steps as possible to accomplish any necessary tasks. In so doing, uneccessary steps are eliminated while those that remain are simplified as much as possible. This results in a very streamlined process that takes less time than was required with the old procedures and, because it has been simplified, is also less likely to generate errors.

To illustrate this, examine the process of sending an in-

Exhibit 4.3 **Tasks That Can Be Automated**

1. Automatically accessing the customer's account information
2. Dialing phone numbers
3. Faxing—creating and transmitting
4. Note taking
5. Prioritizing collection activities
6. Report generation
7. Scheduling the next follow-up date
8. Transmitting problem notices to internal contacts via e-mail
9. Updating the contact listing with payments

voice copy to a customer via a fax. With a manual system, the collector will most likely be talking to the customer's accounts payable contact when informed that the invoice in question cannot be paid because they do not have a copy of the invoice. The collector then asks for the customer's fax number (if he or she does not already have it) and promises to fax a copy of the invoice. After hanging up, the collector walks to the file room to retrieve a copy of the invoice in question. At this point, the collector will probably make a copy of the invoice because multipart invoice copies do not feed well through fax machines, and also to have a copy that can be stored in the customer's credit file for future follow-up. (Credit files are usually situated in a more convenient location for collectors than the files holding invoice and shipping documents.) The collector must now write up a cover sheet, probably by hand, and then take that with the invoice to the nearest fax machine, which may not be situated in close proximity to the credit department. At the fax machine, the customer's fax number must be entered. Many collectors will then wait for the fax to go through rather than make a second trip to the fax machine to confirm a successful transmission and pick up the documents. The cover sheet and invoice are then either (1) filed in the customer's credit file, with a reminder note made on a calendar to follow up in a week or so, or (2) filed in a tickler file.

This whole process can easily take 5 or 10 minutes, or longer if the collector stops to chat by the fax machine. Depending on the collector's individual habits, there are at least eight or nine discreet steps required to send an invoice copy by fax. The worst part is that at the end of the process, the collector still does not know whether the customer will accept the invoice in whole or part. If not, there will certainly be further payment delays.

An automated system allows for the radical redesign of this process. With automated faxing capabilities, when the customer mentions during the phone call that he or she does not have a copy of the invoice in question, the collector is able to pull up the invoice data on the computer screen and then tell the computer to fax the invoice to the customer, all the while still talking to the customer. The collector is then able to confirm the customer's receipt of the invoice, following that up with a demand for a firm payment commitment from the customer before hanging up. The only steps involved for the collector are a few keystrokes to bring up the invoice data and then faxing an invoice copy. The system already has the customer's fax number in the customer's master file in the system's computerized database, so it is able to take care of all the other steps: finding the customer's fax number, dialing, sending, recording the transmission in the collection log, and setting a follow-up date.

What may take 10 minutes manually takes only a few seconds with an automated system. Besides, the collector is getting better and faster results using the automated system, offsetting any extra time the collector might spend on the phone line with the customer. However, a minute or two longer on the line is far better than having to make a subsequent follow-up call. An even more effective process is to routinely fax the invoice to the customer before making the collection call. (See Exhibit 4.4.) This is done by attaching the invoice to a collection letter that is faxed to the customer one day and followed up with a scheduled call the next day. On the one hand, many faxes can be sent automatically in a short period of time; on the other hand, the subsequent calls are shorter and more effective because the customer has been prepped for the call.

It is easy to see that improvements realized from automating a relatively simple task such as faxing an invoice copy can impact a collections operation. If the staff sent a dozen such faxes daily, and automation saved an average of only 5 minutes

Exhibit 4.4 **Manual versus Automated Faxing Processes**

To Send a Manual Fax	*To Send an Automated Fax*
1. Walk to the file room and find the invoice in question	1. Look up the invoice on the customer's outstanding accounts receivable screen
2. Walk to a copier and make a copy of the invoice	2. Highlight the invoice to be faxed
3. Refile the invoice copy	3. Hit the "send fax" key
4. Make a fax cover sheet	
5. Look up the customer's fax number	
6. Walk to a fax machine, dial the number, and send the documents	
7. Wait for the fax to go through and retrieve the confirmation	
8. Walk to the credit files and file the invoice copy, copy, cover sheet, and confirmation in the customer's credit file	
9. Return to desk	
10. Make a note on the customer's call log that the invoice copy was faxed	
11. Note a follow-up date on calendar	

per fax, the collection staff would gain an extra hour each day. Redesign and automate several collection activities, and each collector starts recovering a significant amount of lost time from his or her day.

Besides the time savings that translate into added collection capacity, there are additional benefits from more efficient collection procedures. One direct result of the time savings from more efficient procedures is the opportunity to focus that newfound time on critical activities. Not only is more being done in less time but noncritical tasks are being replaced with productive activities. Instead of filing or faxing or updating calendars, collectors are collecting. This is what makes automating a collection operation a transformational opportunity. Streamlined practices increase capacity, and that added capacity is used to focus on critical tasks.

A more efficient, streamlined collection process will also result in more consistent practices among collectors. This is not to say that essentially the same results will be obtained from each collector, but there will be less deviation from normal practices. With automated receivables and manual collections, there are abundant opportunities for collectors to establish their own idiosyncratic collection practices.

Just in the area of scheduling follow-up activities, there can be a wide disparity among a company's collectors. Some will use a calendar while others use a tickler system. Not everyone will allow the same number of days after a promise to pay before scheduling a follow-up. Some collectors will follow up with a letter while others will make a phone call in the same circumstances.

An automated collection process eliminates much of this inconsistency. This is helpful in training customers to pay promptly. Just as consistent discipline on the part of parents is important for children to be well behaved (and well adjusted), a consistent collection process lets customers know exactly where they stand. With an automated collection process, there is little room for ambiguity, which is often a cause of slow payments. It is easier for customers to delay payment when collectors do not send a consistent message about when they expect to be paid. Customers will take as much time to pay as they are given.

Another advantage of consistent procedures under an automated collection system is that a change in collectors does not result in a loss of intelligence regarding the collection status of accounts. Under the automated receivables/manual collection scenario, each collector knows more about his or her accounts than anyone else does. When a collector is out sick or goes on vacation, coverage of his or her accounts is usually minimal because of the time it takes to get someone else up to speed on the accounts. With an automated collection system, the system tracks previous collection activities, among other information, and since collection practices are standardized, it is very easy for someone else to step in and manage any collection activities consistent with the way the assigned collector would have handled things. With an automated collection system, a company is therefore less susceptible to personnel changes or absences.

This may not seem that important, but if the company has only a four-person collection function and everyone misses on average 3 weeks each year due to sickness or vacation, there are 12 weeks each year that the company will be operating with a staffing shortage. That translates to 480 man-hours, or nearly 25 percent of one worker's time each year. Clearly, even if collection coverage is only moderately improved during that period of time, the result will be a significant improvement in collections. Remember, collection results are proportionate to the time and effort expended on actually collecting. Peripheral activities, though often necessary, do not bring in any money.

AUTOMATING COLLECTIONS REDUCES COSTS

More efficient collection procedures not only give a company more value for each dollar it has been spending but will actually reduce the number of dollars it spends in the future. Automating collections is no small undertaking, and it will cost the company a few dollars, but the payback period can be quite short because future expenses have been reduced. This is why making a half-hearted investment in collection technology or trying to automate collections cheaply does not make sense. If it is done right in the first place, a very reasonable payback on the investment can be expected.

The most immediate measurable savings derives from a reduction in accounts receivable carrying costs. Every dollar left in accounts receivable bears a cost, whether it is interest expenses on borrowed funds or lost profit opportunities because these funds cannot yet be invested in the future of the company. The example given earlier in this chapter regarding the need to set aggressive DSO goals highlighted this issue. Automating collections properly will significantly reduce the size of accounts receivable, giving the company cash to invest in the business and reducing future accounts receivable carrying costs because there will be fewer receivables.

In the example stipulating a 20 percent reduction in DSO, not only is there $2 million to reinvest in the company, but future carrying costs are reduced each year by a percentage of that amount. If that money is used to pay down a loan with an 8 percent interest rate, that translates into a savings of $160,000 every year. That savings alone could probably justify the expense of automating collections, but there are also additional savings.

Over the long term, bad debt expenses will be reduced. As mentioned earlier, automated collections will enable a company to reduce the average age of its accounts receivable, which also serves to reduce the amount of risk in accounts receivable. Down the road, there will simply be fewer and smaller bad debt write-offs. Fifty percent reductions in bad debt expense are not uncommon for companies that have automated collections. Such improvements will add significant profits to a company's bottom line over time. (See Exhibit 4.5.)

Exhibit 4.5 **Cost of Bad Debts**

If Actual Losses Are	And Net Profit Is				
	1%	2%	5%	8%	10%
	Amount of Additional Sales Needed to Offset the Losses				
$1,000	$100,000	$50,000	$20,000	$12,500	$10,000
$2,000	$200,000	$100,000	$40,000	$25,000	$20,000
$5,000	$500,000	$250,000	$100,000	$62,500	$50,000
$8,000	$800,000	$400,000	$160,000	$100,000	$80,000
$10,000	$1,000,000	$500,000	$200,000	$125,000	$100,000

Note: When a receivable is written off to bad debt, it takes many more times that amount in additional sales to compensate for that loss. Carrying doubtful receivables (though not yet turned bad debt) can be a very expensive proposition.

However, keep in mind that these cost savings derive from the opportunity costs recovered as collectors spend more time on collections. The cost from collectors performing clerical tasks and other duties not related to collections is greatly reduced, but the greatest benefit results from the collectors doing what they have been trained and hired to do—collect. In fact, if the collectors handle both credit and collections, streamlining the collection process may have an even greater effect on collections on a proportional basis, as much more time is devoted to actual collections.

The reallocation of limited resources provides the benefits from re-engineering any process, and this certainly applies to automating collections. The collection process needs to be re-engineered and automated because under current conditions resources are not being utilized to their full potential. As a result, substantial opportunity costs are going to waste in the majority of credit departments that have automated accounts receivable but still rely on manual collection systems.

HAPPY CUSTOMERS ARE GOOD CUSTOMERS

A very significant offshoot of more efficient collection procedures is improved customer service. Re-engineering and automating collections causes a number of good things to happen from the customer's point of view, particularly quality issues—not those concerning the products or services the company sells but rather the quality of what are essentially back office functions. Even so, these operations affect customers, and, by any measure, increased customer satisfaction is a corporate asset.

There probably are not many people, if any, who would look at a commercial collection operation as a source for additional sales. However, collections very often serves as the gateway to a number of customer support functions and, as such, can definitely impact sales for better or for worse. More efficient collection procedures have the effect of eliminating barriers to additional sales. (See Exhibit 4.6.)

Collectors frequently encounter problems caused by other departments. Without effective corporate procedures and systems to help resolve such problems, collections suffer. The customers also suffer. They want to get the pricing dispute resolved, the lost shipment found, or the advertising credits issued so they can pay the invoice and move on to something else. The problem is that these types of discrepancies tend to linger, and the longer it takes for them to be resolved, the greater is the chance that bad feelings will result. Problems are compounded when new orders are put on credit hold, often inadvertently, because a disputed item is past due.

Exhibit 4.6   **In Search of the Perfect Invoice**

Of course there is no such thing as a perfect invoice. That would require satisfying the documentation specifications of every customer. There is just too much diversity in that sample for one form to do it all. However, that does not mean trying is fruitless—after all, it does fit the bill of an ambitious goal. In fact, this was a goal of Pillsbury during the redesign of its order processes.

Selling into the highly competitive grocery marketplace involves the use of a number of marketing techniques—coupons, advertising allowances, promotional discounts, and so forth—that create customer payment deductions. Most, but not all, of these deductions are legitimate, necessitating some financial controls to be placed on the deduction management process. This often causes a drain on collection resources. While trying to create a better invoice, Pillsbury realized that promotional allowances had little to do with the billing process and more to do with the process of establishing profitable customer relationships. Its solution then was to remove all promotional incentives from its invoice process.

Creating a separate mechanism for handling promotional funds has greatly reduced deductions. In addition, those deductions that still occur are immediately identified, coded, and charged off to the internal department responsible. The results have been dramatically successful. Pillsbury's collection function has recovered a tremendous amount of time that was being expended on peripheral activities, while customers benefit from a straightforward mechanism focused solely and simply on promotional issues.

The ability of an automated collection system to track and identify recurring problems helps tremendously in bringing these issues to a quick resolution. Being able to track the involvement of people from other departments within the company allows collectors to deal more effectively with customers while encouraging their fellow workers to resolve outstanding issues. The faster these problems are solved, the happier the customers will be, not to mention that payment will be received sooner.

An automated collection system also provides a means for collectors to work with the company's other corporate functions to find permanent solutions to those corporate practices that facilitate slow payments by customers. Most customer deductions and other payment discrepancies are in fact caused by the policies and practices of the selling company. Manual collection systems are inherently poor at identifying and tracking these types of problems. This makes it difficult to identify trends and isolate the root causes behind customers' payment deductions and other payment problems. Automated collection systems can do this with relative ease. This knowledge base becomes a powerful tool for encouraging other departments to improve their procedures and processes. These solutions not only correct existing problems, but they also serve to prevent these problems from recurring. The downstream effect of fewer problems is yet more time to devote to collections.

Besides solving problems faster and preventing them from recurring, the problem-tracking capabilities of automated collection systems reduce the number of people customers must talk to in order to get their billing- and payment-related problems resolved. From a customer standpoint, being handed off from one person or department to another is an extremely frustrating experience. By tracking problems and working out expedited solutions, automated collection systems reduce collectors' guesswork about what to do next when a customer presents them with a problem. Directing customers to the decision maker in the company who can resolve their particular situation will help reduce customer frustration and in turn build additional goodwill.

SUMMARY

Re-engineering the collection process is a necessary component of any automation program that seeks significant productivity gains. On top of this, setting aggressive goals is essential to the re-engineering process. These goals should encompass measurements of cash flow improvement, increased customer contact, and improved customer satisfaction. Critical to the effectiveness of any such measures is an understanding of the underlying cost structure of the collection operation and of other corporate functions affected by collections. The growth or shrinkage of corporate accounts receivable affects investments in other segments of the business; therefore, cost of capital is an important component when planning to automate collections.

Creating more efficient procedures is central to a re-engineered collection process. Many tasks found in a manual collection system that relies upon a computerized accounts receivable system are redundant, counterproductive, or otherwise inefficient. Re-engineering seeks to greatly simplify the collection process through the use of automation tools. By putting all the information a collector needs on the computer screen and combining that resource with enhanced communication tools, such as automated faxing capabilities and auto-dialing technologies, the collection process can be re-engineered to meet the agressive goals that have been set.

Re-engineering collections also requires that consideration be given to collection policy and that those policies be adhered to in the new process. Not only must the process be true to corporate policy, but the participants in the collection system must also adopt the new ways of collecting. Old habits and practices must be set aside in order to ensure the optimal performance of the re-engineered collection system.

5

Problems Inherent in Current Practices

Anyone who has been around a credit department during the last 30 years recognizes this scenario: long hours, constant pressure, one problem after another, no time for planning, and a days sales outstanding (DSO) that just does not want to stay down. Of course, there are exceptions to the rule. Credit departments that have not only been well managed but given ample resources, both in terms of technology and personnel, have performed well. One such example is the credit department with assertive "clerical" managers, whose job it is to start work at 5:00 A.M. making sure all cash is posted so they can schedule collection calls and otherwise plan collection activities for the collection staff by the 9:00 A.M. start of business each day. Unfortunately, more than a few of this type of credit and collection operations have been renderred ineffective other corporate initiatives. Even so, many of the stellar examples that remain would be doing a better job if given more effective tools. The point is that most collection functions give evidence of a system that just is not working very well.

The symptoms of an underperforming credit department

are overworked or burnt-out collectors, constant fire fighting as opposed to prevention activities, and stagnant or declining measures of collection performance. Underlying these symptoms is a long list of challenges facing credit and collection departments (see Exhibit 5.1). When these challenges are not successfully negotiated, there is a decided impact on the collection process, ranging from poor cash flow performance and repetitive deduction problems to damaged customer relationships. These symptoms are, in fact, so universal that for the most part they are overlooked and taken as the status quo. This is just like the example of the lumberjack, (see Exhibit 1.1), who is exhausted and frustrated by every attempt to improve his

Exhibit 5.1   Challenges Facing Credit and Collection Departments

1. Past due accounts receivable balances too high
2. Too few collection calls being made and correspondence going out
3. Priority setting is inconsistent from day to day and from collector to collector
4. Inability to monitor each collector's daily activity
5. Inconsistent performance among collectors
6. Small accounts are overlooked
7. No coverage for absent collectors
8. Volume of adjustments (credit and debits) is too high
9. Deduction follow-up falls through the cracks
10. The same types of deductions keep recurring
11. Inadequate reporting to management
12. Staffing constraints
13. Increases in transaction volume
14. Customer relationships are not being managed

performance so long as he is committed to trying to get the job done with only an axe and his own sweat.

WHEN CREDIT AND COLLECTION RESOURCES ARE STRETCHED TOO THIN

With the lumberjack, time and the elements were constantly working against him. Whether it was an axe that got duller with every swing, stormy weather, or poor health, he never seemed able to quite reach his maximum capacity and faced a great deal of difficulty achieving even incremental gains in productivity. The law of unintended consequences seemed to be constantly working against him. As a result, he was worn out, he was always trying to get caught up, and, not surprisingly, his performance stagnated.

The same holds true for many credit departments. Not only must they deal with the unintended consequences of automating accounts receivable without automating collections, but the business climate has worked against them. It is not without good reason that cost-conscious companies are cynically termed "leaner and meaner." Even those credit and collection departments that have not been subjected to a downsizing initiative feel the effects of the cost-cutting corporate mindset that has become so prevalent in the 1990s. The sister of downsizing is the corporate merger. In this scenario, the administrative arm absorbs the operations of each new division, increasing workload without increasing administrative staff. While downsizing and mergers reduce resources, corporate growth increases the need for those additional resources that credit and collection departments are hard pressed to get. In addition, quality initiatives such as ISO 9000 and Total Quality Management (TQM) often increase the demands on credit and collection departments and their staffs by increasing administrative requirements, especially for understaffed departments that have been cutting corners to get the job done as best they can.

It is no wonder that credit and collection veterans feel stressed out. As sales go up, so do transaction volumes and the number of customers to be contacted. Keeping up would be hard enough without interruptions, but by its very nature, credit and collections involves constantly managing multiple responsibilities so that interruptions are just a way of life. The problem is that, in a fast-paced environment such as credit and collections, interruptions can be overwhelming. In this scenario, long hours are the norm, which makes it all the more difficult to get rejuvenated. Also, there is no buffer to help collectors through those crunch times when they are already working long hours. Psychologists tell us that often it is the little things that cause us the greatest frustration. With credit and collections formulated as they are in this day and age, the little pressures are incessant. It is no wonder that burnout among credit and collection workers shows itself as a symptom of a system that is not working as well as it should.

Contributing to collector burnout is the prevalence of fire fighting as part of the normal routine in many credit and collection departments. Typically, collectors are drawn from one crisis to another in a vicious cycle that never lets up. Pressured by both internal and external customers, these crises include anxious salespeople awaiting orders that have been put on hold by the accounting system and the occasional customer that goes into bankruptcy without warning. In both cases, the credit manager is naturally painted as the demon. In the case of the held order, it is perceived that the credit person should drop everything immediately and contact the customer or just simply release the order. The bankruptcy situation is even more pressing. The credit manager, whether there were any apparent warning signs, is perceived as directly reducing profits by stopping shipments—possibly both before and after the bankruptcy filing—or draining profits with bad debt expenses. The stress this causes manifests itself by the apparent resignation of credit and collection personnel to the way things are done as perceived by those outside the organization and the feeling that "that is just the way he or she is" by those within the corporation.

Always busy, but never able to get caught up, collectors often feel helpless to improve their situation. The problem with being in constant fire-fighting mode is that while a total effort is being put forth to address the crisis of the moment, nothing is being accomplished that will prevent a similar crisis from recurring. Planning and prevention are virtually nonexistent, and so is any chance of improvement.

It is no wonder then that for credit and collection departments, where crisis management is the norm and employees are burnt out, collection performance by most any measure is stagnant or in decline. Of course, collectors cannot be blamed when customers choose to delay their payments, but the fact remains that circumstances have conspired to impede collection performance. If a company is having difficulty collecting, chances are there are problems with its collection systems.

However, slow collections are only a symptom of a credit and collection function that is not performing up to par, just as collectors, burned out from constantly fighting fires and working in a pressure cooker environment, give evidence of an ineffective system. In order to turn things around, the many challenges facing today's typical credit and collection department must be successfully addressed.

PAST DUE ACCOUNTS RECEIVABLE BALANCES TOO HIGH

The primary challenge facing most credit and collection departments is too many past due receivables on the books. When one thinks of a delinquent account, the first image that comes to mind is the customer who, for whatever reason, is just not paying. Large-balance, slow-paying customers are usually given a high priority in terms of a company's collection efforts. However, it should be recognized that past due invoices come in many forms and that a nonperforming asset is just that.

Partial payments, payment deductions, open debits, and so forth can all cause considerable problems. In fact, it is likely that these balances should not be classified as accounts receivable because the vast majority of them will be written off after being researched. Even though the dollars involved are not as high as for the customer who is not paying at all, the number of small partial balances can add up besides taking an inordinate amount of time to resolve. That, in effect, is the problem with all past due balances of all forms: They take away time that could be devoted to keeping the productive portions of an accounts receivable current.

The challenge then is to reduce past due accounts receivable balances so that the bulk of the collection effort can be devoted to helping customers to pay on time. When the bulk of one's efforts are put into solving old problems, most of his or her time is spent in a reactionary mode. Every piece of research is a challenge because neither the collector nor the customer has easy access or recollection to the transactions in question. It is the fire drill scenario that seems to never end. However, once past due receivables are brought down to a more manageable level, the emphasis can be shifted toward prevention. When one is reacting, the same problems end up being solved over and over again. When preventative measures are taken, the system is corrected so that errors do not reoccur, ultimately a tremendously more efficient mode of operation.

TOO FEW COLLECTION CALLS BEING MADE AND CORRESPONDENCE GOING OUT

It seems almost too simplistic to say that to collect more one needs to be completing more collection activities, but it is the truth. Everyone seems to understand this; however, getting people to make the commensurate behavioral adjustments is another matter. The tendency is to give more weight to urgency than to importance. This derives from the prevalent crisis management scenario typical of most credit and collection departments.

Again, the problem stems from the reactive mode that results. Unless the vicious cycle can be broken that has collectors darting from problem to problem and focusing time on releasing orders rather than pro-actively contacting customers, nothing can be done about addressing the underlying causes. In the meantime, current receivables are allowed to become past due, and with a little time and inattention they just add to the crisis situation. Some collectors are buried so deep in this situation that they see contacting customers on credit hold and releasing orders as appropriate as their primary collection function. They have written off the task of pro-actively training their customer base to pay on time as an impossibility not worth focusing on.

The obvious solution is to make more collection calls, send more faxes, and mail more letters. This reduces the number of invoices that become seriously delinquent, which in turn decreases the number of items that become problems. As collectors' attention focuses on the newer receivables in an accounts receivable portfolio, they begin to realize much more value for their efforts. By increasing the number of initial contacts made and by following up diligently on customers' promises to pay, collectors will begin to multiply their collection results as customers get trained in a new set of expectations about the company as a supplier.

PRIORITY SETTING IS INCONSISTENT

When collectors jump from one problem to another, they seldom give thought to the critical demands of the day. They think they are, but in effect they are merely reacting to urgency. The idea that there may be something more important to do than answer the latest distress call is simply not considered. An added problem is that each collector will react differently to the situation at hand, especially when faced with multiple problems. It is not surprising then that priority setting is inconsistent at best and nonexistent at worst.

This inconsistency takes three forms. First is the inconsistency caused by intermittent priority setting. In a fast-paced environment in which little time or attention is given to planning activities, systematic priority setting is not the norm. If setting priorities is not a regular task, it is bound to pick up noticeable inconsistencies. When priority setting is intermittent, it is more likely to be influenced by the current agenda rather than by a long-range focus on collection goals.

The second form is increased inconsistencies in priority setting between individual collectors when priority setting on the departmental level is not managed. The less direction individual collectors are given, the more likely it is that personal preferences and work habits will affect the decisions they make, including how they set priorities. The result is a significant divergence between different collectors in the same department as to how they order their own work.

The third case is a constant shift in priorities. For a few weeks, usually before the end of a fiscal quarter, it is about driving down the over-90-day balances to minimize the firm's reserve requirements. Next, the shift in priorities may be to a specific segment of the customer base because the operations management for that area has communicated distress or disappointment. Then, perhaps the focus turns to large invoices in an effort to pick low-hanging fruit to overcome a short-term cash crunch. Of course, a new fiscal quarter is always around the corner to start the cycle again.

With priorities being set inconsistently, intermittently, and in different directions, it is highly unlikely that any collection effort can be clearly focused for long-term results. Instead, there are piecemeal efforts that breed piecemeal results, with both the collection staff and management resigned to the apparent fact that prioritizing is impossible. One of the requirements for a successful collection operation is a consistent collection effort. With a consistent focus, choosing the proper sequence for contacting accounts matched with the proper collection vehicle followed by systematic follow-up procedures is an absolute must. Consistent priorities are central to persistent collections. The challenge then is to make priority setting as systematic and consistent as possible.

INABILITY TO MONITOR EACH COLLECTOR'S DAILY ACTIVITY

As mentioned earlier, most credit and collection departments today have automated their accounts receivable but are still relying upon what is essentially a manual collection process. Under this scenario, credit and collection managers have access to a wealth of accounts receivable data that allows them to monitor DSO, top-dollar accounts, aging percentages, and so forth. However, these are all snapshot measurements. They tell managers where they are but provide little real insight as to how they got there and what is being done to control the asset.

What is missing is the ability to monitor each collector's activity. This should be available on a historical basis so that supervisors have the flexibility of monitoring longer time spans at their convenience. If supervisors knew how many contacts each collector was making on a daily average, the form those contacts were taking (phone call, fax, letter), and the dollars involved in those contacts, much more could be done to maximize collection efforts. Why DSO went up or down would be readily apparent. Which collection activities were the most effective could be more easily determined. Who was meeting collection goals and whose performance was lagging would be clearly seen. Supervisors would then know where remediation was needed, and other decisions could be made with a high level of assurance that they would be effective.

The fact is, just monitoring these things and letting the collectors know they are being monitored will increase contact volume. It is absolutely true that "You get what you inspect." Monitoring collection activities says, "We care how many customer contacts are made."

This information, of course, can be derived from a manual collection system, but it must be collected and processed manually. That means collectors would be required to log in all their activities, a time-consuming process in itself. That does not even take into account the time needed to manually tabulate and analyze this data. For this reason, few credit and collection departments, already stretched to capacity, have been willing to add this burden to their staffs.

The benefits of added supervisory intelligence are far outweighed by the lost time that could be devoted to collections. A computerized collection system should provide this information automatically. Because the system is recording the information as each collector goes about his or her daily routine, no time is lost. By the same token, supervisors do not have to work with raw data, but can instead review tabulated results.

Supervisors are not the only ones to benefit. The individual collectors have access to their own results. This continuous feedback is a tremendous self-motivator and is usually much more effective than anything a supervisor can say or do. Information about their individual collection activities provides collectors with a much greater sense of ownership in their own contribution to the overall process. Improved performance then comes naturally as daily and weekly goal setting becomes a habit and the impact of diversions are recognized immediately.

INCONSISTENT PERFORMANCE AMONG COLLECTORS

If priority setting is inconsistent and daily collection activities cannot be monitored, it almost goes without saying that there is a high probability that significant performance differences will exist between collectors. Since consistency is one of the keys to an effective collection effort, this is a serious challenge. It is also an opportunity, because if the minimum standards of acceptable performance can be raised, substantial improvements in the total collection effort will be realized.

Poor collection practices create the need for more collection activities. When a collector is not pulling his or her weight, other collectors end up with more accounts to monitor, and the collection supervisor or manager must deal with more accounts that have reached critical status. Continued poor collection practices regularly feed more work into the system.

This is highly counterproductive even before the demoralizing effects on a collection staff are considered. The problem is that everybody knows who is doing his or her job and who is not. Typically, when there is unequal treatment or people feel that some collectors are not carrying their share, staff morale suffers and along with it productivity. Such problems are complicated in that it is hard to deal with performance differences without documentary evidence. Therefore, the challenge of eliminating gross inconsistencies between collectors is tied to the challenge of tracking collector activity on a daily basis.

When collectors are meeting minimum standards, there is less chance for a resentful atmosphere to develop among them. The focus is then directed toward individual achievement rather than what everyone else is doing. By bringing all the collectors into compliance with the methods and procedures that make up the collection system, a greater degree of consistency in how things are done is also created. This too will contribute to more consistent results.

In studying collection departments that have installed an automated collection process, it is common to see a 10 to 15 percent staff turnover just before and immediately after the installation of the new system. Supervisors suggest that a reluctance to work in an environment with heightened accountability is the source of this turnover. With the exception of environments in which downsizing initiatives warrant that resignations translate into reductions in the long-term head count, this turnover is generally perceived as positive.

SMALL ACCOUNTS ARE OVERLOOKED

In the environment that has been described, it is not hard to imagine how small accounts can be overlooked. In the face of high past due balances, collectors do not have enough time to get all their work done. Priority setting is inconsistent, causing subsequent collection efforts to be uneven. It is no wonder that something has to give, and that is often any attention by collectors to small accounts.

When faced with time and staffing restraints, it makes sense to allocate resources toward maintaining adequate coverage of larger accounts. In these circumstances, applying Pareto's law, the 80/20 rule, to the collection effort is backed by good logic. However, that is not something that should be done over the long run. As small accounts drift farther past due, they become harder to collect, and any underlying disputes become much harder to resolve.

The impact of this symptom has expanded as manufacturers, in their search for increased margins and improved supply chain control, have moved away from multitier distribution to the direct model. The traditional solution is increased head count in collections. However, as shown, the initial projections of head count and working capital required fall short once the compounding effect of adding significant components to the workload takes effect.

In a sense, the fact that small accounts are overlooked is a subset of the problem of not enough collection calls being made. However, the challenge is to give them appropriate attention. Small accounts do not warrant the same handling as large accounts, not so much because the dollars involved are lower, but because small accounts are different. While small accounts are how companies build market share, the low balances they require and small profits they generate do not warrant the costs of performing individual credit analyses. As a result, they also require less costly collection strategies (i.e., faxes instead of phone calls). In addition, small customers are often less organized and undercapitalized, so lost invoices are more common as well as their reliance on the vendor as a source of short-term working capital. The added capacity that comes with an automated collection system makes it much easier to allocate an appropriate amount of attention to small accounts.

NO COVERAGE FOR ABSENT COLLECTORS

When a collector is out sick or on vacation, coverage of that person's accounts is typically minimal. Only those accounts that are past due and need an order released have any assurance of being thoroughly attended to. Otherwise, the accounts in question are left to age on their own until the collector returns to work. As mentioned previously, a significant amount of man-hours are needed to make up for this lost work over the course of a year.

The reason more attention is not given to an absent collector's accounts is that, besides being extra work, it is very time-consuming work. Chances are the collector's record-keeping system is not the same as his or her peers, so additional time is required to track down all the information needed to make a call. Just reading someone else's notes on an aging report is a challenge, not to mention understanding their abbreviations, hieroglyphics, and color coding.

Harder yet is establishing any priorities between co-workers' accounts; after all, most of the vital information is in their heads, not in their files and notes. Unless a collector is expected to be out for an extended period of time, it is not only easier just to let the work go until he or she returns, it is probably more efficient. For all the time collectors spend on the absent co-worker's accounts, they are losing even more productivity on their own.

With an automated collection system, this challenge is met by the fact that the status of any account and the next logical collection step is apparent to any collector using the system. When a collector is absent, then, account assignments can be shuffled and collection priorities adjusted so that collection resources are configured to achieve maximum collection coverage. Despite collector absences, life must go on. Automating collections makes this a much easier undertaking.

ADJUSTMENT VOLUME IS TOO HIGH

It is not uncommon for manufacturing firms to have to rebill or otherwise adjust over five percent of their invoices. A 1993 study by the Credit Research Foundation reported that for consumer product companies, between 5 and 15 percent of all receivables end up as customer payment deductions. Besides the fact that there is a serious quality issue if customers believe that one out of every ten of a company's invoices is incorrect, deduction issues are often more time consuming to resolve than an undisputed past due invoice is to collect.

The most damaging consequence of high adjustment volumes is the time and costs expended managing their resolution. Resolving deduction issues clearly takes away from other, more productive credit and collection activities. This is just one piece of the puzzle. Even more costly is the sales time spent researching and communicating with the credit department and the customer about these historical issues. Sales time lost translates into reduced revenues and market share, the highest costs an organization can incur. Besides the carrying costs from having deductions linger on an accounts receivable and the potential bad debt losses they represent, the time spent resolving deductions is the largest cost created by deduction issues.

Because deduction transactions tend to age two to three times as long as past due invoices, only 5 to 15 percent of invoices generated can turn into 10 to 45 percent of a corporation's open transactions. This volume of open issues can become mind boggling, given that customers believe these are items they are under no obligation to pay or even research. It is, therefore, not surprising to find that over 95 percent of deductions are eventually credited or written off, and that many manufacturers outsource or assign collection of these transactions to third parties.

The other significant consequence for companies carrying over five percent of their transactions as deduction issues is the loss of profits. Deductions represent an unproductive asset whose value deteriorates daily. Reducing the adjustment volume will add significant amounts of cash over time to bottom-line profits. However, clearing up a backlog of deductions from receivables rarely produces a windfall, because the effort and specialized knowledge required to research these long overdue, disputed items is monumental. The best solution is usually to outsource; however, the outsourcing service provider then becomes a partner in the recovered profit.

Studies show that the majority of deduction issues are settled in favor of the customer. Even with the large volume of transactions that are not collected because of the inefficiency of researching long overdue disputes, the numbers strongly suggest that the underlying cause of deductions lies with the provider of goods or services. Therefore, an effective deduction management program must identify and correct the internal corporate practices that give rise to deductions. As collections are automated, the problem tracking, coding, and reporting features of the collection software provide the intelligence necessary to identify past problems for the purpose of eliminating future adjustments.

DEDUCTION FOLLOW-UP FALLS THROUGH THE CRACKS

Along the same lines, the biggest hassle in resolving deductions is the time and energy it takes to move a deduction to resolution through a company's own corporate structure. Because most deduction issues are not credit related and are instead related to such things as pricing, shipping, quality, and so on, resolving a deduction typically involves one or two other departments within the company. Deduction resolution is seldom a priority for these other departments; therefore, tactful follow-up on the part of collectors is necessary to prevent these items from being neglected. The longer deductions are neglected, the greater is the likelihood that there will not be any recovery.

In fact, there may even be incentives for other departments not to resolve deductions. Issuing credits to customers can reduce sales figures, so it is not uncommon for a customer service or sales department to put off issuing credits to another period so the current period's quotas can be met. This type of manipulation is clearly counterproductive to both the company and its customers, but unless an effective system for following up on deductions exists, overcoming the corporate inertia that allows this type of shortsightedness to be perpetuated will not be possible.

An automated collection system that includes a deduction management feature makes it much easier for collectors to identify, follow, and resolve deduction issues. Just as with an external customer, it should be made as easy as possible for internal contacts to act on the matter at hand. Automated ticklers, status reports, and access to account and invoice details make this possible. The key here is to monitor the deduction as it moves through the organization, tracking dates and timeliness at each phase of the process.

SAME TYPES OF DEDUCTIONS KEEP RECURRING

Another deduction challenge is the recurrence of similar types of deductions. The reason for this repetition, particularly when the same problems keep recurring but with different customers, is a company's own internal corporate practices. If the systems are fixed, the deductions will go away. It really is that simple. The tough part is convincing workers outside of the credit and collection department that their systems need fixing. This is where the powerful graphic reporting capabilities of an automated collection system can help.

The things a company is doing that cause its customers to take deductions may be quite arcane, though often they will be very obvious. Complicated pricing formulas, unreliable methods for calculating freight charges, promotional programs, the failure to review purchase orders and even poorly designed invoices, to name a few, can cause customers to take deductions from their payments. Often, the company's noncredit workers are aware that these things are occurring, but they believe the cost of getting things right is not worth the effort. Only when the costs of making mistakes are documented can a strong case be made for changing the underlying practices.

Eliminating duplicate types of deductions is not a challenge that is easily attained. It takes political expertise and well-organized data to illustrate the inherent costs and the extent of these problems. Automated collection software makes this much more feasible than does manually compiling the necessary information. Even armed with the necessary data, it is often a long, uphill battle to create the changes necessary to eliminate a deduction. The information the system provides helps prioritize these change activities so that the battle can be focused on the deduction categories with the highest return on time invested.

INADEQUATE REPORTING TO MANAGEMENT

Most companies generate credit and collection reports only after the fiscal close for each month. Until the next period's close, other than tracking how much cash is coming in, it is anybody's guess as to what is happening in terms of credit and collection performance. Also, it may take as much as a week to compile the monthly credit department reports, so that by the time they can be reviewed and strategies set for the coming month, there may be only 2 weeks or so to work with.

Another shortcoming of the traditional reporting methods and metrics is their susceptibility to rise as a result of seasonality, sales trends, and terms modifications. Because collectors realize that these factors affect DSO, aging percentages, and other traditional measurements so that these metrics are not directly indicative of the collector's efforts, traditional reports are for the most part not motivational.

That conventional reporting methods treat all receivables as equals is another major shortcoming. To report receivables correctly, one needs to distinguish the receivables by stage of the collection process. These stages tell much more than standard aging buckets, which lose value, particularly when different customer portfolios have different terms or characteristics. For example, a distributor's receivable that has 90-day terms is quite different from an end user's 30-day invoice, especially when they are both 35 days past due. Additionally, problem transactions in which issues other than inadequate follow-up or slow payment are the cause (i.e., disputed items) need to be segregated.

The lack of reporting on this type of information has created an environment in which financial managers lack the distinctions necessary to truly understand overdue receivables. Because systems do not exist to highlight this information, academia has done little to arm financial managers with information on how to monitor the effective control of receivables. In its place, the emphasis has been on the subject of risk analysis, an interesting but very different discipline designed to monitor the probability of loss, with little impact on speeding collections once a decision to sell has been made.

Improved reporting, however, allows the focus to remain on goals and appropriate adjustments to be made whenever there is evidence of getting off track. Collection automation software enables one to review each day's activities and results, so in addition to seeing what is happening, one can also see what is being done. This added intelligence then provides a sound base for subsequent tactical decisions.

STAFFING CONSTRAINTS

Growth, downsizing, and mergers have left most corporate functions understaffed. Credit and collections have not been immune to this trend that seeks a leaner and meaner organization. Some would even claim that being a back office function, credit and collections has endured more than its share of slights in this area compared to other departments. None of this changes the fact that it is very difficult to convince management to add collectors or other credit staff in this day and age.

Outsourcing and the use of temporary workers provide

some relief, but most organizations have not gone these routes. Both of these options also have their drawbacks. Pragmatically, there is a conflict of interest that could prevent the outsourcing service provider from sharing specialized knowledge with the credit department or, worse yet, the corporation. Neither gets at the underlying causes of the inefficiencies that impede the collecting process. Though outsourcers bring their expertise to the fray, they must still interface with the company's systems, which can be a drag on their performance. In a sense, outsourcers used this way provide a tactical cover for the credit department's weaknesses, not a solution. Strategic outsourcing, however, is built on best practices, so the decision to outsource is more directly related to the most beneficial allocation of resources than to simply trying to fix a problem.

The centralized information source, communication, and reporting capabilities of an automated collection system enable the outsourcing provider, in addition to providing all of the information necessary to collect invoices and research deductions, remote access to the collection system enabled by internet e-mail and the system's own reporting capabilities. This allows the outsourcing provider to work from a physically remote location and still be effective. With this infrastructure in place, the outsourcing provider can be monitored and measured and operate as if they were resident. The distribution of information possibly will become even more dramatic as imaging solutions become common and are put to use capturing remittance advice and other support documents required to research and collect deductions.

The problem with temporary workers is the time it takes them to move far enough along the learning curve to be truly productive. Often, their assignment ends even before they reach that point. One of the reasons for the extended learning curve is the complexity of most companies' credit and collection systems. Temporary collectors may know how to make collection calls, but they probably do not know where to find all the information they need to make those calls and answer customer questions. However, with an automated collection system, that information is at their fingertips and the learning curve is drastically shortened.

The learning curve is also a factor should the company decide to add new hires. They are not going to learn the systems any faster than a temporary collector would, so the increase in collection capacity and the subsequent impact on collection results is gradual. However, when collection capacity is increased by automating the collection process, the impact is immediate. In fact, it is not uncommon in an automated environment to have newly trained staff outperform veteran employees who have been using the manual process for years and are reluctant to convert to the automated environment within a short time span.

CUSTOMER RELATIONSHIPS ARE NOT BEING MANAGED

Much attention is given by sales management to the importance of building relationships with customers. Credit and collections need to share this focus. One hindrance, presumably unintended, is that credit and collections is often separated from sales and customer service both physically and in terms of the corporate hierarchy. Accounting and finance departments, whose control most credit and collection departments come under, rarely interface with the personnel who are the point of contact for the customer's purchase. The role of accounting and finance is primarily one of corporate facilitation and cleanup. Under these circumstances, it is easy to understand why credit and collections has a tendency to overlook the development of customer relationships, instead paying close attention to the more easily quantifiable financial interests of the corporation.

While the numbers cannot be ignored, those who focus on them exclusively are focused on the short term. Building customer relationships, however, requires a longer-term outlook. This is something credit needs to share with the various sales and marketing functions within the corporation, but unfortunately that is too seldom the case.

When building customer relationships becomes a priority for credit and collections, the basis for credit and collection decisions changes. When past dues and bad debts are guiding the decision-making process, the tendency to deny credit and take a hard-line approach to collections takes precedence over the idea of maximizing long-term customer profitability. A credit and collections mindset based on building customer relationships is very different from the traditional credit perspective regarding customers. This relational perspective drives increased communication and speedy resolution of disputes. Frequently, the credit department represents the customer's interests in settling disputes and negotiating workable payment terms when cash flow problems are the acknowledged nonpayment issue.

When credit and collections make this switch, improved customer relationships result in a more amicable and productive collection environment along with increased portfolio profitability. This is because problems are resolved more quickly and permanently when all the involved parties know each other and understand each other's way of doing things.

INCREASED TRANSACTION VOLUMES REQUIRE MORE COLLECTIONS

When a corporation is enjoying increased demand for its products, that growth is putting added pressure on its collectors because of increases in the volume of accounts receivable transactions. When the initial growth is not accompanied by an increase in the number of customers, this can be a subtle challenge. It is not too difficult for most collection operations to absorb a 10 percent increase in transactions. However, if that rate continues over a period of just 7 years, the number of transactions the collectors must monitor will have virtually doubled. Along with more invoices to collect, increased volume means a larger number of short payments, more problems to research, and additional transactions to discuss during each contact.

To respond to growth, there are essentially two choices to successfully manage the situation: add staff or work smarter. In this age of the leaner and meaner corporation, adding staff is a hard sell for the credit manager and his or her manager. This means collectors must learn to work smarter. However, incremental improvements will not facilitate the handling of a workload that has doubled. As a result, growth companies that do not add staff find themselves floundering a little more each year, the symptom of which is a gradual increase in the proportion of receivables that get paid beyond terms. This increase often goes unnoticed because it is sometimes hidden in the DSO calculation that is benefiting by the continual increase in sales.

Automating collections, as opposed to incremental improvements, is the one way to radically improve the productive capacity of a collection department. It is the means by which a credit department can catch up with corporate growth in the face of staffing limitations.

SUMMARY

So far, this chapter has discussed the symptoms exhibited by credit and collection departments in this day and age: overworked or burnt-out collectors, constant fire fighting rather than prevention, and stagnant or declining measures of credit performance. Underlying these symptoms, 14 challenges facing the typical credit and collection department have been identified. How each of these challenges is addressed impacts collection performance. A discussion of these challenges could not help but reflect this cause-and-effect relationship.

However, the impact of a modern credit and collection environment on the collection process can be summarized in just three categories:

1. Cash flow suffers
2. Adjustment volume is too high
3. Customer relations are damaged

This is because the challenges are for the most part all interrelated. Remember, this is a collection process, not a single discreet task termed *collections* nor a conglomeration of tasks that have their prime focus on something other than collections that might still impact collections. The problem is that too many companies share these last two views of collections. For example, some companies see resolving pricing issues as a function of sales or customer service and only peripherally a collection issue, unless it becomes a major problem. By the same token, shipping or billing decisions may be made with little or no thought to their impact on collections. The mindset that recognizes collections as a process is too seldom realized.

All 14 challenges affect cash flow in one way or another. As a result, when credit and collection departments successfully address these challenges, cash flow improves dramatically. Of course, this also means that when any of these challenges are not overcome, cash flow is restrained. This makes a comprehensive solution an imperative. Halfway measures got us into this situation and therefore cannot be expected to get us out. Using automation tools to re-engineer the collection process, however, does meet the challenges collectors face today.

If cash flow is suffering, chances are bad debt expenses are not where they could be either. After all, it has been proven that the older a debt is, the more likely it is to become a bad debt. The level of bad debts, therefore, are also related to how well you are meeting all of these challenges. Automating collections, because it improves cash flow, ultimately reduces a company's bad debt expense and exposure.

The effects of damaged customer relationships are more subtle. Still, most of the challenges do affect customer relationships. For example, staffing constraints will often increase the time it takes to resolve customer problems. A lack of collection coverage can mean small balances do not get cleared from customer statements as quickly as they should, causing customers to spend more time reconciling statements than they would like. This type of "little thing" obviously adds up over time, affecting not only the effectiveness of a company's collections, but also the customer's overall perception of the company. This can depress sales and especially profits since uncooperative accounts are relatively costly to manage. However, when all the challenges facing the credit and collection department are met, a significant upsurge in customer satisfaction can be expected. Efficiency on the company's part comes across as caring in the customer's eyes, and that builds customer loyalty.

That is one of the amazing things about using automation to re-engineer the collection process: A major reason a company collects more, sooner, is that its customers are more willing to pay. It is a classic win–win dynamic. Customers see their problems being resolved quickly and their accounts kept up to date. In return, this makes it easier for them to process subsequent payments to the company and leaves them without any excuses, because of the company's actions, not to do so. As a result, fewer collection calls must be made, and when they are, the discussion centers on recent (if not current) invoices, which are easier for all parties involved to address promptly.

Instead of fighting brush fires, the company is now preventing problems, improving its customer relationships, communicating higher payment expectations to its customers, and, as a result, significantly improving its measures of collection performance. A much more satisfying working environment is being created for the collectors. Instead of facing burnout, the collectors' morale will take a turn for the better, as will their personal productivity. By overcoming the challenges facing today's credit and collection departments, the downward spiral that has dogged the profession for years can be broken and the rewards of a dynamic new way of doing things enjoyed.

6

Manual Collection Process

Before moving on to how the collection process can be re-engineered and automated, a thorough understanding of just what transpires during the manual collection process is required. How the current state of affairs in most corporate collection functions came about has already been explained. What is now necessary is to outline in detail just what that point is. Only then can the task of reconstructing the collection process be begun.

The recent wave of re-engineering initiatives has caused many organizations to examine their order to cash cycle. When the analysis is complete and the figures from the activity inventory are summarized, they are finding that their administrative staff may be devoting over half of their time to postsale activities. This collection and deduction resolution process is burdened not only by its own complexity but also by the inability of corporate systems to get things right the first time during the order fulfillment process. Inefficiency is breeding even more inefficiency and stressing manual systems to the breaking point. This being the case, the collection cycle, described in Chapter 3, is clearly critical to the consummation of the order fulfillment process. If collections are not efficient, a company is left with a constant stream of loose ends resulting from the inefficiencies of its order fulfillment process.

Remember, the cycle is composed of five stages: prioritizing, preparing, contacting, following up, and reporting. Before re-engineering and automating collections is begun, in order to build a higher capacity, more efficient collection process, there must be a thorough understanding of the manual components that presently make up each stage of the collection cycle. Then collection activities can be evaluated from the perspective that the components of the old procedures may or may not live on in the re-engineered process. The importance or irrelevance of all the encompassing discreet tasks that make up current collection systems will then become much more apparent.

PRIORITIZATION

Determining which accounts to work on, who to call first, and when to send faxes is critical to an effective collection system. Prioritization is therefore where the collection cycle begins. The accounts receivable software being used by most credit and collection departments will provide some tools that help complete this task, but the task remains an essentially manual one. Therein lie the drawbacks to the current way of doing things. When prioritization is done manually, it is prone to inconsistency and it takes time.

Inconsistency occurs for a number of reasons. For one thing, different collectors will approach their portfolio of accounts differently. One person might like to call old accounts first while another prefers calling large accounts first. This can create quite different outcomes. Collectors who call their old accounts first will probably minimize the number of very old receivables in their portfolio, but, on average, their other accounts may be paying slower than they should. Collectors who call on large balances first will likely have good cash flow from their receivables, but the smaller accounts could end up accumulating on the aged receivables trial balance in the oldest aging category. Assuming the skill levels and effort put out by these two collectors was comparable, the days sales outstanding (DSO) and the amount of write-offs for each of their accounts receivable portfolios could differ substantially solely because of their different priorities.

In response to the apparent shortcomings in the prioritization of collection activities, some accounts receivable systems have implemented "semi-automated tools." Although clearly a step in the right direction, this type of capability falls far short in its ability to generate a re-engineered collection process. Semi-automatic prioritization is doomed to failure because the information that the accounts receivable system draws on is limited to accounting information.

Accounting is a black-and-white world that is not suited to continual renegotiation and adjustment. Accounting transactions by definition must be able to be audited and reconciled. Collection activities, in contrast, are far more fluid, being subject to human interference and so are affected by the competence of the order taker, the shipper, and the payment clerk, not to mention the financial condition of the customer. The accounting system sees a black-and-white world of open or paid transactions based on the original agreement a supplier has made with its customer. It expects invoices to be paid in full within terms. The accounts receivable system is blind to concepts like the grace period beyond terms that many customers expect as a common courtesy; special payment terms negotiated after invoicing in response to the customer's situation; or errors in the product, service, or price charged on the invoice. The accounts receivable database lacks the data points for a system to include these parameters and therefore cannot generate a prioritized activity list.

The semi-automated tools usually begin with a computer-generated report or list displayed on a computer screen. It includes all customers that meet some criterion or parameter expressed in terms available to the accounts receivable software system. One example might be all customers with balances over 60 days sorted by the over-60-day balance. The hope is that this tool will create a prioritized list for contact. That premise holds pretty close the first day the semi-automated system is put into process. Unfortunately, as soon as the system comes into contact with customers, the tool loses its ability to represent a viable calling plan. This is because as customers make new payment promises, the semi-automated tools have no way of temporarily eliminating those customers from follow-up. The customer that was overdue 3 days ago and committed to payment a week from now will show up on the list daily.

With the semi-automated tool, the collector must verify that each collection entry should be completed by checking notes on-screen, in the aging, on a calendar, or on the last few lists of output by the semi-automated collection tool. Semi-automation therefore falls short of making a significant impact on collections, although it may be perceived to provide token assistance by designers of accounts receivable systems.

Even if department-wide criteria for setting collection priorities are established, and are fortunate enough to be supported by a semi-automated tool, very few collectors will pick the same accounts to call first. The tasks each chooses to complete first depend upon a myriad of personal preferences, such as the following:

- "I have a headache, so I will call my problem customers tomorrow."
- "I am getting close to the end of the quarter and I need to make my numbers, so I will shift my attention to

> some large, easy-to-collect accounts—'*low hanging fruit.*' "

- "This account usually pays later on in the month, so I'll just wait and see and call somebody else instead."
- "I'm tired of making phone calls today, so I'll investigate and document these disputed items instead."

And the list goes on. The point is, with a manual or semi-automated process, each of these personal choices affect how collection priorities are set.

Besides creating inconsistencies, manual prioritization takes time. (See Exhibit 6.1.). Any time spent setting priorities takes away from the time available for contacting past due accounts. In fact, this time can be quite substantial, ranging from a half hour to an hour and a half each day. Because the majority of cash postings are updated at night, this task must be completed first thing each day; therefore, unless the collector is willing to intersperse the prioritization process with contacting activities, early morning contacts with accounts payable personnel—when that function is least harried—is not possible. Additionally, the opportunity of getting right into contacting customers first thing in the morning while the collector is fresh and rested is wholly missed. To see how this can be so, one must examine how most collectors set their priorities.

Most collectors use either a handwritten or computer-

Exhibit 6.1   **Manual Prioritization Steps**

- Check tickler for promises and follow-ups
- Check aging report and notes
- Sort by balance

based tickler or calendar to keep track of the accounts that require follow-up based on previous customer promises to pay. At first, this sounds simple enough, and those using a computerized tickler system may even think it is high tech. However, after today's follow-ups are pulled out of the tickler file, each account must be checked against the accounts receivable database to determine if there is still a need for action. In other words, each account must be looked up on the computer to see if the item in question has been paid, credited, or otherwise dealt with. This may not take a lot of time, but it adds up.

Besides determining those previous commitments that require further collection efforts, those new items that require contact must be selected. This is done by looking over a printout of the accounts receivable aged trial balance, which is a more time-consuming process. It requires working one's way through each page of the aged accounts receivable trial balance, and if there are many customers, that can be quite a few pages. It also requires that each potential contact be checked against the computer record for payments and so forth. This step is where the semi-automated tools can help the manual process.

Some collectors try to get around this last step by recording each day's receipts on their aged accounts receivable trial balance. The problem is that it takes longer to record this information than it does to look up the account's current status on the computer. Even so, this unproductive activity persists and in fact is common. After potential contacts are selected, they still must be sorted by past due dollars. This is another, very time-consuming, manual operation.

Some collectors use semi-automated tools to complete the initial follow-up selection. In that case, the list of past due accounts needs to be purged of accounts scheduled on the calendar. If the calendar is a multipage document, this becomes a real challenge. To offset this problem, some accounting systems allow the user to store a note or follow-up date in the customer master file. (See Exhibit 6.2.) This allows the collector to jump to the main customer screen, review the follow-up date and any notes, then make a judgment as to whether to include the customer in the day's contact list. This is the classic case of automating manual activities without process redesign.

As one can see, prioritization done manually is a complex, cumbersome activity. Halfway steps intended to make prioritization easier, such as descending balance reports and computerized collection records, usually result in additional clerical chores intended to ease the process. (See Exhibit 6.3.) Because they are not fully integrated into the collection system, halfway measures are often counterproductive and are usually ignored a few weeks after introduction. Any improvements in one area of the collection cycle are offset by unintended inefficiencies in another. Complexity, in and of itself, also becomes a burden. The result is that valuable time is spent prioritizing and reprioritizing instead of contacting past due accounts.

PREPARATION

Once the accounts that need to be contacted have been selected and who should be contacted first determined, there remains the chore of preparing for each call or gathering the information to be presented in each piece of correspondence. Effective collectors need to know what they are talking about. If they are not prepared, it is much easier for the customer to throw them off track, which will ultimately result in additional payment delays. Therefore, thorough preparation for each call is essential to a successful collection operation.

For the most part, preparing to make a follow-up call or send correspondence is a matter of gathering data. The better organized the accounts receivable display screens, the less time and effort will be required to get ready. Unfortunately, most systems have two or more screens that must be navigated in or-

Exhibit 6.2 **Aged Accounts Receivable Trial Balance with Handwritten Notes**

12-01-97	Aged Accounts Receivable Trial Balance					
Date	Invoice	Current	1–30	31–60	61–90	90+
ACME Widgets	#2019	Boonton, NJ		201-555-9696		
09/21/97	975201			~~5,024.60~~ *Pd 12/5*		
09/27/97	975324			1,235.43 *—Promised to pay—12/18*		
10/15/97	975652		435.98 *—Promised to pay 12/18*			
10/24/97	975698		2,301.75			
11/11/97	975923	253.53				
Subtotals		253.53	2,737.73	6,260.03	0.00	0.00
Yore Mfg. Corp.	#1853	Yardley, PA		215-555-5444		
06/22/97	973111					121.09 *—Freight & Pricing*
07/02/97	973678					78.44 *—Freight*
08/11/97	974001				108.92 *—Art & Pricing*	
09/08/97	975235			65.56 *—Art*		
09/19/97	975455			66.65 *—Art*		
10/23/97	977212		~~10,434.67~~ *Pd 12/17—deducted $74.36 Freight*			
11/05/97	977688	7,698.54				
11/21/97	977866	12,343.98				
Subtotals		20,042.52	10,434.67	132.21	108.92	199.53

Exhibit 6.3 Descending Aging by Aging Category

					09/30/97			Page 1 of 1
Name	City	State	Phone	Total Due	Current	1–30	31–60	Over 60
Acme Widgets	Ann Arbor	MI	313/555-1234	$47,801.42	$0.00	$0.00	$12,675.44	$35,125.98
Your Lion Heart	College Park	PA	717/555-4321	$39,811.31	$0.00	$1,143.87	$23,467.89	$15,199.55
Hoosier Products	Bloomington	IN	010/555-0798	$15,665.95	$0.00	$546.21	$3,666.39	$11,453.35
Buckeye Manufacturing	Cleveland	OH	181/555-4567	$67,839.18	$20.14	$0.00	$62,786.81	$5,032.23
Wildcat Industries	Evanston	IL	302/555-6785	$39,583.06	$24,895.46	$14,543.67	$0.00	$143.93
Cheesehead Inc.	Madison	WI	333/555-5600	$899.71	$0.00	$0.00	$764.56	$135.15
Gopher It	Minneapolis	MN	444/555-3965	$54,502.10	$0.00	$24,756.43	$29,745.67	$0.00
Spartan Furniture	East Lansing	MI	616/555-9587	$27,541.37	$6,549.68	$11,333.41	$9,658.28	$0.00
Indian Chief Corp.	Champaign	IL	222/555-8585	$66,054.52	$15,665.85	$44,245.42	$6,143.25	$0.00
Boilermaker Tools	Lafayette	IN	678/555-9000	$3,985.44	$1,434.44	$2,353.35	$197.65	$0.00
Wolverine Resources	Detroit	MI	313/555-3255	$107,990.97	$52,567.39	$55,423.58	$0.00	$0.00
Hawkeye Equipment	Iowa City	IA	777/555-4545	$32,198.08	$7,675.74	$24,522.34	$0.00	$0.00
Nittany Knick-Knacks	Pittsburgh	PA	814/555-1000	$99,869.03	$84,357.91	$15,511.12	$0.00	$0.00
Big Ten Enterprises	Chicago	IL	302/555-1010	$7,839.23	$250.00	$7,589.23	$0.00	$0.00
Useless Nuts	Columbus	OH	181/555-2999	$17,064.67	$15,766.33	$1,298.34	$0.00	$0.00
Badger Badges	Milwaukee	WI	333/555-4777	$668.22	$103.99	$564.23	$0.00	$0.00
Corn Country Enterprises	Des Moines	IA	777/555-3535	$33,850.93	$33,554.75	$296.18	$0.00	$0.00
Big Red Sprockets	Fort Wayne	IN	678/555-6300	$75,234.65	$75,234.65	$0.00	$0.00	$0.00
Agricultural Products Co.	Lansing	MI	616/555-7500	$52,456.09	$52,456.09	$0.00	$0.00	$0.00
GETPAID Software	Boonton	NJ	201/555-0024	$31,765.08	$31,765.08	$0.00	$0.00	$0.00
Wiley, Coyote, and Byrd	New York	NY	212/555-3333	$15,156.13	$15,156.13	$0.00	$0.00	$0.00
Fred's General Store	Newark	NJ	201/555-0900	$11,096.84	$11,096.84	$0.00	$0.00	$0.00
Northwestern Consultants	Chicago	IL	302/555-6116	$6,008.11	$6,008.11	$0.00	$0.00	$0.00
A2 Resources	Yardley	PA	215/555-5444	$2,333.66	$2,333.66	$0.00	$0.00	$0.00
Dianna's Supply Co.	Parsippany	NJ	201/555-2424	$509.87	$509.87	$0.00	$0.00	$0.00
Suzanne Associates	Philadelphia	PA	215/555-0700	$153.79	$153.79	$0.00	$0.00	$0.00

der to gather all the details they need. This is a direct result of business information systems that have evolved over the last three decades. Fragmentation follows a number of patterns, though, in general, six types of information are affected. What usually happens is that contact information, stored in five places on the computer, must be consolidated. Historical statistics, transaction details, order shipment records, payment information, and customer data are stored in separate databases. Therefore, before contacting a customer, most collectors must consolidate their prioritized list with notes kept on aging reports, calendars, call log sheets or in tickler files, besides information stored on a number of display screens in the accounting system. (See Exhibit 6.4.)

In a typical collection scenario, a collector starts by checking the customer information found on his or her aged accounts receivable trial balance. This is mostly historical data, although some of it can be quite recent. From the trial balance, the collector can see recent open invoices and possibly some recent handwritten contact notes if this is where they are recorded. If the report was well designed, a contact name, address, and phone number will also be included, but seldom will all the necessary

Exhibit 6.4 **Manual Tasks Performed in Preparation**

- Review latest balance on-line
- Retrieve credit files (and return when done)
- Check status of problems
- Get phone numbers or addresses
- Consolidate notes from aging reports, calendars, call log sheets
- Review open transactions in the order entry system for ship-to and line-item information

contact data be on the aged accounts receivable trial balance. Even if some contact data is on the report, the collector will most likely have to go elsewhere to fill in the blanks. This contact information is usually maintained in a computerized customer master file, but many systems lack the space for a secondary contact or fax and e-mail numbers. As a result, if all the contact information is not on the aged accounts receivable trial balance or displayed on a customer master file computer screen, the collector will resort to a Rolodex or pull the customer's physical credit file.

Once the collector knows who to call, write, fax, or e-mail and the appropriate numbers or addresses, the account balance information on the aged trial balance must be confirmed. This requires a check of the customer's computerized accounts receivable file. Many systems will also allow the collector to look up invoice details such as products sold, quantities, price, purchase order numbers, shipping details, and so forth. However, sometimes the collector will have to get this information from the paper invoice and bill of lading. In such cases, some collectors will go ahead with the call or letter without having these details, and look up the information only if it becomes an issue. Asking a collector for more invoice details is a prime example of an effective customer stall, which in this scenario would effectively render the collector's initial effort a waste of time. In particular, not having purchase order numbers available when the collector initially contacts past due accounts is a serious deficiency in the collection system. For this reason, most collectors prefer to gather as much information as possible prior to calling.

Before calling, sending letters, or preparing faxes, it is very useful if any trends can be detected in the customer's historical payment pattern. Increases in the number of days it takes a customer to pay, whether incremental or sudden, is critical information for collectors to have. This information will drive the questions a collector asks the debtor and will also determine to some extent the amount of time allowed before the next follow-up is scheduled. Most accounts receivable systems will track payments in some manner, often on one of the customer accounts receivable information computer screens. Otherwise, the collector can get some indication of the customer's payment trend from the aged accounts receivable trial balance and his or her best recollection of the customer's usual status. As can be imagined, it is very easy for collectors to miss a good number of important customer trends in these circumstances. Perceptions are often misleading.

The following historical data and information about customer characteristics are also needed by collectors.

- Does the customer take deductions?
- What are the customer's accounts payable procedures?
- How long does it take for the customer to cut a check?
- Who approves and signs the customer's checks?
- What pre-existing problems are still open on the customer's account?
- Does the customer always make the same types of claims to forestall payment?

Assuming that this type of information is documented somewhere, the collector must access it, assimilate it with the other facts about the account, and then return any files or records back to their proper place—all this in addition to making the call or sending the fax or letter. Obviously, the more fragmented the information systems, the longer this takes, and the easier it is to overlook an important piece of information. With a semi-automated receivables and a manual collection process, the alternative to preparation is not preparing. Preparing, however, is clearly the better practice. It is required for good service to customers. Preparation, however, has a high cost, in terms of time that could be spent contacting customers. Even using semi-automated tools, the manual process requires that more time be spent prioritizing and preparing than is usually spent contacting customers.

CONTACT

Contacting customers is the only value-added activity in the collection process. The object is to focus as much of a collector's time as possible on making contact with customers. The more customers contacted the faster the company collects. It is that simple. Unfortunately, manual systems make it difficult to maintain a high level of focus on customer contact activities. Too often, contact activities are minimal because nearly all the available time is consumed by the other four steps in the collection process.

In a manual system, the contact phase is primarily a one-customer-at-a-time proposition. The only exception to this is the processing of statements and possibly past due notices. Many accounts receivable software systems will automatically generate these items, or in-house programmers will create similar facilities. These outputs are usually relatively inflexible and are often ignored by customers. For companies with a significant volume of disputed transactions, the dunning process amplifies the negative impact of the initial error. Once a collector, customer service representative, or salesperson has been informed of an item in dispute, the customer expects the balance to be eliminated from its statement. In this case, the dunning notice only serves as a reminder of the bad service or pricing error, and worse yet, may even motivate the customer to find another supplier who can get it right. The customer will question why the supplier is not concentrating on fixing the problem instead of trying to collect something the customer does not owe.

Just one disputed transaction that keeps showing up on past due notices without being resolved can add to the customer's frustration and may severely impact its attitude toward the supplier.

Even so, past due notices and statements have been an effective tool for contacting large numbers of customers, especially those with small balances. However, that effectiveness is limited. Second- and third-letter series exhibit diminishing response rates, meaning that most of these accounts will eventually have to be telephoned. That brings us back to one-account-at-a-time contacts.

Because of the inherent weaknesses in semi-automated dunning systems, most activities in a manual collection environment will be phone calls, although special situations may necessitate an individualized letter or a fax. Before placing a call to a customer, the collector will have gathered all necessary information during the preparation phase. The collector will also have reviewed the account's status to determine what the nature of this contact will be. The collection call will then fall generally into two categories: first contacts and follow-ups. A follow-up is appropriate to find out why a promised payment has not been received yet, to see if a customer with cash flow problems is now able to pay, or to get back to a customer with more information that will hopefully resolve a dispute of some kind, to name a few situations.

The point is that the types of calls a collector working from a manual system may make often vary from call to call. The manual collection system's prioritization tools are generally not able to differentiate the previous collection activity taken against a past due. Past due accounts have therefore been primarily grouped by amount and age past due. Any groupings by collection stage or type of action to be taken—first fax, second fax, first call, second call to confirm commitment to pay, call to follow up for broken promise, call following the sending of documents relating to a dispute, final demand letter, and so on—are dependent on the collector's memory or a review of notes. This means collectors are constantly shifting gears as they move from account to account. There is therefore very little standardization in their work processes, which generally dampens productivity. This situation is even further exacerbated when, instead of phoning, letters and faxes must be composed. Collectors generally get more done in less time if they are just making calls or just sending letters. Switching between activities generally drops productivity. (See Exhibit 6.5.)

When initial contact is made, the majority of the collector's time on the call is spent reciting the past due items on an account in response to the customer's request for balance details. This frequently results in the collector's obtaining a status update on invoices that are already scheduled for payment. Poorly trained collectors may stop at this point, satisfied that they have expedited some cash, moving on to the next customer without getting payment commitments for every past due invoice. After all, they did get a promise to pay. Fatigue from spending so much time reciting invoice numbers and balances due combined with a desire to move on to the next account contribute to this behavior. When this happens, an informal, unspoken understanding develops between the collector and the customer that

Exhibit 6.5   **Manual Contact Activities**

- Send letters, faxes, and e-mails
- Make phone calls
- Identify and resolve problems
- Leave messages
- Record discussions and action taken
- Schedule follow-up on calendar or tickler

late payment of some of the customer's invoices is acceptable, and that is counterproductive.

Much of a collector's time on the phone is spent identifying and resolving problems. Those collection calls that do not run into any problems and result in a promise to pay or the age-old assertion that "a check is in the mail" are usually quite short. However, calls that uncover problems take time, and the information unearthed must be recorded on a call log, note screen, aging report, calendar, or some other component of the manual system. Of course, the results of quick calls that end up with a promise to pay must be recorded. Busy collectors, pressed for time, merely jot their notes on a calendar or on their aged accounts receivable trial balance. The problem with this, which will be discussed further in the next section on follow-up activities, is that these are not permanent records.

Contact time may also prove unproductive when the contact person the collector is trying to reach is unavailable. This occurs more often than not. If for some reason the collector is not able to reach anyone suitable at the customer's place of business, it becomes necessary to make a second or third call and, if still no contact is made, send a letter or fax. However, in most cases, there will be somebody at the customer's office with whom the collector can leave a message. These events—no contact and left message—need to be jotted down and follow-up calls scheduled. Most collectors will use a calendar or tickler file as a reminder that they need to try again. If the collector left a message or sent a note and the customer calls back, the reminder notes need to be checked off and the results of the call recorded.

With a manual collection system tied to computerized receivables, collectors are constantly retrieving information from one location, and digesting, modifying, and recording it in other locations. This is an overwhelming, extremely complicated ritual for new staff members, which makes it very difficult to get new collectors fully up to full speed in less than several months. This being the case, adding collectors can actually be counterproductive for the short term while existing personnel take time from their collections to provide training for those who are supposed to be providing relief. Once indoctrinated to the intricacies of the manual process, its inefficiency becomes just the way things are done. The law of unintended consequences is a harsh taskmaster when it comes to getting out of the black hole some collection functions have become.

FOLLOW-UP

In the manual process, the contact phase generally creates more work—the more contact, the more follow-up. If the contact results in a promise of immediate payment, there are still follow-up activities, such as logging the promise or sending a confirming fax, that must be completed. Often, however, the initial contact will set off a chain of events that result in many additional tasks. These activities constitute the follow-up phase of the collection cycle.

It was mentioned in the previous section that during the contact phase, some collectors jot call notes on whatever is convenient, calendars and aged accounts receivable reports being their first choices. These records can be kept around for future reference, but trying to find a particular piece of information or compiling a complete record of contacts from them is frustrating and time consuming. Keep in mind that this information is useful for more than just deciding what action to take next. Good call records can provide legal benefits for a claim when an account has become a hard-core debt. They are also useful for evaluating performance in terms of daily counts of calls completed and faxes sent.

One common ritual resulting from semi-automation's being applied to the manual environment involves transferring the notes from last month's aged accounts receivable trial balance to the new aging report. This becomes a once- or twice-monthly drain on a collector's time. While it may actually be a relaxing activity for some collectors, from management's perspective it just means less dialing, less contact, and less collections. Transferring the notes to a call log is better since the call log provides a permanent record, but this still entails a duplication of effort. Anytime call information must be recorded more than once, valuable time is lost.

Credit organizations committed to professionalism will usually insist that call records be kept in one of several more permanent formats. Some companies keep their call logs in the customer's credit file. This has the advantage of consolidating all the information about the customer in one place. Regardless, it is very time consuming to pull the file of each customer to be contacted and then return the file afterward. This also requires a considerable amount of personal discipline, and the unfortunate result of a lack of discipline is that the files end up accumulating in piles on the collectors' desks. If credit analysis and collection duties are segregated, this can be a very messy situation, with credit analysts unable to find customer credit files because they are buried in a pile on a collector's desk and vice versa. Also, it is difficult to file documents when the file never gets back to its rightful place. Besides increasing clerical time, this type of scenario can cause important information to be lost or unavailable when needed.

For this reason, many companies have their collectors keep their call logs in three-ring binders. Current calls are available for any authorized department member to see, and old records can be stored in the customer's credit file. The fact that information is not consolidated does, however, increase research time. This becomes more of a factor when there is a problem with an account that includes documents. Then, the collector ends up searching for information in both the file and call log before the next logical collection step. Again, if filing habits are not disciplined, additional time can be wasted pulling everything together.

When the activity log is kept by customer, there are no daily logs to track performance. Having collectors keep two logs is rarely done as it penalizes performance in the cause of measuring improvement. This alone should be ample justification for a one-write type system for keeping a daily log that could be summarized by customer. A first-step solution is computer-based notepads that provide some added convenience in terms of the collector's being able to quickly access call records. Another quick solution is putting contact management software or PIMS (Personal Information Management Systems) to work organizing this information. They have similar characteristics to call logs kept in loose-leaf binders but, installed properly, can also provide daily logs of calls completed. Computer memory is also a limited commodity, and it is not uncommon for old call notes to either be archived on a magnetic storage medium that is not readily available for lookup or, more simply, to be printed out and filed in the customer's credit file for future reference. The bottom line is that an unintegrated computer-based notepad does not provide much opportunity for significant productivity gains.

Another follow-up activity involves providing additional documentation to the customer. By a great margin, the most common documentation required is invoice copies. More complicated requests include putting together a customer account reconciliation with supporting documents. Even the simple, continually repeated task of providing an invoice can involve going to a file, finding the document in question, copying it, re-filing it, composing a cover letter or fax, copying that, and filing a duplicate of everything in the customer's credit file. These simple tasks quickly eat up a significant piece of a collector's day. (See Exhibit 6.6.)

Exhibit 6.6 **Follow-up Activities**

- Record notes and promises
- Send follow-up letter/documentation
  1. Find documents
  2. Make copies
- Research problems
- Notify other departments

If a complex explanation is required, a collector can spend more than a day just to satisfy a single customer's needs. Researching the customer's problem is made more difficult when data sources are fragmented. This is essentially the same issue that arises during the preparation phase. Unless documents and records are copied and stored in the customer's credit file, it is possible that the same documents will be retrieved from the order or invoice files more than once. Until a collection problem is resolved with a payment or a credit memo, there is a strong likelihood it will need to be re-addressed.

Even producing follow-up letters that do not require additional documentation can take up a considerable amount of a collector's time. Without much clerical support, many collectors must handle their own correspondence, hopefully with a personal computer (PC)-based word processing program and not a typewriter. Form letters can usually be handled without too much trouble using a PC, but personalized correspondence still takes time. Even so, personalized correspondence has proven to be more effective than form letters.

Not only must customers be sent confirmations, reminders, and status reports, but other people in the organization need to be advised of the actions being taken with the company's customers. Sometimes, this will involve gathering

---

documentation in order to solicit a decision, while at other times the intentions are purely informational. Sales needs to know when accounts have been placed on credit hold because the customer is unable to commit to a payment deadline. Customer service and shipping need to know when merchandise is being returned. There are any number of circumstances that require other departments to be apprised of collection activities, and this need generates a commensurate number of memos, phone calls, and other intercompany communications.

REPORTING

Reporting serves a number of purposes. It provides information for upper management that is used to make strategic decisions that are affected by cash flow and to evaluate the performance of the credit and collection department. Collection reports, on an individual account basis, provide valuable information to sales about customer status. Reporting also provides feedback for the collectors as to how well they are doing individually. Last of all, reporting provides the credit manager with a basis for making tactical decisions to improve the performance of the credit and collection department.

Reporting is therefore a very valuable and important component of the collection cycle. Most importantly, the information provided in the reporting phase provides the basis for the prioritization phase of the next collection cycle. Without well-designed, appropriate reports, less than optimal decisions will be made during the next collection cycle. By the same token, otherwise good reports that lack sufficient detail may mask deficiencies or cause opportunities to be overlooked as the next series of collection activities is planned. Without good, timely reporting, collectors are operating blindly. It is that simple.

In a manual collection environment, the number and depth

of the reports that are compiled are limited by the time it takes to put the reports together. Most reporting is done on an end-of-the-month basis, but there may also be some ongoing issues that require timely updates, for example, a major account that has run into some credit difficulties. Since time is such a limited commodity in a manual collection environment, ad hoc reporting often is done as quickly as possible with minimal concern for quality or comprehensiveness. When these qualities are absolutely necessary, the time needed to meet these standards is usually taken from the contact phase of the collection cycle.

At month's end, reporting usually consumes a good portion of at least one day for the credit manager, sometimes more depending on corporate requirements. This causes a necessary break in other collection activities during this time. The bottom line on reporting in a manual collection environment is that the more reporting required, the greater its cost. As such, excessive reporting requirements, despite the information provided in the process, can depress collection performance during the subsequent cycle. Obviously, balance is required. (See Exhibit 6.7.)

Just as the aged accounts receivable trial balance is the centerpiece of the other phases of the manual collection process, it also serves as the main component for the reporting phase. It is

Exhibit 6.7 **Common Reporting Practices**

- Manually assemble account information for reviews
- Use aging to track progress
- Calculate DSO
- Report promises, problems, expected results
- Send to other departments
- Little time spent on analysis

used to identify customers with the largest and oldest balances. From it, the percentage of receivables over 90 days, over 60 days, and within terms as a percentage of total receivables is calculated. Compared to previous aged accounts receivable trial balance calculations, these percentages identify trends.

All of this information is sometimes extracted manually by the credit manager. Most companies, however, have written programs that will help extract some of this information, such as top ten lists or balances over a specified amount. Even better is the capability to create separate aged accounts receivable trial balances by collector, product line, sales division, or some other logical differentiator. This information is then usually compiled on a PC spreadsheet for distribution to interested parties throughout the corporation.

For some companies, this is more or less all the month-end reporting that is required, or possibly that they feel they can afford to accomplish. Others may require additional information such as cash flow projections. Such a report is often based on a compilation of each collector's major promises in conjunction with expected remittance patterns based on the aged accounts receivable trial balance. How this usually works is that on a weekly basis, collectors record in a log all promises above a specified dollar threshold. The credit manager then tabulates the totals from all collectors and factors in the aging trends.

Another common monthly reporting requirement highlights the status of either major accounts or high-risk accounts, or both. Information for each account on such a watch list is compiled in much the same way as information is gathered in the preparation phase of the collection cycle. The major difference when the purpose is reporting is that it must be presented in a standard format. Typically, collectors will provide their credit manager with the details for those accounts under their supervision. The credit manager, in turn, compiles this data in a predetermined format for presentation to management. This can be a particularly time-consuming task.

Unfortunately, for all the time and energy put into this reporting component, relatively little analysis is provided. All the little problems that create a drag on collections are seldom identified. Even if they are, it is difficult to quantify them, and without that information it is difficult to get other functional areas to take notice and agree to making changes that will prevent recurrence. Part of the problem behind a lack of analysis is that the reports that can be easily generated with an automated accounts receivable and a manual collection system tend to focus only on the numbers available from the accounting system. Qualitative information and process details are required if root causes are to be identified and analyzed. That being the case, qualitative, in-depth analysis is difficult because the reports simply do not provide qualitative, in-depth information.

Without qualitative information, trying to determine why DSO is increasing becomes a guessing game rather than an analytical exercise. The fact that collector number 4 is making many less phone calls because he has been asked to serve on a committee to plan the company picnic just does not show up. That may seem like a silly example, but it serves to make the point that there are any number of factors that may affect collection performance. Most companies simply do not have the reporting capabilities to accurately measure the inputs to collection performance. Results get measured to a degree, but that information is derived from the makeup of the accounts receivable, and that necessarily includes the very influential input of a company's recent sales pattern. It is the effect of recent sales that reduces the credibility of DSO as a measure of credit performance. Because of this lack of credibility, DSO never was an effective motivator of team performance or a useful factor for calculating financial incentives.

The final reason that little analysis is performed relates

back to the issue of time. Compiling reports takes a significant amount of time by itself. Therefore, it is easy to understand that when the time comes to analyze these reports, more seemingly urgent matters that have been accumulating during the reporting phase take precedence. The outcome is that analysis is put off, and once that happens it soon becomes irrelevant as the next collection cycle begins.

SUMMARY

As previously discussed, one key to improving collections is contacting more past due accounts. The problem with collections as they are practiced today is that collectors typically spend less than a third of their time making contact with their past due accounts. In some situations, preparation and follow-up time together can consume over half of a collector's day. Add to this the need to allocate significant blocks of time to prioritization and reporting, the front and back ends of the collection cycle, and it is easy to see why contact time is very limited under a manual collection process. Incremental improvements are simply not going to dramatically reduce these numbers.

Exhibit 6.8 provides an example of how a collector, without any other outside responsibilities, will typically spend his

Exhibit 6.8 **Time Allocations for the Manual Collection Cycle**

Collection Phase	Hours Per Day
Prioritization	1.0
Preparation	1.5
Contact	2.5
Follow-up	2.0
Reporting	1.0

or her day. Under this scenario, a collector might send out a half dozen letters or faxes and complete about a dozen collection calls. In addition, messages might be left for another five to ten past due accounts. Considering that half of the past due customers may require a second call, it is impossible for a collector to effectively manage more than 300 past due accounts. If the collector is responsible for more accounts than that, not everybody will be contacted who should be. To make matters worse, many collectors also have credit analysis responsibilities and short-pay transactions to research, further reducing the number of accounts one person can effectively monitor.

In many companies, the coverage requirements are much higher than this. It is no wonder then that credit and collection personnel feel burnt out and are resigned to constantly working in catch-up mode. Very often, their only recourse is longer hours, which will eventually contribute to a loss in personal productivity. It can be a vicious cycle, as the lumberjack in Exhibit 1.1 learned. Sharpening one's axe or hiring extra help does not change the inefficiencies inherent in the current system. Fortunately, buying that chain saw opens up a whole new world of opportunities.

Part Two

Automating Collections

7

Solving the Dilemma

Up to this point, both the rationale and the imperative for companies to commit themselves to a re-engineered, automated collection environment have been explained. Quite simply, with the way credit and collection systems have evolved over the last four decades, too many credit and collection departments are finding it increasingly difficult to keep up with the demands of the modern corporate environment. With things as they are, it is virtually impossible for collectors to become more productive. There is too little time, and their own patchwork systems continue to chew up inordinate amounts of that precious commodity.

The result has been sagging performance. (See Exhibit 7.1.) The solution is new and radically different systems that will save large amounts of time while also creating intelligent tools to further enhance productivity. While the old systems focus on transaction processing, the new systems must provide portfolio management capabilities. The new systems must eliminate non–value-added components of the collection process and in so doing be much more cost effective than their predecessors. That is the promise of the re-engineered automated collection environment. The purpose of re-engineering and automating

Exhibit 7.1 Trends in DSO

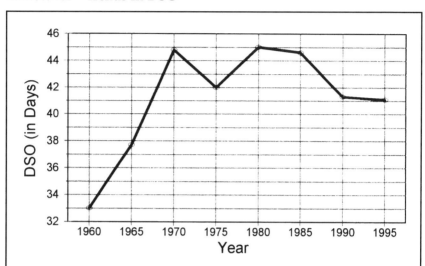

Note: This data was derived from the National Summary of Domestic Trade Receivables compiled by the Credit Research Foundation (CRF), Columbia, MD. The figures are the median DSO for the first quarter of the year indicated. They were reported to the CRF by its members, which range across all industry types but tend to be large corporations. After World War II and prior to 1960, a much larger sampling indicated DSO slowly rose from the low 30- to the low 40-day range. Results for the remainder of 1995 and the first three quarters of 1996 indicated a slight upward trend in DSO from 41.1 days to 42.5 days. In any event, despite computerization, DSO has mostly tended upward.

Source: This information was taken from *Statistics of Income*, a government publication, and was originally published in Martin H. Seiden, *The Quality of Trade Credit* (New York: National Bureau of Economic Research, Inc., 1964), 46–49.

the collection process is to achieve dramatic improvements in performance and results.

Until now, the current state of credit and collections and why there needs to be change have been discussed. In the next five chapters, how to re-engineer and automate the collection process will be examined. The first step in that process is to identify the key features of the new collection system. The

question is: What are the critical components of a collection system? In other words, what are the key activities that must be accomplished to collect a company's receivables both quickly and
efficiently. Quickly, because the ideal goal is to collect every receivable by its due date. Efficiently, because in today's corporate environment, there are simply no resources to waste.

What is being looked for, in effect, are solutions to all the
problems collectors face with today's systems. These problems
tend to fall into the following three areas:

1. Slow payments from trade creditors
2. Not enough time for credit and collection departments
   to get everything done
3. Inconsistencies between collectors in terms of how they
   organize themselves and complete their assigned tasks

Only by devising solutions to these three problems can collectors hope to dramatically improve collection performance. By
the same token, if no answers are obtained in any one of these
areas, the best that can be hoped for is incremental improvements in measures of collection performance because the three
areas are inextricably linked together.

After all, while there are certainly external reasons why
customers pay slowly, there is also a relationship between
slow payments and how much time a credit and collection
staff is able to devote to contacting customers. As the number
of past due invoices increases, there is not enough time to follow up on all overdue accounts. Many smaller customers and
some large ones respond to reduced follow-up by paying
slower. This further increases the follow-up workload. Some
staffs respond to the increase with an increase in productivity
(often by working not just harder, but longer). Many do not.
Inconsistencies between collectors lead to a decline in the
standards of performance in terms of consistency of customer
contact and follow-up. This leads to customers paying slower.

Since these problems are inextricably linked together, so must be their solutions.

CALL EARLY, CALL OFTEN

The best way to attack slow payments is to stay on top of open invoices. That means starting the contact process as early as possible, which in some instances may mean contacting customers before their bills go past due, and then consistently following up until payment is made. Call early, call often may sound simplistic, but that does not make it any less of an effective tactic. The problem is that in today's time-challenged collection environment, it is easier said than done. That is why changes must be made in collection systems so collectors can call earlier and maintain consistent contact.

There are a number of positive results when collection efforts are started sooner. The most obvious is that collecting sooner will accelerate payments. Any experienced commercial collector knows that there are some customers who do not bother paying until they are asked for the money. Other accounts payable departments cut checks for their vendors and then hold those checks until a collector makes contact. In a situation in which the customer is facing a cash shortage, after critical vendors are paid fastest, then it is often the vendors that make first contact who will get paid with any remaining funds, while those who delay will be forced to wait even longer.

Contacting early also educates vendors about a company's expectations. While the published terms of sale may state that the company's terms are net 30 days, if collectors do not begin making collection calls until an invoice is at least 30 days past due, it is implied that the terms are actually 60 days. When collectors consistently call or fax the customer on the thirty-first day, they are sending a very clear and strong message that the terms of sale are in fact net 30 days. While customers may not immediately begin paying on time, or for that matter faster, over time most will start responding to requests for payment by moving the company that makes the early request up in the sequence of payments distributed. (See Exhibit 7.2.)

Another advantage from initiating collection contacts earlier is discovering problems sooner. Problems, whether they are short payment deductions, customer complaints, or a matter of customer liquidity, are all more easily resolved the sooner they are identified. Problems that are not discovered until they are ancient history take considerably more time to resolve, because old problems require that all interested parties have their memories refreshed. Older records have a greater tendency than current records to get misplaced, and important facts can be forgotten or overlooked. In addition, problems that are not discovered early on or resolved promptly tend to create customer ill will, and therefore the customer may not be as cooperative with lingering problems. When collectors call early, problems can be discovered and resolved when the entire matter is fresh in everyone's mind and before resentment becomes a factor.

Because problems are also more quickly resolved when they are found early, the company saves time, money, and marketshare over the long run. This is a case in which ignorance is not bliss. Undiscovered problems will cost a company dearly in time, effort, and customer goodwill.

The same is true with old past due balances. Even if there are no problems involved with the past due other than the customer's unwillingness to pay, it will usually require more effort to collect an older past due balance than an invoice that has just reached its due date. Customers are more likely to ask for duplicate invoices and other documentation on an old past due. Whereas an invoice 5 days past due can often be collected with a single call, an item that is 45 days past due when the collector first calls is more than likely to require subsequent calls. Even though there are more invoices on the accounts receivable that

Exhibit 7.2   **Defeating Accounts Payable Slow Payment Strategies**

Some sophisticated, albeit unscrupulous, companies have turned the art of slowing payments into a science. A practice known as payment timing optimization is the culprit. Implementing such a system can raise substantial sums they can use interest free to invest in their business or to pay down loans. The reference list of vendors of these services includes an impressive list of *Fortune* 500 corporations. The problem is that your company and other vendors are paying the price for this free loan.

Payment timing optimization works like this: Since most credit and collection departments age their receivables in 30-day aging buckets, an invoice that is 1 day past due is lumped in the same aging bucket as invoices that are 29 days past due. In addition, most credit and collection departments do not actively call accounts that are less than 30 days past due. They may send statements or even form letters, but seldom do they push for prompt payment from their customers that are just a little slow. If your company follows this pattern, your implied credit terms would be net 60 days if, for example, your published terms were net 30 days.

By analyzing its top vendors' collection habits, a company is able to identify each vendor's real credit terms. By paying within those terms, these companies are able to stretch out payments without doing any damage to their relationship with their vendor. If the vendor does not see any movement from the 1–30 aging bucket to the 30–60 category, they are none the wiser to what is going on. Meanwhile, the customer has probably added 15 days, and possibly more, to the payment cycle. If the payment cycle goes from 40 to 55 days, that is a 37.5 percent increase. In other words, an accounts payable that previously averaged $1 million will increase by $375,000, and that amount of money then becomes available for investment or reducing debt.

There are a number of ways to protect yourself from payment timing optimization: making your first two aging buckets only 15 days in length or calculating a rolling average of how long before each customer's payments are received help identify trends. However, the best defense is automating your collection efforts. Because collection activities are driven by individualized customer collection strategies, customers cannot hide behind your aging buckets. Better yet, as you work your automated collection system, your best defense will be your offense as you systematically tighten up your collection strategies in an effort to get all your customers to pay according to your published credit terms.

are 5 days past due than there are items 45 days past due, time will be saved in the long run if collection efforts are begun sooner rather than later.

This leads to the issue of follow-up. Once an effort is made to collect a past due, the collector must be ready to follow up that initial action with subsequent collection steps if the customer does not pay as promised. Without consistent follow-up, the initial collection contacts are largely wasted effort. It is the second and third calls, the follow-up letter, or the follow-up call to the fax sent the day before that make the greatest impact on accounts that are more difficult to collect. After all, it is with the difficult accounts that a collector earns his keep, and difficult accounts are more likely to pay, and sooner, when the collector keeps them on a short rope. (See Exhibit 7.3.)

This also goes back to the idea of educating customers as to the company's expectations. If customers think they can de-

Exhibit 7.3   By Gradually Tightening Its Collection Strategies, Dunlop Accelerated Customer Payments

Because of their understaffed situation, Dunlop's collectors were not able to contact every past due account as early or as often as they would have liked when they first automated their collections. As a result, Dunlop initially allowed its customers a generous number of grace days on past due invoices. However, as Dunlop's collectors worked through their backlog, their collection parameters were gradually tightened, including the incremental moving up of initial contacts. The result was a continued shortening of their customers' payment cycles as evidenced by reductions in Dunlop's DSO and percentage of receivables past due. This improvement, which occurred over a period of 6 months and after the initial cash influx resulting from Dunlop's automating of collections, was directly a result of contacting earlier and more often.

lay payment for another 2 weeks or a month by promising to cut a check next week, that is exactly what they will do. Unless the collector is willing to follow up next week to see if in fact that check has been cut, the first call has been a virtual waste of time. However, in making that second call next week, the collector has probably reduced the probability of having to make a third or fourth call and has clearly telegraphed serious intentions to the customer. It should also be pointed out that this works just as well for the eloquent and persuasive collector as for the collector who is merely professional, yet firm in his or her approach to collections. Actions speak louder than words, and consistent follow-up activities will speak very clearly to customers that the collector is competent and determined. (See Exhibit 7.4.)

Consistent follow-up will catch problems that have not been dealt with, regardless of whether the problem lies with the customer or the company. As stated earlier, doing things sooner

Exhibit 7.4 **Even Customers Can See the Difference**

When Dialogic, a Parsippany, NJ, manufacturer of voice processing components, automated its collections, it set a goal of collecting 60 percent of its past due receivables during the first month of operation. In fact, it collected 85 percent. The long-term results were just as dramatic. Despite a 50 percent increase in sales and without adding any credit or collection staff, Dialogic was able to consistently reduce DSO during the 18 months after automating collections.

Even Dialogic's customers could tell something was different, spawning quite a few inquiries about Dialogic's new collection system. This was not a negative response to Dialogic's increased collection efforts, but rather the recognition that this was the type of collection effort Dialogic's customers would like to implement themselves.

---

rather than later saves time and effort over the long run. Consistent follow-up means less follow-up. It also means the company will get its money faster, and that is a high priority. Speedy collections reduce asset carrying costs and bad debts, and create time for even more consistent follow-up. So, if collectors want to collect more, faster, a system must be devised that will allow them to call early and often.

AUTOMATING CLERICAL TASKS

The major problem with having automated accounts receivables while maintaining manual collection processes is the proliferation of clerical tasks necessary to tie the two systems together. The worst part of this is the necessity of recording, and re-recording, information in multiple places. Even without the extra work required to integrate a manual collection system with computerized accounts receivable, there are a lot of clerical duties required on the collection side alone. Compounding this problem has been the loss of clerical support that has accompanied the computerization of the finance function. The result has been that credit analysts and collectors have been forced to push a lot of paper. For collectors, this has meant that clerical duties have severely cut into the time allocated to contacting past due customers. The obvious solution to this dilemma is to automate these clerical tasks.

The key to this is a single interface between the collector and all the pieces of information that are required for effective collections. By putting all this information in electronic format at the collector's fingertips, it is possible to provide the tools to automate most clerical tasks. These tasks are centered around four activities: scheduling, updating account records, duplicating documents, and communicating.

A major problem that occurred when credit departments abandoned ledger cards for the computer-generated aged accounts receivable trial balance was the lack of a good place to record collection activities (see Exhibit 7.5). Whether call logs were kept in a three-ring binder, a computerized customer display screen, or in the customer's credit file, it took more time than before to retrieve files, review previous actions, record contacts, and update records. Even if a computerized call log was created, it probably was not fully integrated with the computerized receivables, and as such was not as efficient a tool as possible.

The automated scheduling and logging of collection calls and other collection activities, and then tying that information to current accounts receivable, is the solution to this problem. With a computer database not only is the information available for instant recall and review, but it can also be used to automatically drive all necessary follow-up activities when it has been tied to the accounts receivable database. With such a system, collectors no longer need to go through a tickler file to see what items have been paid, because the system automatically weeds out the cleared items. An automated system will also cut down on the number of keystrokes necessary to record collection activities, and these recorded actions will then provide a key as to the next collection activity to be scheduled and when. The result is a seamless interface between the collector, the accounts receivable transaction data, and all the accumulated collection information captured by the system, which together are fed back through the automated process as a catalyst for continuous improvement.

Recording collection activities and scheduling follow-up actions are just a part of the clerical monstrosity many collectors face. A large amount of time is consumed by document-handling activities: retrieving, copying, transmitting, and refiling documents. The tremendous amount of time freed up by automating these tasks can then be directed toward contacting past due accounts.

The most common request made by past due customers is

Exhibit 7.5   **Breaking the Habit**

The most common repository for collection information has been the aged accounts receivable trial balance. Collectors have grown attached to these printouts, because when they are well maintained with call notes and updated payments, they are often the best available source of information for making collection decisions. As a result, getting collectors to stop using their agings after an automated collection system has been installed can be difficult.

Part of the problem is that collectors have a strong sense of ownership regarding the information kept on their aging reports. After all, they are their accounts. Information kept in a database is much more public. Anybody with access can thoroughly check the status of any account without consulting the collector. With an automated collection system, the collector can no longer play the role of guardian of the aging, and in a very real sense, has less control over how accounts are managed.

When Sony Entertainment began implementing its automated collection system, it soon became apparent that this mindset would have to be addressed head on. As the system was rolled out throughout the organization, each collection group was required to attend a meeting with the Vice-President of Corporate Credit and Customer Finance. The price of admission for each collector was one accounts receivable aged trial balance and one marking pen. When the collectors entered the conference room, they were instructed to throw their aging reports and highlighters into a trash bin that had been placed in the center of the conference table.

Despite the strong object lesson and the subsequent emphatic instructions that aging reporters and highlighters were no longer to be used, a number of collectors still had trouble kicking the habit. Sony has continued to work with these people to help them transfer the confidence they placed in the aging reports to the new automated collection system. In the end, the best motivator has been the productivity of the collectors who were able to completely adapt to the automated system.

for copies of outstanding invoices. The time it takes to get up from one's desk, go to the file room, find the invoice copy or copies in question, go to the copier, make copies, go to the fax, make up a cover sheet, fax the documents, go back to the file room, return the original invoices to their files, return to one's office, and file the copies in the tickler file has already been discussed. That whole process takes eight or nine distinct steps and quite a bit of time (see Exhibit 4.4). Being able to retrieve an electronic invoice and then readily transmit it to the account is a much simpler process from the collector's point of view. With a good automation system, there are essentially two steps: retrieving and transmitting. A manual task that took many minutes can be done automatically in seconds.

Keep in mind that the key to automating this task is to have integrated the accounts receivable and order entry databases with the collection software. Of course, invoices are not the only documents that past due customers request. However, the same type of automation solution can, with the help of imaging and other document retrieval tools, be used to dramatically improve the handling of any receivables document. Order forms, packing lists, bills of lading, and statements can all be recreated and transmitted electronically.

Even proofs of delivery (PODs) can be expedited with an automated system. Until recently, collectors have had to wait for their shipper to supply PODs, usually by mail or fax. Collectors would then have to fax the POD to the customer. Now that some shippers are making PODs instantaneously available over the Internet or via a direct nightly download, collectors using an automated system can capture the electronic POD for electronic transmission to their customer. What took days can now be done while the collector is still on the phone with the customer. In this case, automation not only provides time-saving efficiencies but also allows more effective procedures.

Tied into the automation of account updating and document handling is the area of communications. Effective collections of necessity requires effective communications. Anything that can be done to automate the communication environment upon which collectors depend should return dividends quickly. Automated document handling loses much of its punch if the communication component is not also automated. This is obvious, as illustrated in the document faxing example just given. Faxing is not the only communication tool that benefits from automation. Letter writing, e-mailing, telephoning, and using the Internet are all communication activities that can be enhanced with properly constructed automation tools.

With letter writing, automation provides both speed and flexibility. Using form letters as a collection tool has long been a standard practice in most credit departments. Sometimes, these have taken the form of a dunning notice in which a program has been written to insert the customer's address and open items taken from the accounts receivable database into a standard text. Seldom can they be addressed to a specific person. Less sophisticated form letters may simply consist of a checklist that the collector fills out with pen and ink before sending to the customer. In either case, speed is the primary beneficial characteristic, but flexibility is limited. These dunning and form letters also have the disadvantage of looking like a form letter rather than a personalized piece of correspondence.

The promise of automation is to be able to generate correspondence based on preset forms that can then be personalized. Ideally, this means that accounts receivable details such as reference numbers and balance information should be integrated into each piece of correspondence, with collection data such as contact names and adjusted balances to account for disputed invoices. In addition, the process must give the operator the option of easily personalizing the message. Individualized correspondence can then be generated with a minimum amount of keystrokes. If the collector has the required information already compiled in a suitable format, it will not take long to add a personalized note or explanation. Such correspondence would then not only be generated quickly, but it would also be in a proven effective format.

This correspondence can then be transmitted with a keystroke as a fax or an e-mail or, if need be, printed out as a letter right at the collector's desk. All appropriate documentation would also be available as attachments to the main piece of correspondence, and therefore available for printing or electronic transmittal. In such a seamless system, a collector could process targeted correspondence very quickly. In the case of e-mails and faxes, receipt by the customer would be nearly instantaneous, eliminating mail time as an impediment to faster collections. In addition, copies of any correspondence, including any postscripts the collector wants to add, can be forwarded electronically to other departments such as sales and customer service. Covering all the needs of the customer and everyone else involved in the process cuts down on the effort required during the follow-up phase of the collection process.

Thanks to form letters, whether automated or not, most collectors will send more collection correspondence than they will make collection phone calls. However, phone calls take up the greater portion of the time collectors spend making contact with customers. For this reason, any automation that simplifies and speeds up the calling process is a benefit. It was previously noted how automating the call-logging process will help facilitate collection calls, but there are a number of other automation tools that enhance the process of calling.

The first of these is auto-dialing. Instead of looking for the contact's phone number and then dialing it, this feature allows the collector, who is reviewing an account's status prior to making a call, to simply press a key and have his or her computer place the call. While the time saved is minimal, the greater benefit is derived from the time and energy saved by not having to look up contacts and phone numbers. This is especially so if the contact information has previously been kept on a manual call log. Reducing energy spent in the preparation phase means allocating more power to making contact. This translates into more customer contacts and improved collector focus on the communication aspects of collection calls, since the mechanical components of collection activities are eliminated.

Also, with many customers, there are other people the collection team may need to periodically call besides the main contact. Maintaining these names and numbers in the computer database facilitates the automated calling of these secondary contacts. As a side note, these secondary contact names can also be incorporated into any correspondence the collector generates. Centralizing this information provides a big payoff when a temporary or permanent change of the person responsible for collecting the account takes place. It also opens the possibility of having more than one person maintain the relationship with the customer. As a result, collectors have the information they need right on their desktop, and the computer can use that information to automate the calling process.

ADOPT CLIENT-SPECIFIC STRATEGIES

Because the manual collection system leaves the individual collector to determine what accounts are called and when they are called, collection results can vary greatly between collectors. Of course, no two collectors will ever get the same results, but performance variations are magnified by the complexity of a manual collection system that relies upon computerized accounts receivables. For instance, the learning curve for a new collector is quite steep because of the complexity of integrating the collection process with the accounts receivable system. Another reason is that in order to solve problems, a new collector has to learn all the ins and outs of data retrieval. However, companies that have automated collections have found that new people can get up to speed in a day or two rather than weeks.

This is in large part due to the simplified process and the easy accessability to information the collector has with an automated system. With a manual system, new collectors must feel their way with every call they make until they learn their employer's systems and processes. Each call presents a challenge in terms of finding out what was done last, what should be done next, and, if the customer has a gripe, how to resolve it in order to get paid. It is not surprising that new collectors end up getting sidetracked, have to ask a lot of questions (sometimes approaching the magnitude of one question for every customer contact), and spend an interminable amount of time in the file room. Because of their lack of insight into the process to be followed for each category of customer, they are not only unsure of what to do next but often take a lot of time doing it. With good reason, a new collector is inclined to consistently err on the conservative side of things, treating every customer contact like a first contact. Demanding payment or any other assertive action against a customer is very difficult, especially so when the collector is unsure of his or her footing, which comes from having easily understandable and accessible information. With time, the collector's productivity increases, but early on a new collector spends a great deal of time learning how things are done rather than collecting.

Under these circumstances, new and experienced collectors alike tend to develop their own unique ways of performing their job. The patchwork nature and complexity of manual collection systems give them lots of options, and everybody has his or her own preferences. It is easy to understand why performance varies tremendously with a manual collection system. The problem is a result of the system as opposed to the people.

The answer to this problem is to develop specific collection strategies for each customer type, and employ the computer to prompt the process. By standardizing how different types of accounts are handled—from when they should be first contacted and how, to the sequence, timing, and nature of subsequent collection activities—much of the variability in collector performance is eliminated. Strategies also help set corporate collection priorities so that all accounts are given attention commensurate with their importance to the business. Key customers and those with large balances will automatically be given more attention than small-balance accounts while allowing for all past due customers to be contacted in an organized fashion.

Taking another look at what new collectors are up against, an automated collection process that uses predefined strategies enables a very different learning scenario. New collectors do not need to learn where or who else to go to in the corporation to get information required for the collection process, because it is already being captured by the collection database. Once collectors gain some familiarity with the collection software, they are off and running. Previous collection activities are at their fingertips so they know what to do and say next. In fact, the system tells them what is scheduled to be done next. (See Exhibit 7.6.)

There are a number of different ways to develop collection strategies. For most companies, it is sufficient to start with broad groupings of customers according to several payment-sensitive issues. These are industry or distribution types, payment tendencies, and risk characteristics. Once classified in each area, it is a simple matter to ascribe a strategy based on the customer's characteristics.

An easy way to do this is to first segregate customers by either their industry or the company's distribution channels. There are usually timing characteristics, such as terms of sale, discounts, promotional programs, or manufacturing lead times, that are unique to different industries or distribution channels.

Exhibit 7.6   **Sony's Temporary Collectors Adjust Quickly to Automation**

> Sony Pictures Entertainment automated its collection system during a period of organizational change. As a result of the realignments Sony was going through, it often relied on temporary collectors to keep collections flowing. It was a pleasant surprise to find that the temps could be easily plugged into the new automated collection system. Nearly all were functional before the end of their first day on the job. In fact, not having preconceived work habits, the temps readily took to the automated collection system whereas some of Sony's old pros found it more difficult to give up their aged accounts receivable trial balances and colored markers.

All these things affect the payment cycle and need to be accounted for in the collection strategies. These categories should probably be subdivided based on size or volume considerations.

The customers in each of these classifications can then be evaluated by their payment history and risk category. It is here the customers will be differentiated from the debtors. The risk of slow payment will be measured against the risk of default. This done, a number of different combinations will be found. Exhibit 7.7 illustrates what some of these might be for any given industry grouping. Collection strategies are then assigned to each unique classification. Obviously, the collection strategy for a slow-paying, high-risk customer will be different than that for fast-paying, low-risk account.

However, some of the other groupings with more subtle differences might be assigned the same strategy. Moderate-risk accounts that fall into the average or good payment categories could rationally be assigned the same collection strategy, which helps limit the number of strategies required. In fact, there may

Exhibit 7.7   **Evaluating Risk versus Payment History**

Risk	Payments		
	Slow	*Average*	*Good*
High	5	4	3
Moderate	4	3	2
Low	3	2	1

Note: Risk in this case is measured on a scale of one to five, with five indicating the highest level of risk.

be only three or four primary strategies from which subtle variations are made as needed. Of course, there is always the option of creating a unique strategy for a unique account. Whatever the case, the specific collection strategy assigned to each customer will then drive the automated collection system, determining priorities and ensuring maximum coverage of all past due balances. (See Exhibit 7.8.)

With strategies in place, the performance differences between different collectors are minimized because everyone is operating from the same set of priorities, procedures, and practices. This is not to say that excellent collectors will not outperform their peers. They still will, but average collectors will do a better job because they are working with a standardized process that works each past due account according to a set of selected criteria. Furthermore, as the automated collection system is used, it accumulates added intelligence not only about individual accounts but also about groups of customers. Over time, collection strategies can be refined, with the goal of further improving customer payment performance.

Proven collection strategies are thereby easily applied to all similar customers, improving every collector's performance. System improvements are thereby multiplied through each collector.

Exhibit 7.8   **Sample Collection Strategy**

Balance < $5,000	Mid-size Distributors	Low Risk
Timing	Form of Communication	Action
End of grace period	PC/Fax	We've noticed you're late.
Next day	Phone	Is there a problem we're not aware of?
8 Days later	PC/Fax	Problem resolved? Notify salesperson.
7 Days later	Phone	Express concern. Notify management.
10 Days later	Priority Mail	Send final demand notice.

Note: The timing of the strategies is based on mail days and the reliability of the customer's promises, which vary with customer location and customer type. The sequencing of communications and actions also flows from the customer type, thus providing for consistent handling of all accounts. Of course, should the customer pay at any point in the strategy, all further collection activities would be halted automatically.

This is not unlike a targeted direct marketing campaign in which the selection of the market and the script are more important to the success of the program than are the telemarketers entrusted with getting the job done. Improving the process—in the case of collections, fine-tuning the collection strategies—will ultimately improve the end results.

SUMMARY

Solving the dilemma created by manual collections and computerized accounts receivable requires addressing three specific problems. First, the issue of slow payments requires a system that will allow collectors to call early and call often. Next, the lack of time faced by collection departments is solved by automating clerical tasks. Finally, inconsistency between individual collectors is minimized by the adoption of client-specific collection strategies. (See Exhibit 7.9.)

Calling early and often produces multiple benefits that serve to accelerate the collection process. Calling early will directly accelerate customer payments. It also serves to uncover problems sooner and to help educate customers about the company's true payment expectations. Calling early also addresses the fact that old receivables are harder to collect than more current invoices. It is also good customer service. The sooner accounts are freed of collection problems, the less opportunity there is for other credit and collection–related customer service issues to arise.

Calling often has a reinforcing effect upon customers. It creates an impact with them. After all, repetition has long been recognized as an effective teaching method, and it reinforces the idea that the company is serious in regard to its payment expectations. Regular follow-up also serves to speed the problem resolution process by not letting issues drag on.

Automating clerical tasks involves implementing a number of technical solutions. Central to these is the single interface that puts all the information a collector needs on his or her

Exhibit 7.9 **Solving the Dilemma Created by Manual Collections and Computerized Receivables**

Problem	Solution
Slow payments	Call early, call often
Not enough time	Automate clerical tasks
Inconsistency between collectors	Adopt client-specific strategies

desktop. Once this integrated collection database, which includes collection contact information, has been created, it is possible to install an automated contact log integrated with the accounts receivable details and an automated tickler, reproduce documents electronically, and automate communications.

With clerical tasks automated, client-specific collection strategies can then be used to drive the automated collection process. These strategies serve to standardize the type, sequence, and timing of collection activities, besides clarifying contact objectives. These collection strategies also address specific customer characteristics and are therefore assigned to accounts based on customer type and risk class.

A collection process that enables collectors to call early and often, that automates clerical tasks, and that is driven by client-specific collection strategies is fundamentally different from manual collection processes that have been linked to computerized accounts receivable systems. Automating individual tasks without changing the process will not achieve dramatic improvements in collection performance. Redesigning the process and then automating its components will.

8

Objectives of an Automated Collection System

There are nine primary objectives that should be achieved by automating the collection process. Throughout the exercise of streamlining the collection cycle, it is important to be mindful of these objectives. The tasks that are automated should directly contribute to at least one of these objectives and should never hinder the cumulative success of the automation program. There is no room for counterproductive activities in an automated setting. After all, that is the legacy that followed the computerization of accounts receivable.

There is one interesting common denominator between these nine goals: Every single objective is intrinsic to every collection department. Everyone wants to increase collections, reduce days sales outstanding (DSO), reduce past due balances, and reduce expenses. It is entirely appropriate that an automated collection system should espouse these same objectives. Any collection department making progress toward these goals merits commendations. However, when automating the collection process, the objective is not to just make progress toward these goals but rather to make substantial progress on all fronts.

Incremental gains are not acceptable for an automated collection system. (See Exhibit 8.1.)

Therefore, it is necessary that a broad set of initiatives be undertaken toward the attainment of each of these nine goals. Both the individual and cumulative effects of automating multiple tasks within the collection process are necessary to achieve substantial improvement in all measures of collection performance. Automating just a few critical tasks will not be sufficient. Breakthrough performance gains require integrated processes, not disjointed tasks.

INCREASED COLLECTOR PRODUCTIVITY

Increased collector productivity has been the central premise behind automating collections. The whole idea is to help collectors do more. The best way to do this is to create more time by automating as many of the clerical-type tasks that collectors perform as is possible.

Probably the biggest single aid for collectors is the daily work list. Nearly all the time collectors spend prioritizing their

Exhibit 8.1 **The Nine Goals of an Automated Collection System**

1. Increased collector productivity
2. Increased contact quantity
3. Increased contact quality
4. Increased customer satisfaction
5. Improved measurements
6. Reduced DSO
7. Improved cash flow
8. Reduced bad debt
9. Reduced collection expense

work can be automated. In addition, the daily work list provides additional utilities so that collectors can work through the list in the most efficient way possible. In particular, the ability to sort the list a number of different ways provides the collector with a flexible tool that addresses varying needs.

The initial computerized sorting of the daily work list should be by broken promises and then largest outstanding balances in descending order. This ensures that prime exposure is given to the most critical and largest collection issues. Broken promises should get top priority because follow-up activities need to be done promptly to avoid giving the customer the impression that additional payment delays will be tolerated. Also, when a customer breaks a promise, the chance that its account will not be paid, or at least that payment will be delayed, increases. This immediate rise in the risk factor for that customer demands the collector's top priority. Then, after all broken promises have been addressed, logic dictates that collection efforts proceed against the debtors with the largest overdue balances first.

However, it is not always possible for a collector to contact every account on the daily work list. This is where flexibility becomes important so that the collector is able to contact as many accounts as possible. An extremely important subset of the daily work list breaks out the accounts to be contacted by their current stage in the collection process. This allows the collectors to concentrate on one type of collection activity at a time. For example, newly past due balances may be slated to receive a faxed reminder along with a duplicate invoice. Being able to group these accounts together allows the collector to process many more reminders than would be possible jumping between different types of collection activities and from account to account. At another point in the day, the collector might work through all the accounts requiring follow-up phone calls and, when those are done, move to initial phone contacts.

The idea is to keep collectors working as efficiently as possible throughout the day. By being able to group similar tasks together, collectors are able to always be concentrating on a task that they are able to perform effectively at that point in the day. Another subset of the daily work list breaks out accounts requiring phone contact by the account's time zone. This ensures the highest number of connections, since leaving messages is a low-productivity task. Thus, a collector on one coast can work across the country, calling overdue accounts at the most opportune times.

While the innovations discussed so far in this section have dealt with prioritizing communications, the automatic recording of collection notes addresses the results of those communications. The problem with notes in a manual system is that recording and retrieving them is time consuming. Using a computerized notepad addresses these issues but does not go far enough. The biggest payback comes when the computerized notepad is integrated into the other elements of the collection process.

Because individual customer collection strategies are driving the process, the system already knows what type of action is being taken and who is being contacted, so this data should automatically be recorded in the contact log. Also, requests for payment usually receive a standard answer; for example, check number 123 for $123.45 paying invoice #12345 and #67890 was mailed last Monday, or a check for $987.65 paying all past dues will be mailed next Friday. By prompting the collector for the salient details, unnecessary keystroking is eliminated, and the collection system can then use this information to schedule the next appropriate collection step. If a customer promises to put a payment in the mail tomorrow, the system knows to schedule a follow-up 5 days later if the funds are not received.

As a result, much of the time collectors spend jotting call notes on their aged accounts receivable trial balance and desk calendar is eliminated by the automated note-taking features of the collection software. This is critical, because this customer-specific collection data is a key driver for the entire collection process. With a manual system, the format and contents of the notes taken are unique to each collector, but with an automated system this is standardized. The disjointed nature of the data resources available to collectors working with a manual system is both a result and a major cause of the inefficiencies of those systems. The close integration of the collection notepad with the other data elements of the collection process is essential to dramatically boost the productivity of collectors.

INCREASED CONTACT QUANTITY

In addition to providing collectors with a prioritized calling and contact schedule, an automated system should also have auto-dial capabilities. After all, the contact telephone number is already in each customer's master file. This may seem like a small thing, but if the contact information is right on the collector's screen, how long can it take to dial a phone number? However, dialing does take time, and it diverts attention. If an auto-dialer enables a collector to make two more phone calls per day, that translates into 10 more calls per week and more than 400 additional collection calls per year. That amounts to roughly a month of calls for a collector working with a manual collection system, which is a substantial increase in capacity.

The advantage to this is that the collector can focus on preparing to speak while the telephone is dialing and connecting. For larger collection teams, a predictive auto-dialer is an even more powerful dialing alternative. This device takes the prioritized call list, dials the telephone, and listens to the line. The computer detects busy, voicemail, or actual person, and responds as programmed. Usually, connections are directed to the collector while at the same time displaying the customer's collection screen on the computer. Such a device can increase contact volume during an uninterrupted calling period by up to 30 percent.

Along the same lines, but with even greater impact, are the productivity gains derived from putting a fax/modem in each collector's personal computer. Being able to send and receive faxes from their desktops is a tremendous time saver for collectors. In the example of a collector faxing an initial reminder along with duplicate invoices, that task takes considerably more time when each invoice is printed out, a fax cover sheet manually written out, and then everything physically run through a fax machine. The ability to seamlessly process the fax on the collector's desktop allows many more accounts to be contacted daily.

Automated faxing capabilities also provide collectors with the benefit of immediacy. For example, should the accounts payable clerk on the other end of the phone line claim that an invoice was never received, the collector is able to transmit a copy while still on the phone line, and then stay on the line until the customer has committed to paying the bill. This eliminates the need to make follow-up calls after manually faxing the invoice. To appreciate the value of this, you need to remember that at least 50 percent of these follow-up calls would reach voice mail. Keep in mind that return phone calls are low-productivity tasks. This feature, in contrast, makes the initial phone call that much more effective.

To a similar extent, e-mail capabilities also increase collector productivity. This is true for communicating not only with customers but with internal contacts as well, especially when trying to resolve deductions and other problems. Rather than becoming engaged in seemingly perpetual games of phone tag, an e-mail can be accompanied by documentation or an image of the customer's remittance advice. Because it is so easy for the salesperson (or whomever) to reply to the well-documented message by just pressing the reply button in the e-mail program, this is a very effective tool for resolving routine matters. As the Internet grows and gains wider acceptance, there will be additional opportunities for utilizing e-mail as a problem resolution tool.

These developments are tied into technological progress in the field of electronic imaging. Links between the collection software system and external imaging applications provide collectors with valuable information resources right on their desktop. The ability to view and then retransmit electronic images of original documents greatly enhances the use of automated faxes and e-mails in addition to expediting the problem-resolution process. The collection software system has downloaded invoice details from the accounts receivable software module, but purchase orders, packing slips, bills of lading, freight bills, and so forth must still be obtained from paper files. The Application Program Interface (API) protocol now allows imaged documents to be viewed in standard formats from within Windows-based collection software, and to then be either faxed or copied onto a word processing document. From the collector's point of view, such electronic linkages provide quick and easy access to information that can then be just as quickly and easily forwarded in an appropriate format to both customers and internal contacts. The result is many more contacts being made by collectors as well as more productive contacts.

INCREASED CONTACT QUALITY

Closely aligned with increased capacity (the ability to make more contacts) and gains in productivity is the issue of contact quality. Contact quality can be loosely defined as getting the most out of collection efforts. It stands to reason that the higher the quality of a collector's contact efforts, the greater the payments that will be promised and the fewer payment promises that will be broken. This will lead to more cash coming from each contact. Problems will be resolved quicker, and the overall level of customer satisfaction will increase.

Specifying collection strategies for each customer is crucial to the objective of increasing contact quality. Strategies that are tailored to each customer's characteristics and industry type ensure that collectors are taking the right actions at the right times. This ensures a consistent and appropriate performance standard for all customers. Strategies fashioned after best practices provide consistency between collectors and across a company's entire accounts receivable portfolio.

By having assigned a collection strategy to every customer, the automated collection system can then prompt collectors to make sure that all call objectives are achieved. For example, an automated collections system will identify the specific invoices on which the collector should obtain payment commitments. Such invoices could be highlighted in red on the collector's computer screen so that there is no mistaking the items in question. Without such prompting, it is common for collectors to get promises only on the oldest past due items or the transactions the customer readily commits to paying, often to the neglect of items recently beyond terms. This sends a message to the customer that past dues are tolerated.

For each step of the collection strategy, the system should clearly identify appropriate objectives for the collectors to follow. The objectives of a follow-up call are different from those of an initial call, and both are different if a previous problem is being addressed. An automated collection system can be relentless in terms of holding collectors to the task at hand, without the negative effects associated with close human supervision. It is much better to have the system prompt the collector rather than the collection manager.

Closely aligned with call objectives is excuse prompting. A completely automated collection system maintains a database of excuses and appropriate responses. As collectors work through each call's objectives, requesting payment on every past due item, customers will often raise objections. The collector can then simply press a few keys and navigate a list of effective responses. In effect, the system provides a script for the collector to follow that is designed to keep the collection call on track with its objectives. This also allows the automatic recording of the customer's excuse in the contact notepad, which later helps prevent recurring excuses.

Even experienced collectors benefit greatly from being prompted to attain call objectives and to respond appropriately to customer excuses. These features also greatly benefit new employees or temporary workers who are not familiar with a new employer's products, systems, and policies. These tools also send a message to customers that they are dealing with a thorough, professional organization. Nothing is haphazard or left to chance, and contact quality is enhanced.

This also holds true for collectors working with the problem-solving component of an automated collection system. Since many deductions, disputes, and other problems fall into standard categories, a database of customer service issues helps collectors provide answers to customer inquiries and resolve problems faster. Getting problems out of the way as quickly and effortlessly as possible helps keep collectors focused on purely collection issues.

The thinking behind all these tools is to help keep the collector on the attack. Customer excuses and internal company issues can sidetrack collectors. Therefore, an automated collection system uses call objectives, excuse prompting, and the customer service issues database to help collectors work both quickly and thoroughly through each collection issue. Tied to these tools is the ability to quickly and easily send multiple faxes and e-mails to both the customer and any other internal corporate problem owners, which helps collectors quickly get back to their core collection chores. Being able to send electronic copies of documents and correspondence helps collectors keep all interested parties informed of the status of a situation without taking additional time from the collection process. Collectors also need to be able to simply flag problems for later follow-up so they do not have to interrupt the collection process. It all comes down to the fact that a single-minded focus on collections is essential to superior quality and performance.

INCREASED CUSTOMER SATISFACTION

Much of what has already been discussed in this chapter ultimately impacts customer satisfaction. The customer's accounts payable staff has their own work to process, so it is in their best interests to handle vendor invoices only once. Much of the re-engineering movement has focused on the order procurement process, which runs from purchasing through payables. People working in a streamlined payables operation are therefore appreciative of collectors who have their facts together and can get things done.

For one thing, the heavy reliance on faxes and e-mails by automated collection systems for routine matters is regarded as less intrusive than phone calls, though still eliciting some sense of urgency from the receiving party. Accounts payable personnel are just as pressed for time as anybody, so phone calls often become just another interruption. Faxes get around this issue and provide additional benefits when accompanied by documentation such as duplicate invoice copies.

By the same token, quick action on customer inquiries and the speedy resolution of problems such as deductions can also make life easier for the customer's accounts payable department. They do not want to explain more than once why they cannot pay an item or are able to send only a partial payment.

With an automated collection system, that information is recorded the first time the explanation is given and then permanently linked to the invoices involved. If necessary, this information is readily available to also be passed along to the problem owner, regardless of his or her corporate function or location. Keeping everyone on the same page and resolving problems quickly the first time they arise is appreciated by customers. Resolving problems quickly also helps keep unnecessary clutter out of the customer's account; things like partial payments, unapplied credits, and debit memos, which can cause additional problems or delay the payment of nonproblem invoices—another feature that benefits all parties.

Another tool some companies are using to increase customer satisfaction and forestall problems from impacting payments is the customer service call. This contact can be incorporated into a customer's collection strategy and is especially effective when used with larger-dollar invoices. Very simply, before an invoice comes due, a collector calls the company a specified number of days after the invoice date to see if everything was delivered as promised and that the paperwork is being processed for payment without incidence. If there is a problem, the collector has the opportunity to resolve the issue before it can delay payment. From the customer's point of view, it is a courtesy call that is well received, not a collection call. The call does, however, put the customer on notice that if there are no problems, payment is expected by the due date. (See Exhibit 8.2.)

Looking at the big picture, a professional collection operation that is both fair and firm will be respected by customers. Automating collections raises the standard for a company's collectors, and this will be noticed by customers. Even more than that, a collector's ability to quickly and equitably resolve problems encourages the customer's accounts payable clerks to bring problems to the attention of the collector without hesita-

Exhibit 8.2   Customer Service Calls Speed Collections and Build Goodwill

With five percent of their invoices accounting for roughly 50 percent of their receivables balances, Ortho Clinical Diagnostics, a Johnson & Johnson company, made customer service calls part of its collection strategy for large invoices. Five days before a large invoice is due, a collector gives the customer a courtesy call to make sure the invoice has been received and is approved for payment. If an invoice copy or other documents are needed, they are immediately faxed. If there is a holdup in getting the invoice approved for payment, the collector asks to speak to the person responsible for resolving any problems, in this case often a lab supervisor who is having Ortho's equipment installed. In another situation, a customer gets a one percent discount for payment within 10 days, so the courtesy call also serves to help the customer pay on time to get the discount. These calls require a collector with tact, but they have been very effective in building customer goodwill and helping Ortho get its cash in faster. With some invoices reaching $1 million, a few days' improvement can mean a lot. In Ortho's case, DSO has dropped 20 percent since collections were automated, and part of that reduction is certainly due to using customer service calls in its collection strategies.

tion, which is to all parties' benefit. Such open communication between customer and supplier creates a sense of goodwill that, while intangible, is still an extremely valuable commodity.

IMPROVED MEASUREMENTS

One of the weaknesses in manual collection systems is a lack of satisfactory measurement and assessment tools. Reams of articles have been devoted to the sales bias inherent in DSO. Likewise, looking at aging buckets and dollars past due must take into account sales trends and other corporate issues such as quality problems and manufacturing or distribution weaknesses. No matter how good their collection processes, collectors cannot squeeze money out of stones, which are what some customers become when they feel a supplier is not serving their needs.

Another measurement problem is that while such measurements can be applied to individual collectors as well as entire divisions or companies, they provide only a snapshot of results and give little insight into causes. Because this snapshot is usually taken at the end of the month, the information is provided after the fact and cannot be used to impact the present. Unless collectors working in a manual collection environment are instructed to record all their calls and letters on a log sheet, it is impossible to really know how individual collectors spend their time. Few companies go to this trouble, because maintaining such a log sheet ultimately takes away from the precious little time available for collections. Automating collections provides opportunities to overcome these deficiencies.

Having only month-end numbers can create a distorted view of collection performance. For one thing, collection departments are focused on making their month-end numbers look as good as possible, so a big push to get collections in during the last half of the month is not uncommon. In addition, monthly reporting is often not completed until after the first week of the next month has passed. The upshot is inconsistent collection efforts, and thus results, over the course of the monthly cycle. Since the size of the receivables and collections can affect borrowing, it is difficult to see the costs that are accruing during the month by looking only at the month-end numbers. When collections are automated, with data collected in a centralized database, it is possible to perform much more sophisticated calculations than month-end DSO. Collections software can provide a number for days beyond terms (DBT) or sales weighted days outstanding (SWDO), which remove the sales bias inherent in DSO.

On the one hand, DBT gives a reading of how many days the entire accounts receivable is past due. Extended terms are factored out, as are sales and current receivables, so that an unbiased reading of the average age of a past due invoice is rendered. This provides a fixed mark for comparative purposes that can be accessed at any time during the month.

On the other hand, SWDO calculates the average age of all receivables. It weights each invoice by the dollars involved to provide a reading of how old the average dollar of receivable is. Whereas DSO can actually drop if current invoices are being paid while all other invoices are going further past due, SWDO reflects the actual account receivable aging trends.

However, these two measures do not give an accurate measure of the risk inherent to a particular accounts receivable portfolio. They tell how old items are, without the bias of sales, but they still do not explain why. An automated collection system can explain why by showing the dollars outstanding for each stage of the collection process. What has been done to try to collect an invoice is a good indicator of the risk that invoice will not be paid, or that payment will be further delayed. Items that remain open despite a number of attempts at their collection are obviously matters for concern. Accounts that require more collection than the norm are also candidates for more aggressive collection strategies to compensate for their riskiness.

The ability of automated collection systems to compare DBT, SWDO, and dollars by stage of the collection process between collectors, sales regions, product lines, corporate divisions, and so forth, provides collection managers with powerful analytical tools for better understanding the dynamics that are causing changes in the composition of their accounts receivable. Is a particular type of deduction causing serious problems? Are there an abnormally high number of bad accounts in a particular sales territory? Are different product lines or corporate divisions experiencing different receivables patterns? Are the collectors with the best receivables portfolios making more customer contacts than the other collectors? These powerful questions can be asked of an automated collection system.

It is extremely important that these types of drill-down capabilities exist. An automated collection system will accumulate a tremendous amount of information in its database in a surprisingly short period of time. It is essential to continued productivity improvements that this data be accessible for analysis and evaluation. Being able to look at collection data in new ways has the potential to release previously unrecognized synergies that can help improve not only collections but the performance of other corporate functions as well. This cannot happen without powerful reporting tools.

TRADITIONAL MEASURES OF COLLECTION PERFORMANCE

While the goals discussed so far relate to operational capacity, productivity, and quality, the remaining goals of an automated collection process are the traditional objectives of every collection function. This does not make them any less important. Success in implementing an automated collection process will be assured by dramatic improvement in these measures. However, the means for attaining these objectives is found in implementing programs and procedures that address the operational goals just discussed.

By automating collection tasks and implementing procedures that increase individual collector productivity, contact quantity, and contact quality, and that enhance customer satisfaction, the goals of improving cash flow and reducing DSO, bad debt, and collection expenses will be achieved. The automated tasks and new processes designed to accomplish the first four goals will also serve to achieve these last four. In a somewhat different sense, improved measurements will also enhance collection performance according to these traditional measures. The ability of improved measures to better identify trends within an accounts receivable portfolio, as well as their causes, ultimately results in improved management of collection activities and subsequent improvements in the traditional measures of collection performance.

SUMMARY

The performance objectives to be realized from implementing an automated collection process are identical to the objectives of any collection operation. Only the expected degree of improvement is different, the expectations for automated collections being much higher. By devising automated tasks and processes to meet the prime operational objectives—more collection contacts, better quality collection efforts, and more productive collectors—the desired performance standards should also be attained.

To this end, the following tasks, processes, reports, and utilities are critical to successfully automating the collection process:

1. Specific collection strategies assigned to each customer are at the core of any automated collection system. The strategies drive the collection process by determining what activities should be completed and when.

2. Call objectives are derived from the strategies that help focus collectors on the specific task at hand, and ensure that nothing is overlooked.

3. An automated collection system must also provide excuse prompting so that customer objections can be readily answered without the collector's being deflected from the purpose of the call.

4. The system must contain a customer service issues database that is used by collectors to expedite problem resolution.

5. Who to call first is always an important issue, so creating an automated daily work list is a top priority for an automated collection process. Customers who have broken promises should be listed first, followed by customers with overdue balances in descending order. The capability to then break this report out by each account's stage in the collection process (derived from the collection strategies) or by time zone gives collectors valuable planning and productivity tools.

6. Collection notes need to be recorded automatically to reduce keystroking by collectors—after all, they are collectors, not data-entry clerks. The computerized notepad that contains these customer- and invoice-specific notes then must be integrated into the collection process in order to ensure follow-up and progress through each customer-specific collection strategy.

7. Auto-dial capabilities save time, so collectors can make more calls and send more correspondence.

8. The installation of a fax/modem in each collector's personal computer, or at least as part of the collection department local area network, also enhances productivity in regard to both incoming and out-going communications. These devices allow the faxes and e-mail to be integrated into the collection process.

9. Electronic document imaging puts more information on the collector's desktop quicker. Documents can then be distributed to both internal and external customers, along with other collection correspondence.

---

10. Improved measures of collection performance help answer the question why, as opposed to merely providing an estimate of where we are. Automated collection systems can readily calculate DBT and SWDO, in addition to providing reports on the dollars outstanding by stage of the collection process and other drill-down scenarios in order to pinpoint problems and areas for further improvement.

Automating the collection process requires a redesign of current collection practices if aggressive performance goals are to be met. Automating current practices only serves to further institutionalize the current collection habits of most companies, which are a mixture of computerized receivables processing and manual collections. Such scenarios produce only incremental improvements in collection performance at best. Automating only some parts of the collection process will not achieve the desired results. It is the integration of the whole process that creates the synergy to attain dramatic gains in collection performance.

9

Automated Collection Cycle

The automated collection cycle has the same five elements as a manual collection cycle: prioritization, preparation, contact, follow-up, and reporting. However, the time and effort required of the collector during each stage of the process is quite different. Most notably, the collector spends much more time making many more contacts per hour with an automated collection system as compared to a manual system. This fact alone makes an automated collection system much more efficient and with a considerably higher production capacity than any manual system.

Also, the tasks the collector performs during each stage of the collection cycle are often different from those undertaken with a manual system. Remember, in automating collections, and to achieve peak efficiency, it is necessary to re-engineer the collection process. To automate and not re-engineer the collection process will result only in lost opportunities to realize dramatic breakthroughs in collection performance. To continue performing many traditional collection tasks and routines only perpetuates the inefficiencies inherent to manual collection systems that rely on computerized receivables.

While some traditional tasks and routines remain, many

nonproductive activities have been either eliminated or automated. Besides changing the way traditional tasks are performed, automation has also created a new set of computer-based tasks that empower automated collection systems. The elimination of many clerical tasks that were duplicative or otherwise minimally productive provides the impetus for the performance gains realized with automated collections. (See Exhibit 9.1.)

With manual collection systems, collectors can never find enough time to make all their calls and catch up on all their paperwork. That is no longer the case with an automated collection system. As collectors work their automated collection systems, they can realize the previously unheard of situation in which all reminders have been sent and follow-ups made. Being able to feel in control is empowering in itself, and collectors using automated systems not only enjoy their job more but also enjoy seeing ongoing improvements in their collection efforts.

PRIORITIZATION

The prioritization stage is profoundly affected by the automation of collections because setting collection priorities can be entirely automated. With manual collection systems, prioritization uses up anywhere from a half hour to a full hour of the col-

Exhibit 9.1 **Time Allocations for the Automated Collection Cycle**

Prioritization	0 hours	0%
Preparation	$\frac{1}{2}$ hour	7%
Contact	$6\frac{1}{2}$ hours	79%
Follow-up	$\frac{1}{2}$ hour	7%
Reporting	$\frac{1}{2}$ hour	7%

lector's day. With an automated collection system, prioritization takes no time at all, from the collector's standpoint. This time savings is subsequently re-invested in the productive stage of the collection cycle when the collector is making contact with overdue customers.

With an automated collection system, collectors do not need to spend any time prioritizing their work because the software is able to do all the work. By relying wholly on a computerized algorithm, collection departments also gain the benefit of consistency between collectors. Using the computer to handle the prioritization task ensures that each day the collectors first concentrate on broken promises and then the largest overdue balances, thus maximizing collection results. This keeps all collectors following company priorities rather than their own.

By first concentrating on broken promises to pay, the number of accounts that become serious problems is kept to a minimum. This is true whether the reason for nonpayment is due to a complaint, the customer's financial condition, or simple intransigence. Whatever the excuse, the system forces the collector to deal with the issue sooner rather than later. Consequently, the underlying receivables are not given a chance to get old before appropriate action can be taken. It is equally important that, by showing customers there will be follow-up on their payment promises, there is a higher probability that future promises will be kept.

After broken promises are dealt with, an automated collection system will prioritize subsequent activities based on past due balances, largest dollars first. This ensures that as collectors work through their assigned receivables, making initial contacts for payment of past due balances, each day the accounts with the largest outstanding balances are contacted first. If a collector is unable to get completely through his or her work queue on a given day, the accounts that have not yet been contacted are reprioritized on the next day's work queue, again with largest dollars first, if the overdue balances have not yet been paid. By giving each day's collection priority to the largest past due balances, cash receipts are maximized.

Besides providing a prioritized list of customers to be contacted, an automated collection system also recommends the next collection step to be taken. These recommendations are based on the client-specific collection strategies that have been programmed into the collection software. Again, this ensures consistency between collectors since company standards are being followed by everyone in the collection department. Each time a collector calls up the next account to be contacted, the required action is displayed by the collection software. There is no need for the collector to review previous collection activities in order to determine what to do next. The system makes the next action step obvious to the collector, who can get right to work on the task at hand.

PREPARATION

Unlike a manual system, preparation time with an automated collection system is minimal. In a manual process, most of a collector's preparation time is spent gathering information. Actually reviewing that information does not take much time. With an automated system, all the information a collector requires is kept resident within the computerized database. Gathering information is no longer an issue because it is literally at the collector's fingertips. All that is left for the collector using an automated system to do is to review each customer's situation before taking action. For most accounts, this takes only a few seconds.

One of the information activities that consumes a significant amount of a collector's time is verifying the amount due for each account to be called. The problem with manual collection systems that rely upon a computerized accounts receivable is that prioritization is typically done by reviewing a printed receivables aging report. Collectors might work from the same report for a week or two and, in many cases, an entire month. That means that most of the time they are working with dated information because payments are made and credits issued daily. Therefore, collectors working under these circumstances must of necessity verify account balances before initiating any collection activities. This is most readily done by looking up the customer balance on the collector's computer terminal and noting any differences from the aging report. The other, even less efficient alternative is to manually post payments on the aging report, even though remittance details are already being entered into the accounts receivable software.

If the collector finds an open dispute, even more time is required. The collector's notes will indicate the existence of a dispute but are unable to provide information regarding efforts to resolve the dispute after the note was recorded. Subsequent actions to resolve a dispute are very often undertaken by other internal parties. Evaluating the status of a disputed balance begins with a determination of whether the dispute has been settled by someone else. This often leads down a path of discussions with internal contacts from other departments. The time required to do this dramatically reduces the collector's ability to make outbound contacts.

With an automated collection system, account balances are updated at least daily from the accounts receivable software to the collection software being used. As a result, accounts are prioritized with up-to-date information that requires no verification. A collector moving through the automated work queue can count on the balance information displayed to be reliable. This automated update clears paid items out of the work queue, so no time is wasted by the collector's checking for payments or credits. It has all been done by the collection software.

As a result, the collector is reviewing only the accounts

that will actually be contacted, not accounts that might be contacted if they have not yet paid. Working with a single-minded focus is part of the strength of a fully automated collection system. Extraneous activities have been re-engineered out of the collection process, so the collector is fully focused on collecting.

One extraneous activity that collection software can address is the matter of time zones. Aging reports do not contain this information. Sometimes, the customer's city and state listing will be on the collector's report, but often there will be only a phone number. Since it is hard enough to memorize the location of every area code (especially since they keep changing), collectors usually have an area code map handy to determine the customer's time zone. Determining when is the best time to make a call is another of the collector's prioritization tasks that cuts into the time allocated for contacting customers. An automated system easily addresses this issue so that calls to a specific time zone can be grouped together and made at the most opportune time for reaching the desired contact. Many credit organizations partially address the time zone issue by assigning collectors by geographic region. Of course, this means the collector on the East Coast who covers the West Coast cannot make phone calls for most of the morning. These types of situations continually chip away at productivity, but with an automated system that no longer needs to be the case. Automation permits new organizational priorities, such as assigning collectors by product line, customer type, or even stage of the collection process.

Grouping work by collection step allows for a more productive work flow since the collector can concentrate on the same sort of issues that are inherent at each stage of the collection process. For example, say it is late in the day and the collector is getting tired from having been on the phone for much of the day. By requesting the work queue to list all the remaining

customers requiring a reminder notice—by descending overdue balance, of course—the collector can then maintain a high
level of output by focusing on a type of task that requires less
mental energy than the problem solving that goes along with
phone calls. By the same token, a collector might be all fired up
and in a frame of mind to work through some problem accounts, and can accordingly request the work queue to list the
day's problem accounts—achieving more consistency, higher
productivity, and better collections.

Whether used with a strictly descending dollar prioritization or in a grouping type of scheme, the work queue serves as
the entry point to the customer's collection data screen. A single
keystroke from the work queue screen brings up complete customer details. Previous collection steps taken, account history,
contacts, phone and fax numbers, payment trends, and details
on all overdue items, including a recommendation for the next
collection step based on the customer's assigned collection
strategy, are all displayed for the collector's review. By having
access to collection, customer, and accounts receivable details
from just one screen, collectors can get up to speed on each
delinquent customer's status very quickly. Preparing for collection activities therefore takes very little time at all.

CONTACT

With prioritization completely automated and preparation reduced to brief reviews, collectors are freed to get right into the
contact phase of the collection cycle. No longer can collectors
complain that they are so busy with clerical tasks that they do
not have enough time to collect. More time spent making contact with overdue accounts translates directly into more dollars
collected faster.

Automating collections eliminates the distractions that in-
hibit collectors from contacting more delinquent customers. In

this sense, automating collections is not so much about automating collections, but rather automating all the support tasks that make an effective collection program possible. Streamlining and automating all these peripheral activities allows collectors more time to do what they do best, and that, of course, is to talk on the phone with customers and assist them in paying overdue balances. Automation serves the collector, not the other way around. Collection software does not replace the collection professionals, it makes them better. Automating collections allows collectors to move to a significantly higher level of performance, and the key to that stems from allowing the collector to make many more contacts of a significantly higher quality. That translates into more effective results and more work accomplished. Both capacity and quality improve, and can be measured by dramatic improvements in all measurements of collection performance.

With automated collections, the contact phase is initiated earlier in the billing/payment cycle and is more consistent. Not only are customers being contacted sooner after they go past due (or even before going past due if a customer service type call is part of the assigned strategy), but they are also being contacted sooner as each invoice ages.

With manual collection systems where prioritization is done off an aged receivables trial balance that is sorted by company name, initial contacts are scheduled if an account's delinquent invoices fall within a specified aging category. In many companies, a collector's initial phone calls are made to accounts that have hit the 31 to 60 days past due aging bucket. The problem with this is that while some accounts with balances 31 days past due are being called, other accounts have balances that are already a month older than that at the 60-day parameter. Worse yet is the problem that customers whose names begin with the letter "A" are called early in the month, while those accounts that fall at the end of the alphabet, and so are called later in the month, can wind up getting their first phone call as their balances approach 90 days past due. As time goes on, customers sometimes are called earlier and sometimes later, depending on the follow-up required for each monthly collection cycle. This does not send customers a consistent message regarding payment expectations.

With an automated collection system, customers are always called earlier. This consistency also serves to help train the customer to pay sooner. The inconsistency of manual systems often gives the customer the opportunity to get away with slow payments. With an automated system, that will not happen. In fact, the opposite is possible. As delinquencies are brought under control with an automated collection system, it is possible to gradually decrease the initial contact date in the collection strategies. By doing this over time, customers can be trained to pay even sooner.

Another advantage of training customers to pay on time is that as they begin to do so, there is a decrease in the amount of collection effort required. In turn, fewer past due customers means more time can be devoted to serious and chronic past due problems. Consistency in collection policy and procedures contributes more than any other factor to improving the effectiveness of the collection environment.

Tied into the consistency aspect are the customer-specific collection strategies that are a part of a fully automated collection system. By segmenting an accounts receivable into different customer types and assigning an appropriate collection strategy to each type, the sequential consistency and effectiveness of the collection process is assured.

One of the fundamental tenets of collections is that the pressure on the customer to pay be increased with each subsequent step taken during the collection process. The idea is that each account will eventually reach its trigger point and pay. By programming a collection strategy for each customer, this process of increasing the pressure to pay is institutionalized rather than left to the whim of the collector. As the strategies are followed, it then becomes readily apparent what a particular customer's trigger point is. Then, it is a simple matter to devise a new collection strategy that employs the triggering activity very early in the collection process.

For example, many companies simply throw all statements and dunning letters in the trash and will only respond to a collection phone call. As these customers are identified through the automated collection process, it is a simple matter to reassign them to a collection strategy that starts with a phone call or a fax. To do anything else as a first step is a waste of time, money, and effort. Such an approach may seem obvious, but that is not always the case with manual collection systems. An automated system makes it much easier to identify opportunities to collect faster because of the consistency inherent in automated processes.

The value of the enforced change of environment an automated collection system provides cannot be overstated. From the customer's point of view, initial contact with an automated collection system does not fit the parameters of business as usual. Collectors often resist the language proposed in collection scripts and on automated faxes provided by the system, because the automated system is not affected by the tone of voice a specific customer may exhibit in response to being contacted just a few days after an invoice comes due. Installing an automated collection system is management's way of saying, "We expect all customers of the same type, polite or impolite, to pay by the terms set out on the invoice." Consistency is thereby enforced on the collector and customer alike by an automated collection system.

Past due customers that fall outside of the norm for their customer type can be easily recognized with an automated collection system. This provides the collector with the opportunity to identify exceptions sooner and take corrective action. By the same token, changes in customer behavior are more readily apparent, allowing the collector to respond to the negative changes before they get out of control. Without strategies for each customer type, collectors manage their receivables portfolio on an ad hoc basis, severely limiting the opportunities for substantial improvement. With strategies, opportunities to improve both collections and the collection process naturally arise from the oversight responsibilities of collection management. The more the strategies are used, the easier it is to fine-tune them to improve collections even further and to identify accounts that are out of compliance and thus in need of additional collection efforts.

Not surprisingly, many of the ways customers are contacted are automated, but it need not be a mindless automation. An automated system can create letters or faxes with a few quick keystrokes. This correspondence can include complete invoice and account details because all necessary information is resident within or accessible by the collection software program. What makes this correspondence powerful is the ability of the software and the collector to quickly and easily personalize the message. The software displays data and text in one of several formats that the collector can then change (or not change) to get the attention and meet the unique needs of the customer in question. The collector sends a personalized piece of correspondence rather than a form letter, addressed to a specific decision maker employed by the customer. Unlike dunning notices produced by the accounts receivable software, the correspondence from the automated collection system knows the customer contact last contacted; whether that contact was via telephone, fax, or letter; the specific promises made; and the date the next contact is scheduled. Additionally, because the collection software is focused on having correspondence appear personalized, dates are printed in common language such as "last Thursday," enabling some degree of tone to be imparted, based on the collection strategy and the current juncture of that strategy as it affects the transactions in question. Form letters get thrown out. Personalized correspondence gets read. (See Exhibit 9.2.)

In the time it takes to process form letters, the collector can transmit personalized correspondence. While letters will be used, collectors using an automated system rely much more heavily on faxes. There are two reasons for this. First of all, faxes convey a sense of urgency, which is a message collectors want to get across to their past due accounts. Second, with an automated collection system, faxes can be created and transmitted almost instantly, eliminating mail time from the collection cycle. In some situations, collectors will actually fax their contacts while they are still on the phone with them. This capability is a powerful tool for getting problems resolved and customers to pay. (See Exhibit 9.3.)

In addition to automatically generating letters and faxes, an automated collection system includes e-mail capabilities. This provides the collector with a means of sending quick notes or messages to both internal contacts and external customers. The ability to pull information from the collection database into an e-mail message is a powerful collection tool. E-mail is useful for keeping other departments informed of the status of customer problems and for requesting assistance from other departments in resolving collection issues. The alternative is to make phone calls, which take more time, cause interruption, and often result in frustrating episodes of phone tag. E-mail is direct, quick, and to the point. As a result, everyone can get more work done.

Another tool that benefits the contact phase is automatic dialing. As a collector reviews the customer's status screen, the computer can be dialing the appropriate contact. Though dialing does not take much time (however, it eventually does add

Exhibit 9.2 **Automated Faxes and Letters**

- Merge customer data with collection records
- Use professional and proven texts
- Allow customization
- Enable correspondence to be sent directly from the collector's PC as a fax
- Copies can be sent to other departments via fax or e-mail

Sample Fax Before Customization

Dear Mr. Smith:

This is a reminder that invoices for your account #42536 are overdue. We expected to receive payment after our phone conversation last Wednesday. Your account has an overdue balance of $634.15 and some invoices are over 53 days old.

Our records show the following invoices remain unpaid on your account.

Invoice	Date	Purchase Order	Amount	Balance
23967	7/18/97	3254667-756	195.65	195.65
23989	7/19/97	3254667-756	195.65	391.30
25273	8/10/97	3258454-756	242.85	634.15

Your total account balance is $957.75. Please mail your check today.

Sincerely,

Sample Customized Fax

Dear Jeff:

This is a reminder that invoices for your account #42536 are overdue. We expected to receive payment after our phone conversation last Wednesday. Your account has an overdue balance of $634.15 and some invoices are over 53 days old.

Our records show the following invoices remain unpaid on your account.

Invoice	Date	Purchase Order	Amount	Balance
23967	7/18/97	3254667-746	195.65	195.65
23989	7/19/97	3254667-756	195.65	391.30
25273	8/10/97	3258454-756	242.85	634.15

Your total account balance is $957.75. Please mail your check today.

Sincerely,

Bob

PS: Hope you had a great vacation . . . but it's back to work!

Though the difference between these two samples is not great, the effect of customization is significant. The customer knows the customized fax has been created by a real person and not just a machine.

Exhibit 9.3 **Do Not Let the Message Affect the Medium**

Though the ability to edit correspondence is important, collectors need to keep that capability in perspective. Specifically, collectors should not be spending a lot of time editing form letters. Adding a quick personal touch, yes, but editing text, no.

After Liener Health Products installed collection software, it found that although output was up, its collectors were not sending as many faxes as expected. The reason was excessive editing. This required getting the collectors to understand that they needed to trust the wording of the form letters and expedite their processing. The message was "Don't think about it, don't edit it, just do it."

While format is certainly important, nuances in wording have only a superficial impact on collections. Creating the perfect collection message is not critical. Getting the collection note in front of the customer at the appropriate time, without expending a lot of time and effort, is the key to effectiveness. Once the issue of editing was addressed, Liener's collectors' output jumped dramatically, as did subsequent cash receipts.

up), the big savings comes from not having the distraction of looking up contact names and phone numbers. An automated collection system stores multiple internal and external contact names and addresses in addition to phone and fax numbers for each contact name.

Once the intended party has been reached, the collection software can assist the collector in meeting the call's objectives. This is done through scripts that are tied into each account's preprogrammed collection strategy. If this is a first call, the collector is prompted to simply ask for payment. However, if it is a call following up on a promised payment, the collector is directed to ask more probing questions not only to get a new commitment but also to find out why the payment was not sent as promised. (See Exhibit 9.4.)

Exhibit 9.4   Sample Scripts

Sample #1:   Customer Service Scenario

1.	Greeting	I am calling to make sure your order that was billed on invoice #1234 was okay.
2A.	If okay	Good. Do you have a copy of the invoice?
2A1.	If they say yes	It's late. When will the check be mailed? (Record date and amount)
2A2.	If they say no	I'll fax it to you. When will it be paid? (Record date and amount)
2B.	If not okay	What is the problem? (Listen carefully)
2B1.	If you can solve it	I'll take care of that.
2B2.	If not	I'll report it to customer service (Press N and type short note describing the problem)

Sample #2:   Fax First Scenario

1.	Greeting	I'm following up on the fax we sent yesterday. I'm very concerned. Your account balance is $3,456 and it's late. Some of it is 47 days overdue. Is there a problem?
2A.	If they say yes	What is the problem?
2A1.	If you can solve it	I'll take care of that.
2A2.	If not	I'll report it to customer service (Press N and type short note describing the problem)
2B1.	If you do not believe them	I would like you to speak with my manager. (Transfer call)
2C.	If they say no	When can we expect payment on the open invoices? (Record dates and amounts)

Sample #3:   Common Excuses

If the customer says . . .	The collector responds . . .
• The check is in the mail.	What is the check number, invoices being paid, amount, and when was it mailed?
• I cannot pay you this week.	How much are you short? What can you send?
• I do not have an invoice copy (or other document).	I am faxing that to you right now. When can you send payment?
• That invoice has not been approved for payment.	Who approves the invoice, and can transfer me to them?

The second role of the automated scripts is to help the collector respond to customer excuses. This is especially useful for less experienced collectors, but even the best can sometimes draw a blank. The collector is able to move from the customer's status screen to a screen that displays the scripts. If a customer gives an excuse, the collector can just click on it to get suggested responses. In this way, the collector is able to control the course of the conversation with the debtor for a much more focused and effective result. The proper response to a specific reason for not paying is one part of the unwritten corporate culture that collectors need to learn before they can proceed with confidence. Scripting maintains consistency and management control of the culture besides helping new collectors adapt quickly to their new environment.

As the collector works down through the work queue, all collection activities are automatically recorded. The system knows who has been called or faxed and what invoice balances were addressed. It is little extra work for the collector to enter the customer's response. From that information, the automated collection system then schedules the next collection step. Contact notes can be recorded against either a particular invoice or the account in whole. This allows item-specific issues—a dispute on an invoice, for example—to be reflected against only that item. On the other hand, if the customer is facing a seasonal cash shortage, that information is recorded as an account issue and will be shown whenever the account is reviewed, not just when the invoices in question are investigated.

The invoice-specific customer notes are critical to the collector's need to track problems. An automated system, in addition to these contact notes, also allows for a problem category (sometimes called a deduction or reason code) to be recorded against specific invoices. With this information, collectors now have the means to effectively track and resolve problems, using e-mail and faxes to share information with their internal contacts and external customers.

This permits the collector to separate problem invoices from routine past due balances. Routine collections continue while problems are being resolved. It also allows problems to be grouped together for handling. As was mentioned in the section on preparation, the collector has the option of ordering the work queue by the collection stages. This helps the collector maximize collection results by concentrating on similar collection activities rather than always jumping from one type of collection situation to another. Working on problem items is no different. It is especially important that invoice problems and deductions be handled efficiently, since they usually involve smaller balances but traditionally consume a disproportionate amount of a collector's time. By identifying, isolating, and tracking problems, automated collection software allows the collector to remain focused on maximizing collections.

Perhaps the most important factor accounting for the increase in collections that derives from automating the process is the added time that is spent on the contact phase of the collection cycle. With a re-engineered and automated collection process, collectors typically increase the time spent on contacting overdue accounts by a factor of two and a half to three. This is a pure and simple increase in collection capacity. However, on top of the time being spent contacting overdue accounts, the actual process of doing so is also more efficient. Therefore, there is a productivity component that complements the capacity improvements. This explains why automated collection departments are able to survive downsizings and hiring freezes to do more, usually much more, with less human resources.

FOLLOW-UP

The time spent on follow-up with an automated collection system is significantly lower than for manual collections. Traditionally, gathering and disseminating documentation took up the bulk of a collector's time during the follow-up phase. Since an automated collection system maintains a database of invoice details that is linked to automated letter, fax and e-mail tools, much less time needs to be devoted to this phase (see Exhibit 9.5). Word processing templates merge the data customers require for processing payments into useful formats. This is a transparent process from the collectors point of view. Collectors need to do little more than select the document required. (See Exhibit 9.6.)

When working with a manual system, collectors often

Exhibit 9.5 **The Power of Automated Customer Contact**

- Customer contact starts sooner
- Collections follows a strategic process for each customer type
- Customer promises are consistently followed up
- Personalized, automated faxes and letters are quickly created
- Notes and documents are e-mailed to internal customers
- Automatic dialing saves time and increases focus
- Scripts help collectors meet call objectives and answer excuses
- Activities are automatically recorded
- Time zones are taken into consideration, improving connection percentages
- Calls with similar objectives can be grouped for higher productivity
- Customer problems are automatically tracked

Exhibit 9.6   **Imaging Complements Collections Software**

Imaging programs can be an excellent supplement to collection software. One reason for this is that for capacity reasons, collection software cannot maintain a comprehensive historical database of paid or otherwise closed billing documents. An imaging system can.

For this reason, Sony Entertainment began archiving images of all invoices and other billing records on CD. Using Windows-based imaging software and an LAN (local area network) to store the CDs has given Sony's collectors near immediate access to virtually any billing and shipping document they might require. By using the Windows operating system, the collectors are able to cut and paste entire documents into word processing software. Because each collector also has a fax/modem in his or her PC, these documents can be quickly disseminated to both external and internal customers.

The big advantage to Sony's collectors is the time saved from finding and retrieving paper documents, which are many times located in another department that can be in a distant part of the building such as on another floor, copying original documents, refiling documents, and manually faxing correspondence. Essentially, the collectors do not have to touch any paper, only information, and that is an imminently more productive scenario, especially in terms of reducing the time spent on the follow-up phase of the collection cycle.

---

group their calls and, having made a number of calls, then go back over the results to address any follow-up issues. With an automated collection system, follow-up activities are usually quickly handled, often during the course of the call itself. In particular, duplicate invoices and confirmation letters are easily sent to the customer during the course of a collection call. When paper documents do need to be retrieved, the problem-tracking feature of the software helps ensure that the information needs of all interested parties have been met so that a quick resolution of the problem can be achieved. In particular, problem reports and notices can be quickly and easily sent to internal customers such as sales, customer service, shipping, etc. Also, once a document has been faxed or scanned into an automated collection system, the facsimile of that document is then available to be faxed to anybody else who needs it.

REPORTING

The changes an automated collection system brings to the reporting stage are transformational. With a manual collection system, most of the time spent on reporting is taken up with compiling reports. As a result, the analysis and evaluative components of the reporting phase are typically short-changed. However, an automated collection system reverses these two components of the reporting phase. Reports are generated much more easily with an automated collection system, putting the focus on analysis and evaluation. The time thus spent better serves the objective of continually improving the collection process.

The reports that can be generated are also more useful in evaluating collector performance. With a manual collection system, it is very difficult to measure a collector's performance, and because the measurements used are not usually available until after the close of a month of business, the results are not useful for changing the current collection month's trends or otherwise changing collector performance. It is virtually impossible to accurately measure an individual's collection results on an objective basis. At best, companies are able to calculate a sales-biased days sales outstanding (DSO) number and print out an aged accounts receivable trial balance for each collector. Because an automated collection system compiles its own centralized database, many more useful reports can be generated and made available daily, reflecting the last few days' productivity or lack of it.

With automated collection software, there is no longer a need to wait until the end of the month to generate reports. With a database that is updated daily, performance criteria are always available for review. Also, because the database contains more information than the typical accounts receivable software program can provide, the reports an automated collection system provides measure a variety of factors that have not been available with traditional systems. (See Exhibit 9.7.)

One group of daily reports provides summaries of balances by collection stage, customer type, and receivables age. Only balance summaries by receivables age are generally available from an accounts receivable software package, and then

Exhibit 9.7 **Improved Reporting Does Not Just Benefit Management**

Liener Health Products is using the reporting function from its collection software to document individual collector productivity when they conduct collector performance reviews. Prior to automating, determining whether collectors were getting their work done was primarily based on perceptions, because there was no hard data to reveal what was actually being accomplished. Automating collections now allows Liener to track each collector's performance.

The greater benefit, however, is that just by having performance statistics and sharing those numbers with all the collectors, individual productivity has improved. Being able to compare their performance to everybody else's in the department is motivating Liener's collectors to do more. Even though everybody will not aspire to be on top, nobody wants to be left behind on the bottom of the pile.

Collectors also had their own perceptions as to how hard they were working. Being able to consult hard facts will shatter any such misconceptions and also serve as positive reinforcement as performance improves.

not usually on a daily basis. However, the balance summaries by collection stage and customer type are more valuable for recognizing trends and identifying problem areas. Balance summaries by receivables age provide an overview of the entire receivable and its dynamics; however, such a report will not clearly reveal the underlying fundamentals driving changes in the composition of the receivables. Being able to break out the same information by collection stage and customer type will.

For example, a successful sales promotion can create a short-term increase in accounts receivable, and as these receivables age they will affect the past due percentages for the various aging buckets. The movement of these receivables through the aging report is somewhat reminiscent of the proverbial pig in the python. Hopefully, the receivables that result from the sales promotion will be collected in a relatively timely matter, so that the pig is pretty much digested by the time it reaches the older aging buckets. However, as time elapses after the sales promotion, there are other factors affecting the receivables. To blame any increase in the older aging buckets on a sales promotion that occurred several months ago is therefore a logical stretch if the only report being evaluated is an aged accounts receivable trial balance.

A balance summary by customer type will in fact shed more light on such a phenomenon. It might reveal that there is a payment problem with only one type of customer. If the sales promotion was directed at only one type of customer, the balance summary by customer type could show that the collection problem is actually centered in another customer group. This type of information is not revealed by viewing only a receivables aging.

By the same token, a balance summary by collection stage will shed light on which collection steps are ineffective or being overlooked. If balances are not being cleared up until a follow-up step is taken, there is good reason to re-evaluate the initial contact activities built into the collection strategies. Likewise, if a sizable portion of the accounts receivable are reaching the more advanced collection stages, the overall collection strategy being employed may be ineffective, or possibly there is a serious industry trend developing. By using these various types of daily summary balance reports, it is then much easier to establish a collection strategy that will achieve corporate goals. (See Exhibits 9.8 through 9.11.)

Exhibit 9.8 **Reports Available with an Automated Collection System**

- Daily balance summaries (sortable by collector)
    By age
    By collection stage
    By customer type
- Exception reports
- Ad hoc reporting
- Cash receipts/Cash flow forecasts
- Customer service/Deduction reports

Better reporting enhances evaluation. This is especially true with deduction management, in which identifying the causes of deduction issues is critical to success. In order to identify the root causes of deductions, which are usually the result

Exhibit 9.9 **Sample Exception Reports**

- Customers of a specific type who have invoices over 50 days that exceed $8,000
- Customers who have invoices outstanding that exceed their average payment days by 5 or more days

---

of internal practices, good information is absolutely essential. Because automated collection software allows for the entry and storage of deduction or reason codes, reports can be generated to help evaluate the situation. These customer service reports provide insights for other corporate departments as to the problems customers are experiencing. Being able to easily gather and organize this information about deductions or other problems evaluation is rendered much less difficult.

The big advantage gained from an automated and computerized collection process, however, is that more time can be spent on evaluation because the system automatically tracks the underlying data. Successful deduction management does not depend on how well deductions are managed, but rather upon eliminating the root causes. By being able to spend more time on evaluation, more effort is subsequently spent on the elimination process. This in turn frees up more time for working high-dollar collections as opposed to the small-dollar dilution that results from the accumulation of redundant deduction issues.

Exhibit 9.10 **Sample Ad Hoc Reports**

- All customers with invoices from a specific sales promotion who have invoices in dispute and, although they were excluded from the sales promotion, still believe their balances should have been included.
- All customers whose 12-month high credit has exceeded $50,000 and whose average payment days have been more than 15 days past due.

SUMMARY

The most visible changes that result from automating collection processes relate to the amount of time dedicated to the different

Exhibit 9.11   **Cash Receipts Forecasting**

12/01/97 Page 1	Yore Manufacturing Corporation Projected Cash Receipts Forecast				
		Week Of:			
Customer	*Acct. #*	*9/8/97*	*9/15/97*	*9/22/97*	*9/29/97*	*10/6/97*
STELL Unpromised	2940		1244	255		
COAST Promised	2941		250076		52586	
TRIDE Promised	2944	125786	223634			
MICRO Unpromised	2945			2512	1809	1206
SAVAN Unpromised	2950	1348				
QUOTE Promised Unpromised	2952	245376	124624	22347		
PROMA Unpromised	3232		196	5104	17634	
SAVAN Promised Unpromised	4096	24340 33167				
CHRIS Promised Unpromised	4097		609 2450	15354		
QUEST Unpromised	4102	11763	192058			
Grand Total Promised Unpromised		441780 269716 172064	794891 474319 320572	45572 15354 30218	72029 52586 19443	1206 0 1206

steps in the collection cycle. A cursory review of Exhibit 9.12 shows how dramatic these changes are. Obviously, differences of this magnitude indicate fundamental changes in the conduct of collections. By significantly reducing the amount of time spent on prioritization, preparation, and follow-up, a tremendous amount of time is freed up for contacting overdue accounts. Combined with streamlined processes, automation provides a powerful engine for credit departments to collect more and faster.

Underlying these changes in the amount of time allocated to each of the different stages of the collection cycle is the automation of clerical and repetitive tasks. This is what creates more time for the collectors and in a sense increases the capacity of an automated collection process over a manual system that relies on computerized accounts receivables. Many of the automation tools that drive a re-engineered and computerized collection process are in turn enabled by the consolidation of accounts receivable and collection information within a single database. Thus, the time spent accessing and manipulating data is drastically reduced so that collection efforts can be directed toward increasing the quantity and quality of contracts made. As a result, automating collections increases a credit depart-

Exhibit 9.12 **Automated and Manual Collection Compared**

Activity	Manual	Automated	Savings (Increase)	Percentage
Prioritization	½ hour	0 hours	½ hour	100%
Preparation	1½ hours	½ hour	1 hour	67%
Contact	2½ hours	6½ hours	(4½ hours)	(160%)
Follow-up	3 hours	½ hour	2½ hours	83%
Reporting	½ hour	½ hour	0 hours	No change

ment's production capacity besides increasing the individual productivity of collectors.

Further productivity is derived from an automated collection system through the generation of added intelligence that can be brought to bear on the collection process. Not only does an automated collection process consolidate information resources for presentation in highly intelligible formats, but computerized collection software also both captures and creates information that has never before been available. This reporting power can then be used to make further modifications and tactical adjustments to the collection process in order to wring even more cash flow out of the accounts receivable by better allocating limited resources. Time spent compiling reports with a manual collection system is now spent evaluating a larger selection of automatically generated reports that integrated collection software makes possible.

The bottom line is that automated collections result in more time (capacity), more effective collections (quality), and much more insight into the trends and dynamics affecting accounts receivable (which can then be translated into increased productivity). Because of these three factors, automated collections provide a tremendous improvement in performance over manual collection systems, even those that rely on computerized receivables software. Perhaps best of all, collectors are empowered by automated collection systems to retake control of their work and are therefore able to concentrate on improvement rather than survival.

10

Automation Pitfalls: What Not to Do

There are a number of pitfalls that can impede a collection automation project or send it down a path that will eventually lead to discarding the effort. These are usually either misguided activities or solutions that will significantly diminish the capacity of an automated collection system to get the job done. At worst, these impediments will render a new collection system as inefficient as the old one. Exhibit 10-1 lists the four things to be avoided when automating collections. Most of the time they result from trying to come up with a quick fix rather than a comprehensive solution. Incrementalism, rather than process re-engineering, is a sure way to achieve incremental improvements at best rather than dramatic performance enhancements.

Keep in mind that in order to achieve dramatic improvements in collection performance, collectors must be more productive, and they also must demand a system that is easier to work with and that provides considerably more collection capacity than is presently offered. The goal is to collect more dollars in less time, and that cannot be done without the full buy-in and involvement of the collections staff. Automation

Exhibit 10.1   **Beware These Automation Pitfalls**

1. Automating ineffective processes
2. Installing a simple notes organizer, tickler system, or contact manager
3. Add partial solutions that add keystrokes
4. Affect the A/R software directly

projects that do not address the human factor are destined to fall short of the mark.

AUTOMATING INEFFECTIVE PROCESSES

One of the biggest mistakes a company can make when it implements a new software system is to automate its old manual processes without any thought to whether there might be a better way of accomplishing the task at hand. In so doing, ineffective processes are institutionalized. The result is systems that do not have a significant impact on the metrics they were intended to influence. Very often, besides not providing the productivity gains that were expected, these systems are cumbersome, overly complex, and expensive to maintain. There is no strategic benefit to the user in further institutionalizing the old manual collection process through computerization. Sometimes it is easy to adapt "the way we've always done things" to computerization, but the results will almost always be disappointing. Automating re-engineered processes, on the other hand, provides all the advantages of a streamlined series of tasks: speed, accuracy, throughput, reliability, and improvement in the targeted metrics on an entirely new scale.

One example of an ineffective process is the practice of many collection departments to send a series of dunning letters to their past due accounts before other collection steps are taken. If collectors are working with a manual collection system and have more accounts than can be personally contacted in any given month, a mass mailing of dunning letters will provide blanket coverage. Collection departments can even outsource this activity to a dunning letter service, freeing their staffs to concentrate on calls. Companies that have chosen this approach will typically send two to five letters before they begin making collection calls. By that time, there are fewer past due accounts, albeit they are now probably 30 to 45 days past due.

The letters do have some positive effects on cash flow, but the percentage of effective letters goes down with each subsequent mailing. Because many customers choose to pay a set number of days slow, typically 15 to 30, many times the letters are ignored. The letters make no difference to these accounts but get sent anyway. Other letters go out to accounts that have made partial payments or have otherwise indicated a problem with their outstanding bills. In these cases, the continued receipt of dunning letters can be quite annoying to these customers.

How mass-produced dunning letters are generated can also create problems. They are sometimes created from a computer program that identifies invoices within a specified date range. In this case, a single customer may get several dunning letters at one time because several invoices fall within the date range. Dunning letters created in this fashion may contain a fair amount of invoice details to help the customer research the past due balance, but if the dunning letters are generated from an aging report, often less supporting information is provided. Companies that employ a dunning letter service often turn over a diskette or tape of their accounts receivable each month. The dunning letter service then begins sending letters to every account with balances in the 1- to 30-day aging column. This means letters sometimes go out to balances only a few days old, but sometimes by the time the first letter arrives, the balance is over 30 days past due. Letters generated in this fashion may also only reflect a balance due with few other supporting details.

The point is that while mass-produced dunning letters can have a place in a manual collection system, despite their weaknesses, to then integrate mass-produced dunning letters, as they are generated today, into a fully automated collection process would be a grave error. To send the same letter to every past due account simply because they are past due the same number of days produces no strategic advantage over current practices. The best that can be hoped for is generating the letters more efficiently, but that overlooks some of the inherent flaws of mass-produced dunning letters.

One large flaw is that, unless done manually, disputed balances, with the potential of upsetting the customer, are not excluded from the dunning letter run. Automated dunning systems also ignore the fact that utilizing client-specific strategies in any automated collection process is a requirement. Another problem arises when collectors use statements or dunning notices to drive or schedule follow-up calls. This causes the bulk of call activity to fall during only one time period each month. The rest of the month does not get the consistent calling activity that is needed, and during crunch times it is hard to make all the follow-up calls because there is only so much time in a day. One last problem with automated dunning notices is that there is no possibility of including an invoice with the letter if appropriate. Automating mass-produced dunning letters merely automates an ineffective practice, and will not result in dramatic improvements in performance and productivity. (See Exhibit 10.2.)

In the case of dunning letters, the solution is to create a

Exhibit 10.2 **Automation Needs to Address These Inefficient Practices**

Inefficient Practice	Explanation
1. Statements	Most companies do not pay from statements. Statements create unnecessary requests for duplicate invoices, and the inquiries that result when a large number of statements are sent early every month can interrupt more critical collection activities.
2. Dunning letter series	Each series of letters is significantly less effective than the previous letter. Mass-produced dunning letters also requireing significant clerical resources that are not always available to collectors, who must then do it all themselves or pay for an outside service.
3. Not identifying and coding problems	Customers then get dunned for disputed items. Besides aggravating customer service issues this practice increases collection costs by causing redundant efforts. In addition, reports do not accurately reflect A/R status.
4. Not linking A/R updates to the tickler file	When invoices are paid or credited, cleared items should be cleared from the follow-up list. Otherwise, the collectors have to review their computerized to do list to see what has been paid.
5. Linking reporting to the end-of-the-month closing	When collections is put on an accounting cycle, collection activity is affected by month-end closing activities, both delaying the compilation and therefore the analysis of reports and interrupting collection activities.

process whereby appropriate form letters may be readily customized and quickly transmitted to the past due account as part of the collection strategy for that account. Such letters would be sent at an appropriate time in conjunction with other collection steps to ensure early payment of past due balances. Automated correspondence then becomes a targeted tool rather than a scatter gun, hope-we-hit-something approach. The ability to produce many, much more effective letters in a relatively short period of time, and in most cases deliver the correspondence electronically via fax or e-mail, is a much more effective process than simply adding more automation to the typical dunning letter system.

Of course, it takes more time and effort to devise a system that can generate correspondence that is both automated and customized, but the benefits far outweigh the costs. In automating repetitive tasks, the benefits of automating are mitigated by any inefficiencies built into the system. To look for the quick fix, then, is extremely shortsighted and much more costly in the long run.

INSTALLING A SIMPLE NOTES ORGANIZER, TICKLER SYSTEM, OR CONTACT MANAGER

Many collectors schedule follow-up calls on a desk calendar or day timer. With manual collection systems, this is a common-sense practice that allows collectors to not only keep track of upcoming follow-up calls but to also manage future work-loads—they do not want to schedule too many calls for one day. Having scheduled the follow-ups on the calendar, most collectors will also cross off those accounts who pay as promised. This takes a fair amount of clerical effort. Even if the collector waits until the actual day the follow-ups are scheduled, to review who has paid and therefore does not need to be contacted, quite a bit of time is required.

With the growth and acceptance of Personal Information Management Systems (PIMS) and the availability of off-the-shelf calendar and contact manager programs for personal computers, using such programs in a commercial collection environment would appear to provide a quick and easy automation solution to the task of maintaining an effective tickler system. From the standpoint of the individual collector, using such a program might be of some assistance, especially if the manual tickler system was subpar. However, these programs are to a certain extent only as good as the information and effort put into them, because the data that drives the automated calendar program must be entered manually. Instead of recording the information on a paper calendar, it is now being recorded on a computerized calendar, which is not necessarily faster to do.

If that is personally preferable to the individual collector, there will probably be some benefits. Some of these programs will dial the phone, launch a word processing program using a macro to fill out the header for a letter with the contact's name and address, or perform a number of other nifty utilities. As such, they can provide some incremental benefits to the collector who is competent in using the software. However, they fail to deliver dramatic improvements in productivity because they are not integrated with the accounts receivable database.

Just having a program list the accounts that require follow-up on a particular date is not enough. When a tickler file indicates that action is required on an account, the collector must still look up the account on the computer to check open transactions and dates as part of the process of deciding whether the account really needs to be contacted (invoices could have been paid) and, if so, just what type of contact is appropriate. Having decided to initiate a contact, the collector may still need to gather specific account information to complete the preparation stage.

Many corporate programming departments will write a simple tickler or note-taking program as an adjunct to the accounts receivable software module. While these programs might have some integration with the receivables database, they probably lack some of the personal productivity features that come with the off-the-shelf calendar or contact management software. Unless the in-house programmer has been willing or able to spend the time, a simple tickler or note-taking program will not appreciably automate the collection process. Unless such contact management software is able to

- Prioritize a collector's daily work
- Determine the next collection step to be taken based on client-based collection strategies
- Update itself when invoices are paid
- Automatically record the collection activity just completed
- Generate customizable correspondence
- Dial the phone, send the fax, or transmit the e-mail
- Code and track problem items
- Provide reports on collector productivity

it will not have a dramatic impact on collections. If it did all this, it would not be contact management software, it would be automated collections software.

Automated collections software in essence is a contact management program that integrates the whole collection process, not just a piece of it. Contact management software merely automates a task—recording and scheduling contacts—it does not automate the collection process. Companies that previously had a notes organizer or tickler system as part of their accounts receivable software module still realized dramatic performance gains when they fully automated collections and got rid of their old ticklers (see Exhibit 10.3). In fact, it appears that the productivity improvements for companies that formerly used some form of contact management software in their collection process were as sizable as for those firms that had relied on manual ticklers and calendars before fully automating collections.

Worse yet, some tickler systems built into accounts receivable software modules are counterproductive. One major accounting software company has put a follow-up date on every transaction, but few collectors are willing to use it. If they do, most of their time is spent advancing the dates on high-transaction-volume customers. Also, when a transaction comes up for follow-up, the collector must still perform a search to find out if any other items are past due. This tickler system only compounds the clerical burden faced by the collectors, and it is no wonder that they fall back on manual methods.

DEVELOP PARTIAL SOLUTIONS THAT ADD KEYSTROKES

There are many partial solutions that are tried by credit and collection departments to automate collection tasks. Some can be as simple as having the corporate programming department create a hot key so collectors can flip quickly back and forth between a computer screen displaying a customer's outstanding receivables and an invoice details screen. Others can be much more complicated, requiring data to be pulled from a number of files to create useful information screens or search utilities to help research issues raised by past due accounts. Done well, such automation utilities can stimulate incremental improvements in collection performance.

Often, companies upgrade their accounting or business system software only to find that the new accounts receivable software that came as part of the package does not do the job as

Exhibit 10.3 **Automated Notepads Fall Short**

One of the reasons Nalco Chemical of Napierville, Illinois, turned to a dedicated collection software package was that its accounting software, despite having much better than average collection utilities for this type of software package, still did not provide a complete automation solution. On the accounts receivable side of the ledger, Nalco was realizing a 95 percent hit rate from the software's auto-cash function (see Chapter 14, "Automated Cash Applications"). Flowing from the cash application features, the software also provided some sophisticated deduction management tools (see Chapter 13, "Deduction Management"). However, without the proper collection automation tools, this software failed to provide the productivity gains Nalco desired.

A major problem with the accounting software package was the fact that its mechanism for recording customer contacts was limited to one action deed per account rather than being able to drill down to an invoice-by-invoice level. Because of this, Nalco's collectors still had to track invoices individually, using accounts receivable agings to monitor payments and broken promises. In essence, the notepad automation features of this accounting software package merely duplicated existing manual processes. Also, because this notepad was linked to the customers' accounts and not their invoices, it could not provide any intelligence to drive automated faxes or letters, a critical fault.

To correct these deficiencies, Nalco installed a dedicated collection software package that addresses these issues. The collection software downloads accounts receivable information from the accounting software. Nalco's collectors then work from the collections package, without the need to refer to manual notes or paper reports. As a result, the collectors have been able to substantially increase, on a daily basis, the number of customer contacts being made.

well as the old software system. This does not necessarily mean the new receivables software is not as good as the old, but is more a reflection of the enhancements that were written for the old software. The loss of these piecemeal system improvements, in aggregate, is often not completely made up for by any improvements the new receivables software may offer. Only after the new software has been thoroughly tested and assorted enhancements written to address any loss of utility in terms of credit and collections does the company get back to square one.

Also, it should be kept in mind that accounts receivable software is primarily just that and not credit and collection software. Most enhancements therefore tend to be written to provide additional credit or collection functionality. This being the case, nearly all companies, no matter what accounts receivable software they use, will find it essential to create at least some software solutions to address needs within their processes affected by credit and collections. While there is a potential for improvements in doing this, there is also the potential to create an array of Rube Goldberg–like software patches that in the long run complicate the collection process and accordingly restrict the capacity to collect more.

In today's competitive environment, there is no place for poorly thought out solutions. The tendency of understaffed and overworked corporate programming departments, however, is to look for quick fixes rather than system improvements. While automating tasks can provide incremental benefits, their long-term payback is much less than that of system improvements. Worse still are partial solutions that are inadequate to the task at hand and suffer from design flaws. They subtly perpetuate inferior processes and complicate future system improvements.

One way to identify those partial solutions that will negatively impact a collection system is by the number of keystrokes they require. If a partial solution adds keystrokes, it is better to leave things unchanged. Effective solutions have the opposite characteristic of significantly reducing keystrokes. After all, the purpose behind automation is to reduce the scope and quantity of manual tasks. Replacing a manual task with data-entry duties is not automation.

The number of keystrokes, however, is just the tip of the iceberg. Keystrokes are a symptom of poor design. For example, say that a company wants its collectors to be able to fax an invoice while they are talking with a customer. Requiring the collector to get out of the primary collection screen, navigate to a reprint screen, type in an invoice number, a fax number, a contact name, and the collector's name is not an effective automation solution. There is too much data that must be rekeyed (increasing the chance of an error), and once the collector has done all this, he or she may need to navigate back to the primary collection screen to address the next open item. Even though adding automated invoice faxing capabilities to the system is an improvement over manually retrieving invoices or even simply reprinting invoices on a collection department printer, it does not meet the standards of a fully automated function.

A better solution is a fax key that will automatically send a copy of all marked invoices. After all, the computer system should already know who the collector is, the contact person called, and that person's fax number. The extra time and expense of programming a total solution right from the start will reduce costs and improve efficiency over time. The bottom line is a manifold increase in productivity.

AFFECT THE ACCOUNTS RECEIVABLE SOFTWARE DIRECTLY

To some, this may seem like an obvious warning. However, it needs to be stated and clarified because it is very common for corporate programming departments to make repeated minor changes to the accounts receivable software, none of which have a negative effect on the original functionality of this software, that is, until it is decided that an upgrade or major changes are required to be made to the original accounts receivable software. At this point, carrying forward all these little programming changes require a major time commitment from corporate programmers.

Also, the more of these minor changes that are made, the greater the chance that something will inadvertently affect the functionality of the original accounts receivable software program. From an audit standpoint, as soon as changes are made to a proven program, the integrity of that program, whether or not it is actually compromised, is called into question. With today's integrated software, small problems are not necessarily isolated and therefore have the potential to affect other areas of the system.

Anything that adds to the complexity of accounts receivable software should be avoided at all costs. Trying to reprogram accounts receivable software so that it also automates collections simply adds complexity. Making accounts receivable software do something it was not designed for is counterproductive. Such a system will never achieve the peak efficiencies of a system designed specifically and solely to automate collections. (See Exhibit 10.4.)

The alternative to affecting accounts receivable software is a collection system that draws information from the accounts receivable software being used but never changes the information in the accounts receivable software's databases and never uploads any information to the accounts receivable software. The only relationship the collection software should have with the accounts receivable software is download and look-up capabilities. All collection activities are then done within the confines of the collections software, as are all accounts receivable activities such as billing, adjustments, and

Exhibit 10.4   Interfacing Accounts Receivable to Collections

AR to Collections Interface

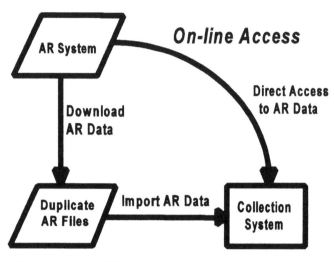

On-line Access

Download Method

The chart shows how collection software takes accounts receivable data, combines it with collection-specific information, and then presents it in a collection-sensitive format. The installation and update process for these systems is relatively straightforward because the transfer of data is one way—accounts receivable to collections.

Data is moved from accounts receivable to collections either by downloading or via on-line integration. The download method calls for a periodic (typically nightly) download to the collection system. The software then manipulates this updated accounts receivable data relative to the collection data that has been accumulating through the collection process. In the on-line method, collections directly accesses the information stored in the accounts receivable system, continually redefining the collection process as cash and new invoices are posted. The on-line method requires an AR system that stores its data in a client–server environment so the collections software can get direct access to the accounts receivable data.

cash posting kept within the working capabilities of the accounts receivable software.

By not affecting accounting software, automating collections is both simplified and concentrated solely on the collection process. When information contained in the accounting software is downloaded to the collection system, or retrieved through a simple look-up screen, there is no risk of affecting accounts receivable records. Processing information within the collection software is therefore not complicated by the need to preserve the integrity of the accounting system. Data retrieved from the accounting system can then be re-arranged, manipulated, and added to without consequence.

It is also possible to build a data format that is better suited to collections than to accounting. Limitations in the field and file structures of accounting software pose no impediment to the design and function of the collection software and the process it serves. For example, collectors often find that they have multiple contacts at a single customer. Usually, there is a primary contact, but depending on the nature of the customer's business and the vendor–customer relationship, there can be several other people who are contacted fairly regularly. All these contacts may have their own phone, fax, and e-mail numbers, not to mention different titles. Most accounts receivable software will provide for only one credit contact. Chances are, adding several more contact data fields to the accounts receivable software's customer master file is not possible and certainly not practical. Setting up a contact master file is a possible solution, but that involves programming links to both the customer master file and the contact master file whenever the collection process requires this information. It can be made to work, but it ends up creating a complicated process that demands a significant amount of programming support. Confining this data within a separate collection software module allows for more flexibility and ease of use from a programming standpoint.

Besides contact information, collection software requires efficient links that allow the tickler program to react to changes in accounts receivable details (paid invoices, etc.), the prioritization process to integrate the customer-specific collection strategies with the tickler and the accounts receivable details, item-specific problem tracking, the monitoring of collector activities, and so forth. To build these functions on the back of an accounts receivable software module is a daunting project. Greater functionality, however, can be achieved by keeping these activities within the parameters of a stand-alone collection module that does not require changes be made to any accounts receivable software.

SUMMARY

Automating collections requires more than just a quick fix or a few incremental improvements to the current accounts receivable software. As tempting as seemingly easy solutions may appear, they often result in inefficiencies or lost opportunities. Shortcuts very often restrict the long-term productivity benefits that can be achieved through a re-engineered collection process.

First, automating ineffective processes merely institutionalizes unproductive activities. While a repetitive task may seem like a prime candidate for automation, the more important issue is to determine whether the task can be eliminated and, if not, how it can be accomplished more quickly and easily. Only then should it be automated in the context of a re-engineered collection process. The goal is to implement process changes that will result in dramatic productivity improvements. That objective cannot be achieved though incremental improvements that otherwise maintain the status quo.

Second, installing a simple notes organizer, tickler system, or contact manager is not a collection automation solution. These programs require the collector to manually enter all data and, as such, are only as good as the information recorded. Thus, they create an added clerical burden on overtaxed collectors who may not always be disciplined enough to stay up to date on this data-entry chore. An automated collection system both makes decisions based on the information in the tickler program and feeds updated information to the tickler file. A stand-alone contact manager cannot do this.

Likewise, any automation solution that adds keystrokes defeats the purpose of automating. The idea is to create more time for collectors to do what they do best: collect. Data entry is not their forte and therefore is an inefficient use of a collector's time besides being susceptible to errors. Keeping keystrokes to a minimum improves both the efficiency and the accuracy of the automated collection system.

Finally, accounts receivable software should never be affected by collection automation. To do so brings into question the integrity of accounting data and creates an overly complex programming environment with limits on its potential to produce significant productivity gains. Stand-alone collection software that works with downloaded accounts receivable details within its own parameters has far more potential and flexibility than a collection system built on the back of an accounts receivable software module. The latter will forever be limited by its underlying architecture, which was designed for accounts receivables, not collection. Collection software requires its own information structures if it is to provide maximum functionality.

11

Developing Collection Strategies

There is really only one way to find out why an account is overdue, and that is through contact with the customer. This may sound simplistic, but the truth is that many collectors do not make contact for 30 or 45 or even 60 days after an invoice has passed its due date. Worse yet are the collectors who then do not ask why. Many collectors focus on getting overdue balances paid without bothering to determine why the invoices were not paid when they came due. Without knowing why customers are overdue, it is impossible to design an effective strategy to accelerate their payments. Without an informed strategy, the best that can be hoped for is hit-or-miss tactics.

The first priority of any collection strategy, then, is to find out why the invoice is not being paid. With that knowledge, steps can then be taken to accelerate payments. Determining why accounts are overdue from the start of the collection process has no dampening effects on near-term collections while improving long-term efforts. This is not to say that customers will always provide collectors with an honest answer to the question of why they are late. As in life, it is true with collections that actions speak louder than words. Honest customers can be identified by the fact that they keep their payment commitments. Customers seeking to further stall the payment process will show their true colors when they do not pay as promised. Broken promises then provide the collector with another opportunity to confront the customer with the truth so that eventually the customer's reason for delaying payment will become apparent.

Collection strategies effectively drive this dual process of truth gathering and cash accumulation. (See Exhibit 11.1.) As reasons for delayed payments are uncovered, an automated collection system, through the vehicle of customer-specific collection strategies, may be subject to continued refinement in order to maximize collection efforts. This is not to say that initial collection strategies can be designed and implemented in a vac-

Exhibit 11.1   Creating Effective Collection Tactics

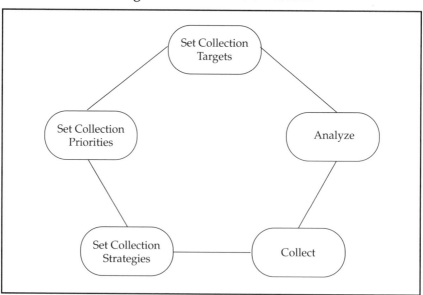

uum. It is first necessary to set collection targets applicable to the entire organization and observe the regularity and timing of the follow-up process to which customers have been acclimated. Collection priorities can then be derived from these targets and observations. Following the priorities are the customer-specific collection strategies. Strategies represent the tactical implementation of the collection targets and priorities. Once collection strategies are set, the actual collection cycle begins, followed by an analysis of the results. From the analysis, new or revised targets, priorities, and strategies are set as this cycle begins anew. (See Exhibit 11.2.)

Exhibit 11.2 Can Collection Goals Be Too Aggressive?

As already mentioned in Exhibit 3.1, when Dell Computer implemented its automated collection system, the goal was to contact each past due customer five times (two faxes and three phone calls) within 60 days of switching on the system. For most accounts, the preliminary contact activity was a fax. The unexpected result was that a much higher percentage of customers responded to these faxes than had been anticipated, and these phone calls and return faxes demanded immediate collector attention. Collectors found themselves spending almost all of their time responding to these "good" interruptions at the expense of scheduled collection activities.

In order to stay on track with its contact goal, Dell carved out calling blocks for its collectors to make outward-bound contacts without interruption. For an hour and a half in the morning and again in the afternoon, the collectors were focused solely on systematic collections. In so doing, customer collection strategies were advanced as scheduled, customer inquiries were answered, and the goal of five contacts within 60 days was met. The bottom line from all this was literally millions of dollars added to Dell's cash flow during these 60 days.

SETTING COLLECTION TARGETS

The process of implementing effective collection tactics begins with the setting of collection targets. This process requires answering the question, "Where are we going?" Targets address corporate-wide objectives regarding cash flow and expenses. There are two elements to such objectives. The first is corporate needs. As credit managers and collectors know from their experiences with customers, cash flow is the lifeline of the corporate entity. Therefore, there is a need to generate a specified level of cash flow within commensurate expense parameters. The second element in setting corporate objectives deals with that which is possible.

The great advantage of an automated collection process over most manual systems is the ability not only to shoot for and attain much higher performance levels but to also be able to better program, and in greater detail, the strategies and tactics that will result in collection targets being met. Essentially, this is the ability to see more ways to achieve aggressive collection targets. Making incremental improvements to a manual collection system is not a viable means of attaining significantly better collection results, so that really is not an option. That leaves adding more people as the only way to achieve significantly better collection results, short of automating the entire collection process. However, this option merely adds capacity and does nothing to improve productivity. Also, hiring more collectors, whether permanent or temporary, is not an acceptable option in most tightly staffed corporate finance departments. Third-party outsourcing as another alternative, but even outsourcing providers agree that outsourcing has its greatest impact in an automated collection environment.

When collections have been automated, setting collection targets is no longer weighted down by limited possibilities. With a new automated collection system, targets are still limited by previous experience, and so some gut-level assumptions must be made about what goals are attainable. Having once gone through the target, priority, strategy, collection, and analysis cycle, revising and resetting targets becomes a much more informed process. Initial goals for days sales outstanding (DSO), overdue balances, and bad debt will then become much firmer targets the second time around. From that point on, future targets can be tightened even further as the collectors work the automated collection system, adding intelligence to the goal-setting process.

However, even initial collection targets for an automated collection process can be derived from more definitive elements than from a manual collection system. Setting goals by customer type and individual collector gives the subsequent corporate-wide goals a much more solid base. When setting collection targets, having a strong sense of the underlying components is vital to subsequently setting logical collection strategies.

SETTING COLLECTION PRIORITIES

Setting collection strategies in the context of creating a framework of effective collection tactics is quite different from the prioritization step that leads off the collection cycle. Setting collection strategies is instead a matter of determining how collection targets will be met. It involves identifying the critical areas of the accounts receivable portfolio so that the appropriate collection strategies can then be implemented.

For example, a company that sells to a few big accounts and many small accounts all within the same industry is going to have different collection strategies than a company that has many customers in a number of different industries and no dominant customers. The former will have to pay special attention to its biggest customers from a collection standpoint, because any serious collection problems will have a very deleterious effect on cash flow and the attainment of the chosen collection targets. By contrast, the second example requires a completely different set of strategies that is dependent on the unique characteristics of the industry or customer for each accounts receivable segment.

Setting collection strategies is therefore a task that must take into account the makeup of a company's customer base. The operative question then is, "Who are we dealing with?" A thorough knowledge of the company's customers and marketplace greatly facilitates setting appropriate collection strategies. With this knowledge, it is a simple matter to determine which types of accounts will require the most attention early on in the process and who else can be handled via a less staff-intensive front-end activity without harming collection results.

Available human resources are a critical factor to consider when planning collection strategies. The most important component here is collectors. How the accounts receivable portfolio is allocated between a company's collectors goes hand in hand with the setting of strategies. Those segments of the portfolio that require the most attention on the front end of the process should be allocated the most manpower. From this point, decisions made about how the different portfolio segments will be worked become primarily tactical considerations.

SETTING COLLECTION STRATEGIES

A company's collection strategies are at the heart of its collection process. Even when collections are a manual process, the collection strategies that are employed will to a large part determine how effective each individual collector is. The better a collector's strategies, the better will be that collector's results, and vice versa. This is one of the weaknesses of manual collections, which are extremely dependent upon the individual skills of each collector.

Because collection strategies in an automated collection process are system based rather than collector dependent, they serve to make all collectors better. They do this by intelligently driving the entire collection process. Collection strategies determine when different types of overdue accounts will be contacted, and they strongly influence the prioritization process. Because collection strategies specify the type of action to be taken with an account, under various circumstances they define the preparations required before initiating contact. Collection strategies outline the objectives for each contact; therefore, they strongly influence the conduct of that phase. Because collection strategies are tailored to how customers respond to each collection step, they affect the course of subsequent follow-up activities. In the end, the reporting process helps companies refine their collection strategies for maximum effectiveness.

There are a number of considerations to take into account when setting collection strategies. First, the customer collection types must be determined. Every accounts receivable portfolio is different, so a good amount of thought must be put into this identification process. The second issue is also dependent on the accounts receivable portfolio's characteristics but must additionally consider the number of available collectors. A low-balance threshold allows for different strategies for low- and high-dollar accounts while a grace period determines when collection activities begin. Finally, strategy elements must be selected and assigned to each customer type.

CUSTOMER COLLECTION TYPES

No accounts receivable portfolio is homogeneous. There will be large accounts and small accounts, good-paying accounts and slow-paying accounts, and key accounts and less important customers. It is also common for companies to sell customers serving different marketplaces. A healthcare clinic, a hospital, a pharmacy, a physician, and a healthcare products distributor will all have very different characteristics, although they may all buy the same product. This diversity must be addressed by differing collection strategies once the various accounts receivable portfolio segments are identified.

Identifying the various segments is not a difficult task, but it does require careful consideration. In particular, the collection priorities that have already been established and the current paying characteristics of customers need to be reviewed. This is especially true when the company is selling into different marketplaces. Not only can terms of sale be different, but there may be significant seasonal variations, unique document processing practices, varied competitive conditions, or other quirks, for lack of a better term. Sometimes, there will even be significant differences within the same segment of customers such as between large and small contractors and large and small retailers. There are also the marginal accounts or other special accounts that require special attention.

A sampling of the most common customer collection types is presented in Exhibit 11.3. These categories are neither overly broad nor too narrowly defined. It should be noted that categories such as manufacturers, distributors, and service providers can readily be broken down by industry or further segmented by size. In addition, it does not matter if different segments end up with the same collection strategies. There is always the possibility that the strategy for one of the segments will change over time, besides the fact that different segments also provide points of comparison. What is important is that each segment should be unique. Whatever the final scheme, once the accounts receivable portfolio has been broken down into unique segments, it is possible to start making tactical deci-

Exhibit 11.3 **Sample Customer Types**

• Small retailers	• Small contractors	• Manufacturers
• Large retailers	• Large contractors	• National accounts
• Local government	• Foreign customers	• Service providers
• National government	• Foreign distributors	• Healthcare providers
• Hospitals	• Nursing homes and clinics	• Promotional accounts
• High-volume distributors	• V.I.P.	• Other equipment manufacturers (OEMs)
• Small distributors	• Schools and universities	

sions about how to best collect each segment in order to attain the established collection targets.

One very important factor that will affect these tactical decisions is the human resources available to the collection effort. It is always better to underestimate the collection staff's ability to make phone calls, send letters, and generate faxes. This is especially important immediately after the implementation of an automated collection system. The problem arises from the fact that automation allows many more contacts to be made. When a large number of these are letters or faxes, allowances must be made to handle the subsequent customer responses, which can be surprisingly high. In effect, a collection department's newfound capacity to generate a high volume of initial customer contacts can overwhelm its resources to subsequently follow-up on those contacts.

THRESHOLDS AND GRACE PERIODS

As mentioned earlier, the low-balance threshold and grace periods are used to determine respectively how low- and high-dollar balances are treated and to determine when collection activities begin against an overdue account. These are additional parameters that affect the scope and character of a company's automated collection efforts.

As such, it is critical that Staffing resources be taken into consideration when setting these parameters. Too low a threshold and too long a grace period will cause many more overdue invoices to fall into collection strategies that require significant collector activity. If the collection department is not staffed to handle this level of activity, individual collectors will find it extremely difficult to come anywhere close to finishing their daily work lists. In determining the optimal grace period, the proportion of initial calls to be made as compared to faxes or letters must be considered. Sometimes less call-intensive strategies can be as effective as an aggressive phone-based approach. By the same token, setting the threshold too high and the grace period too long results in opportunities to accelerate payments from some of the company's more sizable customers being missed. The key, then, is to find a good balance between thresholds, grace days, and staff resources.

The low-balance threshold allows for different strategies when customers owe either above or below that amount. Generally, balances under the threshold will initially be contacted by letter or fax with some lag until a call is made, while balances above the threshold will get a follow-up phone call much sooner. However, this is not to say that the same strategy could not be used both above and below the threshold. Thresholds can be set differently for each customer type, because what is considered a low balance can vary greatly between the various customer types. For example, it is expected that the low-balance threshold for a national account would be quite dissimilar to that for a small retailer. For national accounts, the threshold could be $5,000, while for a small retailer, $500 would make more sense.

The reasoning behind grace periods works much the same way. The grace period defines the number of days after an invoice is due that collection activities will be initiated. An industry or customer type that exhibits generally reliable payment characteristics will be assigned a shorter grace period to expedite collections from that segment, while a traditionally slow-paying segment might start out with a longer grace period. It might be advisable from a customer service standpoint, for example, to give V.I.P. accounts a few extra days before collection activities begin, as opposed to small contractors or, better yet, marginal accounts, in which a very short grace period is called for.

One key factor to consider is that when the automated collection system is being implemented, reasonable grace periods should be established so as not to overburden collection department resources. The grace periods should be tighter than traditionally given with the old manual system, but not too tight. Over time, as the collection strategies are worked and receivable balances reduced, the grace periods can be shortened to motivate customers to pay even sooner. It is clearly preferable to have to tighten grace periods rather than loosen them. After all, the idea is to coax customers to pay promptly, so steady, uninterrupted progress toward that goal is desirable.

STRATEGY ELEMENTS

Each collection strategy is composed of a sequence of events. Each event involves a specific collection activity to be performed at a specified time, assuming the invoice or invoices in question have not yet been paid or otherwise cleared from the customer's account. The logic behind the timing of this succession of events is also part of the strategy. Two different collection strategies could include exactly the same events but with very different timing. For example, a strategy relying on minimal intervals between events is much more aggressive and serves a different purpose than a collection strategy that is spread out over time.

When formulating the timing element of collection strategies, there are a couple of factors that must be considered. First, mail times will vary from customer to customer depending on their distance to the company's remittance addresses and the efficiency of the postal service between those two points. Also, timing strategies should take customer characteristics into account. For example, priority might be given to known promise breakers and other high-risk accounts.

All possible strategy elements, that is, the specific collection activities that make up the events and their timing, should be considered when devising appropriate collection strategies for each of the customer types that have been identified. This requires a knowledge of what works and when, in terms of convincing customers to pay. The following general collection principles should be kept in mind:

- Phone calls have more impact than faxes, which have more impact than letters, which also take more time to be delivered. Therefore, if a customer has a fax number, there are very few occasions when a letter is appropriate.

- In a series of faxes or letters, subsequent faxes or letters will have less impact than the preceding fax or letter. You should expect a second letter to have only half of the impact as the first letter, and the third to have only half of the impact of the second. Because of this, it seldom makes sense to send more than two letters or faxes before making a phone call.

- Follow-up is critical. Delaying follow-up activities, if only for a day or two, serves only to encourage the customer's accounts payable department to take care of other vendors first. In contrast, timely follow-up procedures send the message that the company means business. Accounts payable staffers save time by withholding payment to vendors that may not make a follow-up call and by paying those that are likely to call. Make no mistake, accounts payable personnel do not want to receive collection calls that interrupt their busy days as well as pose an emotional burden. If they expect a company to be a squeaky wheel, that company is more likely to get an on-time payment.

- Pressure should be increased with each time a customer fails to respond to collection activities with a payment. Collectors need to get progressively tougher in their efforts until a customer finally does pay, and collection strategies should reflect this. The contents of the faxes and call guides for each step assist collectors to have less tolerance for further delay with each subsequent contact. By systematically eliminating reasons for delayed payments, each step gets closer to the ultimate goal of either 100 percent payment or referral of the customer a third party for collection or legal action.

- It is important to note that every customer has a breaking point, so to speak. With an automated collection system, this point becomes apparent over time, and collection strategies can be adjusted accordingly to decrease the time the customer takes to pay. In other words, begin, as early as possible, the collection strategy with the activity that is the most likely to resolve the reason for nonpayment. For example, if a lost invoice is the most common reason, include an invoice copy with the initial follow-up fax.

Collection strategies consist of a sequence of stages and a preferred method of contact for each stage. Together, the stages, their sequence, and the forms of contact for each stage comprise the collections strategy elements. Once these are defined, different collection strategies can be created to address the established collection priorities and to achieve the collection targets within each segment and at each balance threshold.

The different contact methods that can be incorporated into a collection strategy are identified in Exhibit 11.4. Each collection stage must necessarily be associated with a contact method. Exhibit 11.5 defines the most common collection stages. Because each business is different, not everybody will use all these collection stages, and some collection departments will find it necessary to modify some of these stages or create entirely new stages.

Once the collection stages and contact methods have been put in sequence, the timing of each stage must be considered. One important consideration here is mail time. Mostly, this relates to the time it takes a customer's check to reach the company's bank. However, since there will be occasions to send letters, the time it takes this correspondence to reach the customer must also be taken into account. An automated collection system should make these calculations, allowing only a day for mail to be delivered to or from the company's own zip code and up to 5 business days for mail going cross-country. Therefore, when setting up the time intervals between collection stages, only the number of working days it should take the customer to respond should be taken into account; the system will calculate the rest.

This includes accounting for weekends and holidays. With an automated collection system, the time intervals between collection stages are measured in business days rather than calendar days. This is necessary because if calendar days were

Exhibit 11.4   **Collection Strategy Elements: Contact Methods**

Contact Method	Usage and Benefit
Telephone call	Provides an opportunity to directly confront customers with all overdue invoices, determine why these items have not been paid, and arrange for their payment. May be used as the primary means of contact for large-dollar balances with some customers.
Fax	An effective means of contacting customers without the interrupting effect of a phone call while still maintaining some sense of immediacy. Very effective means of transmitting corresponding documentation, such as invoice copies. Should be used as the initial means of contact whenever possible. Also valuable as a backup when collectors are unable to reach their contacts by phone.
Letter	When a customer does not have a fax, letters provide a substitute but convey less of a sense of urgency because delivery is not immediate. Next-day and second-day courier services can mitigate this effect but are relatively expensive. Letters are appropriate for formal or sensitive matters such as final demands.
Customer visit	Not a part of the collector's daily collection routine, but can be extremely valuable in resolving problems and building long-term relationships. Sales personnel should always accompany credit and collection personnel on customer visits. For some companies (usually distributors), salesmen are asked to make customer visits and collect overdue balances as a step in the collection process.
E-mail	As the Internet gains broader acceptance and utility, its use as a collection tool will grow. With customers who have e-mail, the Internet provides a useful communications tool with similar impact to a fax, though with somewhat less of a sense of urgency. E-mail is already proving particularly useful in problem solving and internal communications. One key advantage of e-mail is the ease of response for the customer. Given that the text of the e-mail sent is frequently incorporated in the response, e-mail provides a self-documenting process that provides a history of follow-up activities unlikely to be disputed by the customer or salesperson.

Exhibit 11.5 **Collection Strategy Elements: Collection Stages**

Collection Stage	*Usage and Benefits*
Customer service call	Used primarily with large customers and key accounts to ensure that there are no problems that will delay payments. Such calls are usually made at least a week before an invoice is due.
Reminder	Used for initial contact with the customer. If correspondence, may be accompanied by documents such as invoice copies or proofs of delivery.
Follow-up	Can be a phone call that follows a letter or fax, or a letter or fax that confirms the results of a phone call. Useful for reinforcing the preceding collection activity, it is most effective when confirmation of the new payment agreement is faxed.
Problem resolution	If initial collection activities uncover a problem, or if a partial payment (deduction) is received, this stage is used to resolve the matter in order to resume routine collections as quickly as possible.
Serious reminder	If customers do not respond to initial contacts, a serious reminder is used to try and get their attention.
Serious demand	This stage increases the pressure on unresponsive customers, short of making a final demand for payment. May be accompanied by the holding of orders.
Hold orders	Holding orders is usually an effective motivator. It gets customers' attention and gives them an economic reason to pay.
First sales notice	Used in conjunction with collection activities against the customer, this stage notifies sales that the situation is deteriorating and that stronger steps such as holding orders are forthcoming. May also be used to advise sales of a problem that must be resolved before payment will be forthcoming.

Exhibit 11-5 (*Continued*)

Second sales notice	When a customer is totally unresponsive and orders have been placed on credit hold, sales needs to be updated. Sales is hereby put on notice that a final demand is forthcoming if the customer does not pay.
First notice to management	Management (for example, Controller, Chief Financial Officer, Treasurer) needs to be informed of deteriorating situations or problems that require input from other corporate functions. May be limited to larger overdue balances.
Second notice to management	When a customer is totally unresponsive and orders have been placed on credit hold, management needs to be updated. Sales is hereby put on notice that a final demand is forthcoming if the customer does not pay.
Final demand	This is the last notice the customer receives before being referred to a collection agency or an attorney. The demand is most effective as a letter sent by certified mail or via courier service. It should include a grace period of 10 to 15 days, after which the claim is immediately sent to the third-party collector. It is the second-to-last stage of every collection strategy.
Free demand period	Many third-party collectors offer a free demand period, typically 7 to 15 days, during which any payments made by the debtor will not be subject to commissions. This stage is usually initiated by a letter to the debtor on the agency's letterhead, though it may be mailed by the creditor.
Third party	This is the final stage of every collection strategy. Accounts referred to a collection agency or an attorney have a better chance of collection if they are turned over between 90 and 150 days after going past due. Even so, they still need to be tracked.

used as the determinant, collectors would find 3 days of work on their daily work list every Monday morning—not a very auspicious or motivating way to begin each week. Worse yet, a long weekend could conceivably put a collector behind by a week without his or her having missed a day of work.

Several examples of collection strategies are listed in Exhibit 11.6. These are in no way comprehensive because every company faces a different collection environment. However, they provide an overview of the variations that can be achieved with different collection strategies. Of course, the purpose of designing different collection strategies is to address various circumstances and needs in order to maximize results.

There may also be separate strategies for deductions and other dispute resolution scenarios. These are best tied to the corporate problem owner, whom the collector continues to follow up with from an internal customer perspective. Once a problem is identified, the invoices involved are given a reason code that, among other things, identifies such invoices with an appropriate problem-resolution strategy. These invoices are clearly marked as problems on the collector's computer screen, though the collector should have the ability to remove these items from the listing of past due invoices when trying to collect any other invoices not involved in the problem or dispute. The collector is thus able to work on problem-resolution issues separately from routine collection matters.

INTERFACING WITH SALES AND CUSTOMER SERVICE

An important feature of the collection strategies is that communications with sales and customer service can be programmed into the process. This is extremely important when there is a serious collection problem that threatens to interfere with future sales. Both sales and customer service need to

Exhibit 11.6 **Sample Collection Strategies**

Fax-First Strategy— Large Balance	Call-First Strategy— Large Balance	Small-Balance Strategy	International Strategy
Grace period: FAX Reminder	Grace period: CALL Reminder	Grace period: FAX Reminder	Grace period: FAX Reminder
1 Day: CALL Follow-up	Same day: FAX Follow-up	5 Days: FAX Follow-up	6 Days: CALL Follow-up
3 Days: CALL Problem?	3 Days: CALL Problem?	1 Days: CALL Serious reminder	6 Days: FAX Serious reminder
3 Days: FAX Follow-up	3 Days: FAX Serious reminder	3 Days: CALL Hold shipments	Same day: E-MAIL First sales notice
Same day: CALL Serious reminder	Same day: E-MAIL First sales notice	Same day: E-MAIL First sales notice	Same day: E-MAIL First notice to management
Same day: E-MAIL First sales notice	3 Days: CALL Serious demand	3 Days: FAX Serious demand	6 Days: CALL Serious demand
3 Days: CALL Serious demand	Same day: E-MAIL First notice to management	Same day: E-MAIL First notice to management	6 Days: LETTER Final demand
Same day: E-MAIL First notice to management	3 Days: CALL Hold shipments	3 Days: LETTER Final demand	Same day: E-MAIL Second sales notice
3 Days: FAX Hold shipments	Same day: E-MAIL Second sales notice	8 Days: LETTER Refer to third party	Same day: E-MAIL Second notice to management
3 Days: CALL Serious demand	Same day: E-MAIL Second notice to management		8 Days: LETTER Refer to third party
Same day: E-MAIL Second sales notice	3 Days: LETTER Final demand		
Same day: E-MAIL Second notice to management	8 Days: LETTER Refer to third party		
3 Days: LETTER Final demand			
8 Days: LETTER Refer to third party			

know these things, but when a company has a lot of customers and a manual collection process, very often problems are communicated only when things are at a critical stage. Such notifications late in the process are often received by sales and customer service as unpleasant surprises and tend to justify some people's opinions that credit and collections is really the "stop sales department."

However, with an automated system, sales and customer service are in the information loop very shortly after problems are identified. With faxing and e-mail capabilities, it is a very quick and simple task for collectors to provide status reports and send copies of important communications. This has the added benefit of enlisting sales' and customer service's support in the problem-resolution process. Should a problem move to a critical stage, these departments will have already been part of the effort to set things right and will be on top of the facts, rather than being taken by surprise.

These types of communication benefits also apply when invoices are tagged with a problem code and moved into a problem-resolution strategy. Depending on the problem, any interested person or department can be given updates. An added effect of keeping everyone in the loop is increased awareness throughout the company of repetitive issues that ultimately require the affected business processes to be either fixed or redesigned.

SUMMARY

Collection strategies drive the collection process, especially as part of an automated collection system. Therefore, it is extremely important that they be well thought out and carefully devised from the start. In order to do this, collection targets first need to be set from both a company-wide and, if necessary, an individual business unit perspective. When it is possible to identify unique segments of the accounts receivable portfolio and project attainable collection targets for each of these segments, the overall corporate targets can be closer to the mark and subsequently subject to more intelligible analysis. Segmenting the accounts receivable portfolio also serves the purpose of setting collection priorities, which must also consider staffing resources. Once the collection targets and the collection priorities have been established, the tactical process of devising collection strategies can be begun.

Another benefit from segmenting the accounts receivable portfolio is the identification of different customer types by their payment characteristics. It is to these customer types that the various collection strategies are assigned. Each customer type is also assigned a unique grace period, which will determine when collection activities begin, and a low-dollar threshold that enables different collection strategies to be used whether the account is showing a high- or low-dollar amount past due.

The collection strategies themselves consist of a sequence of collection activities, also known as collection stages. Each stage is assigned a contact method, and the timing between each stage must be set. Together, these collection elements—the collection activities, the contact method, and the timing of each event—constitute a collection strategy. With an abundance of possible variations, collection strategies can then be geared to address the particular collection issues common to each customer type.

After a set of collection strategies have been used and results obtained, their effectiveness can be analyzed. If necessary, the strategies can then be refined to better attain the specified collection targets. Over the long term, the analysis process will provide data to help set more definitive collection targets and better collection priorities. The goal of this effort is continued improvement in the collection process, driven by the intelligence gleaned from the automated collection process. This intelligence extends beyond the collection function to include all corporate processes with links to credit and collections, particularly sales and customer service. The ability to incorporate automated internal corporate communications as stages in every collection strategy is key to improving the efficiency and effectiveness of such corporate processes.

Part Three

Working with
an Automated
Collection Process

12

Monitoring Accounts

One of the most powerful tools provided by automating the collection process is the ability to comprehensively monitor customers. With a manual collection system, accounts are essentially monitored one customer at a time. It is difficult to evaluate different segments of the accounts receivable portfolio and then make comparisons among the customers within that segment, because the resources to collect such data and the tools to analyze it simply do not exist. This, however, is not a problem for an automated collection system. For such a system, it is the merging of accounts receivable and collection data that drives the different elements of the collection process. All that is required then are some analysis tools to bring the big picture into focus and to magnify the details. With a manual collection process, the byword was account management. In the case of automated collections, accounts receivable portfolio management is the operative term.

Not surprisingly, this requires a change in perspective. Many credit and collection managers see themselves as accounts receivable processing supervisors. They are in the business of servicing the financial transactions of their internal customers. Becoming an accounts receivable portfolio manager requires both a change in attitude and the acquisition of new analytical skills. The good news is that the skills come easy. It is the change in attitude that sometimes takes a little extra effort.

Returning to the analogy of the lumberjack and the forest (see Exhibit 1.1), accounts receivable portfolio management provides credit and collection professionals with the tools to clear out the underbrush so that resources can be focused on felling the most valuable trees. Clearly, the purpose of this is to produce, with limited resources, the most value from the forest of accounts receivables. Portfolio tools make it possible to set up processes that identify exactly where more days can be cut from the collection cycle. Without portfolio management tools, one is left to wander around the forest looking for opportunities to increase productivity. With these tools, collectors can immediately focus on the critical accounts and portfolio segments to ensure maximum utility.

Most manufacturers and distributors will benefit from implementing a portfolio management approach to credit and collections. For them, credit and collections is a cost of doing business, and the implementation of portfolio management techniques will help reduce costs by optimizing processes across the entire portfolio in order to get the maximum reduction in interest carrying cost. This is accomplished one segment of the portfolio at a time, using available resources. Those companies that face high transaction volumes and many customers will benefit even more by adopting portfolio management techniques. For these companies, monitoring accounts individually is simply an impossible task for credit and collection management. Portfolio management provides the only viable means of maintaining control.

SEGMENTING THE ACCOUNTS RECEIVABLE

In the previous chapter, customer collection types were discussed in the context of matching them to appropriate collec-

tion strategies. Customer collection types are simply the identification of useful distinguishing characteristics to segment a
company's accounts receivable portfolio into logical components. This provides the basis for portfolio management techniques to be employed by an automated collection system.
Some of the most common differentiating criteria are identified
in Exhibit 12.1. Not included in this listing are alphabetic-
based qualifiers. Though many companies assign credit and
collection responsibilities based on such guidelines, such seg-
mentation usually has nothing to do with the customer's characteristics and so serves no purpose in terms of portfolio
management.

It should be noted, however, that accounts receivable
portfolio management provides utility for both credit analysis
and collections. Portfolio-based credit analysis software provides a framework and tools for credit analysts to establish risk
models. The risk score calculated is sometimes used as a con-

Exhibit 12.1   **Accounts Receivable Portfolio Segmenting Criteria**

- Company size (based on sales or worth)
- Distribution channels
- Product lines purchased
- Industry classification
- New customer/Established customer
- Growth expectations
- Risk assessment
- Customer profitability
- Geography
- Payment habits (discounts, prompt, slow, takes deductions, service problems)
- Customer importance (purchase volume)

trol for the collection process; however, that is the extent of overlap at this point. Companies that have extremely large portfolios and high transaction volumes often outsource credit analysis to service bureaus.[1] Firms that distribute through a highly dedicated and limited-in-number customer base are more likely to complete their own analysis, and many turn to a credit analysis software package to help with this, as the cost of failure of a single large customer would have significant impact. The first type of company uses the credit analysis data to manage its huge credit database, while the second type is concerned with closely monitoring every customer.

In contrast, collection software makes use of portfolio management concepts to accelerate collections. However, as a by-product of the collection process, a considerable amount of internal data is accumulated by this software that is useful to the credit approval process. The ability to identify customer payment trends and to compare those trends to the standard profiles for companies in that particular portfolio segment is extremely useful to credit analysts. In terms of statistical credit scoring, such internal performance data contains the highest predictive qualities.

It is sometimes appropriate, then, to bring a broad perspective that encompasses both collection and credit analysis issues to the task of segmenting the accounts receivable. Customer collection types may be the primary criteria, but there are advantages to identifying subgroups based on other factors. By using more than one segregating factor, it is possible to create distinct subgroups for each collection type. For example, a new customer might be classified by its industry type but also identified as a new account for a period of time. After paying satisfactorily for a specified period of time, this customer could then be reclassified as an established customer of a particular industry type. The "new" subcategory serves to contain the risk posed by the unfamiliarity inherent with new customers.

Another consideration when segmenting the accounts receivable involves matching collectors with segments. A segment made up of national-type accounts will require different handling than a segment of small retailers. Collecting from a national account requires an attention to detail since it is primarily an administrative activity, while collecting from small retailers requires more persuasive skills. A collector assigned to oversee a portfolio of small retailers can handle a much higher account load than the person monitoring national accounts. Matching the collector to the accounts receivable segment, based on the collector's working style and experience, will yield higher individual collector productivity as collectors get to do the work for which they are most suited. Additional benefits are better employee and customer satisfaction. Employees get to do that which they are best at, which in turn results in better customer service.

ESTABLISHING NORMS

Once the accounts receivable has been divided into logical segments, the process of establishing comparative norms can be begun. In terms of an automated collection process, these norms will be based primarily on collection data. In order to be able to use significant data, it is necessary that the collection software be allowed some time to accumulate this information. Once customers have been through the collection cycle several times, which will probably take at least 10 weeks, enough information will have been collected to generate meaningful comparisons. Exhibit 12.2 lists the internally derived collection data that an automated collection process should create, store, and track.

At this point, a number of customer characteristics can be

Exhibit 12.2 **Norming Criteria Derived from the Collection Process**

- Average days beyond terms
- Sales weighted average days to pay
- Percent current/past due
- Average balance due
- Percentage of portfolio disputed
- Balance due by collection stage
- Percentage of portfolio by collection stage

---

established. By finding the averages for these measurements within each accounts receivable portfolio segment, a profile of a typical account can be created. It is also useful to identify the top and bottom quartiles so that accounts substantially above or below the norm can be dealt with accordingly. For any segment based on general characteristics such as size or industry classification, most customers will fall in the middle two quartiles. The exceptions will be at either end of the spectrum.

The specific purpose for establishing norms is to identify exceptions. Those customers that fall within the normal range can be handled routinely, and much of the decision-making process can be automated. The same is true for significantly above-average customers. Below-average customers obviously require close monitoring by the automated collection system and by collectors and their managers.

Automated collection software should also have the capability of storing some limited external data. In particular, credit ratings and credit scores can be extremely useful when used in conjunction with internal collection data. They do not require any complicated analysis, so their utilization in a high-transaction-volume, low-dollar-per-transaction environment can be very informative and useful. Since most companies have many more small customers (which account for a limited amount of the company's total sales volume) than large accounts, credit ratings and scores in conjunction with internal data can efficiently drive much of a credit and collection department's decision making. Processes such as account approval, order approval, and risk classification and collection prioritization can be easily and safely automated when the results of simplification are looked at from the perspective of the total portfolio. Small individual write-offs or referals to third-party collectors in this environment are far outweighed by the overall reduction in bad debt and interest carrying costs created by the efficiency of the portfolio approach.

Without computerized systems, normative data is difficult and time consuming to calculate, much less collect and store. Collection software therefore provides the tools necessary to segment the receivables in order to establish meaningful norms and then begin looking at the accounts receivable details from a portfolio perspective.

RISK CLASSIFICATION

Once norms have been identified for each segment of the accounts receivable portfolio, it is a fairly easy task to assign risk classifications. These can be as simple as high, moderate, and low, but may also be more sophisticated depending on the nature of the accounts receivable portfolio. Customer risk classifications provide a means for evaluating the overall risk contained in the accounts receivable and for identifying accounts that require extra attention.

This is quite different from assigning credit limits, which serve as an upper level threshold for order approvals. Credit limits do not say much, if at anything at all, about a customer's likelihood to pay slowly or default. Of course, balances in excess of assigned credit limits might be considered at greater risk than those within limits, especially if the customer's primary product is the one the company provides, or is dependent on a critical component supplied only by the company, and great care was used in determining the credit limit. In other words, credit limits are usually a very poor measure of risk. The tendency is to set credit limits conservatively for good customers and liberally for marginal accounts. Creditworthy customers can be expected to pay reasonably promptly even when balances due exceed their assigned credit limits, while marginal accounts are at risk of defaulting or delaying payment, no matter how little they owe.

Although accounts may pay slowly and are assigned an appropriate risk score, this does not necessarily mean that they are not worth doing business with. A good business plan will increase the margin on products aimed at slow-pay portfolios and therefore offset carrying costs. Risk classifications recognize these factors and provide a mechanism for evaluating overall portfolio risk with a mind to keeping it within manageable parameters. Too little risk in the accounts receivable portfolio suggests that sales opportunities are being missed, while too much risk will result in excessive payment delays and bad debt losses. The idea is to find a balance that maximizes profits. Risk classifications used in conjunction with a portfolio approach to accounts receivable management help achieve this goal.

Risk classifications also provide a mechanism for targeting at-risk accounts for added collection efforts. This is done by assigning aggressive collection strategies to higher-risk customers or by giving priority to higher-risk accounts in the scheduling of collection activities. By being able to identify and then concentrate collection efforts on higher-risk accounts, payments can be accelerated, which reduces the potential for receivables to turn into bad debts.

PORTFOLIO ANALYSIS

The heart of a portfolio approach to accounts receivable management is the analysis of the portfolio. Establishing norms and risk classifications, essentially analytical tasks, serves to provide a broader framework for subsequent analytical functions. Norms and risk classifications make the quantification of credit and collection management decisions much more feasible, by removing the decision-making process from the one-customer-at-a-time mindset. The result is better justification for the decisions made and more consistency across the entire receivables portfolio.

In a manual collection process, many decisions are heavily influenced by qualitative or subjective factors. Experienced credit and collection managers are often forced by the fast pace of the credit and collection environment to rely on their experience and intuition. Decisions are made because they seem right and have a measure of precedence based on historical activities. While many such credit and collection pros do an extremely good job of "shooting from the hip," that does not mean they are always on target.

In fact, there is an easy-to-appreciate, natural bias toward making conservative decisions. Without a basis in fact, there is a price to be paid for excessive risk taking, so the tendency is to take less risk than would be taken if all the facts were available. The result from being overly restrictive of credit and collections is missed opportunities to add to the company's bottom line. This mindset asks, "Why work with a clearly marginal account?" The collection department has all the work it can handle, and such accounts consume an inordinate amount of precious time and have high failure rate.

Portfolio analysis might reveal that such accounts do not fail as often as expected. In addition, portfolio analysis may show that overall risk levels are low and that gross margins justify the additional extension of credit in order to increase sales and profits despite the added efforts this will require of collections. Through portfolio analysis, the ability to compare a customer to its peers provides intelligence that can be used to maximize returns, from both a corporate and a collections standpoint. Hands-on credit and collection management in a manual environment cannot generate such information.

From a collection standpoint, the benefits derived from portfolio analysis can be broadly identified in the following three areas that may occasionally overlap:

1. The identification of underperforming segments of the accounts receivable

2. Better definition of credit and collection management needs

3. Increased market intelligence regarding the characteristics of desirable and undesirable accounts

These benefits cannot even be recognized without an infrastructure capable of accounts receivable portfolio management. It is this in-depth knowledge, which is the hallmark of accounts receivable portfolio management, that has always defined any best-of-class credit and collection function. Generally, the more collectors know, the better they are at their job. What is true for the individual is also true for the entire function.

The importance of identifying underperforming accounts receivables is self-evident. The easier it is to pick out the bad guys, the more likely it is that future results will improve. Even without portfolio management tools, over time—and often after only a short period of time—collectors learn to recognize the laggards and other problem accounts. However, by comparing portfolio segments and individual customers within portfolio segments, trends, tendencies, and commonalities can be identified, making the process of identifying underperforming receivables much easier and more comprehensive. By using portfolio management techniques, identifying these receivables is much less a random process.

By taking randomness out of the identification process, the answer to the question "Why?" becomes much more meaningful. When an individual account pays slowly, collectors expect the cause to be the customer's cash flow situation or some sort of system problem. However, when a group of similar accounts show similar slow-payment tendencies, the pool of possible causes is much larger and not limited to a single account situation. Industry trends, structural deficiencies, seasonal attributes, and so forth may explain underperforming customers. Why does one portfolio segment have a higher percentage of returned orders than another? What common factors identify the small customers that have gone out of business? What are the differences between prompt-paying and slow-paying accounts? These types of questions lead to potentially valuable answers.

For example, portfolio analysis might show that the overwhelming majority of a particular class of customers that pay promptly turn their inventory within an optimal range, but those paying slowly have a corresponding slower inventory turnover ratio. This information can then be shared with the customer base to help improve their operations and subsequently their payments. This is powerful intelligence, and credit and collection departments that have adopted such a portfolio mindset are using this intelligence to add value to their companies while also increasing their department's visibility as a contributor to corporate goals.

Identifying underperforming receivables requires an outward focus, while better defining credit and collection management needs is indicative of an internal perspective. *Why* is still the operative word, but the answers being sought lie within the credit and collection department or in weaknesses in other corporate processes. Why is a particular sales territory experiencing so much slowness? Is one collection strategy more effective than another? Why are pricing deductions increasing in a particular receivables segment? The answers to these questions might be found to be a new salesman who does not know the ropes yet, particular collection practices, and a change in pricing for one product line, respectively. The point is that portfolio analysis can lead to structural improvements in internal practices that will then positively affect collections.

The third benefit was added marketing intelligence. Accounts receivable portfolio analysis techniques can reveal valuable information that can help companies sell more to the right customers. Identifying portfolio segments or types of customers that are capable of handling higher credit lines provides marketing with the opportunity to increase market share with established customers. Providing sales with profiles of top-quartile and bottom-quartile performers can help them target their efforts toward those prospects that offer the lowest credit risk and best potential for long-term relationships and profits.

The key here is the sharing of intelligence in useful formats. In a manual collection system, it is either impossible or very difficult to accumulate such data, much less formulate it into useful reports. Again, it is the "drill-down" features of automated collection software that makes this an easy, highly beneficial process. By repeatedly slicing and dicing the accounts receivable portfolio in new ways, credit and collection managers can document (or disprove) their hunches, and then share this information with their corporate peers. They will also be able to identify receivables trends and customer characteristics they might not have otherwise noticed. In the end, it comes down to a better understanding and knowledge of one's customers, and that information is as relevant to sales as it is to credit and collections.

ACCOUNT ANALYSIS

This discussion of portfolio analysis should in no way diminish the importance of account analysis. Rather, the portfolio analysis techniques enabled by an automated collection system are in addition to the traditional role of account analysis. Trends in the entire receivables portfolio need to be recognized, but, having done so, collectors are left to still focus on individual accounts, albeit in a more efficient and better prioritized fashion.

Credit and collection managers, along with other top financial managers, have always had an interest in the performance of individual accounts, particularly key customers and slow-paying or otherwise problem accounts. One routine that has emerged from this need to know has been account reviews. These often monthly review sessions consume a considerable amount of the credit and collections manager's time in addition to that spent by the collectors. The more customers and collectors involved, the more time consumed by this task. Much of this time is consumed by searching for data found in different sources: the collectors' notes, the accounts receivables aging, the computer screen for current activity and payment history, and so forth.

However, with an automated collection system, the credit and collection manager is able to review individual accounts without heavy involvement from each collector, saving much valuable time. This is because the automated collection system has recorded every activity taken against each customer. In addition, payment and aging trends are calculated and displayed by the collection software, so it is very easy to see the progress being made with each customer. One particularly useful measure comes from reviewing the debtor's status in the collection process. Since each strategy has steps, the customer's stage in the collection process provides valuable insight into receivables risk that is not apparent from just looking at the aging buckets. Conversations between the manager and the collector are then limited to the most important cases or those few that require additional research.

Having all customer account information on the collector's (or manager's) desktop makes account monitoring a much easier and quicker process. The added metrics and collection details that an automated collection system provides makes account monitoring a much more comprehensive exercise. The result is better tactical decisions for the handling of each account in question and therefore a better focus on improving collection performance. (See Exhibit 12.3.)

SUMMARY

With an automated collection system, taking a portfolio approach to accounts receivable management will generate intelligence that is simply not available from manual collection systems. Automated collections also provides for much more comprehensive individual account monitoring while also saving time. Account monitoring is a process by which credit and collections data is reviewed and analyzed to create information that can be used to better manage the accounts receivable.

The key to effective portfolio analysis is a well-thought-out segmenting scheme applied to the accounts receivable. Logical differentiators such as customer size or industry type provide each receivables segment with common characteristics. By identifying these characteristics and developing structural and

Exhibit 12.3   **Simplifying the Monthly Account Review**

The installation of an automated collection process dramatically reduced the time spent by Landmark Graphics, a Houston, Texas, based supplier of oil and gas exploration software, on account reviews. These reviews had become a valuable component of Landmark's manual collection processes, providing comprehensive monthly collection oversight for the manager of customer financial services and his superiors. However, the account reviews process was very time consuming, taking up more than a day of this manager's time every month. In addition, each of his three collectors was giving up half a day or so from collection activities.

This was because, under the manual system, collectors had to gather up their notes to meet with the manager of customer financial services, who then asked questions about those accounts he deemed important to upper management. The collectors could only guess at the accounts the manager would choose to discuss; therefore, they regularly overprepared for this meeting. Also, there would be the occasional item they missed, which would require additional research after the account review meeting. The manager subsequently prepared a report for his managers, which was reviewed in another meeting.

With an automated collection system, Landmark's manager of customer financial services was able to reduce his preparation time to less than 3 hours. All the information needed was available in each customer's collection activity log and payment history screens. Each collector's involvement in this process was now limited to providing additional background on only those few customers with whom the manager was not comfortable. The resulting time savings amounted to about 20 man-hours every month—time better spent on direct collection activities.

performance norms for each segment of the receivables portfolio, standards are created for the purpose of comparing accounts and identifying portfolio trends.

The establishment of norms also enables the assignment of risk factors to each customer, based on quantifiable criteria. In a manual collection system, any risk assessments are a judgmental function of the analyst's experience. Accounts are usually only assigned a credit limit that is based on the customer's individual creditworthiness without any consideration for that account's ranking in the accounts receivable portfolio.

By establishing norms and assigning risk factors, it is then possible to comprehensively analyze the accounts receivable portfolio. By so doing, underperforming accounts and segments of the receivables can be identified so that remedial action can be taken, weaknesses in both credit and collection procedures as well as other corporate process can more readily be identified and improved or corrected, and information that marketing can use to increase the quantity and quality of the company's sales effort can be extracted. Subsequent actions, based on portfolio analysis techniques, are justified by quantifiable facts rather than derived from intuition or an otherwise subjective decision-making process. Portfolio analysis provides an in-depth understanding of a company's customers. When shared throughout the company, such information has benefits beyond the credit and collections department.

Unlike portfolio analysis, individual account monitoring is customer specific. With an automated collection process, account reviews benefit from there being a single source for all necessary details. Anybody using the collection system can readily see an account's current status and payment history, and review a complete record of collection activity taken against that account. Additional customer-specific reporting features such as the stage of collections paint a more complete picture of any individual customer's status. With a manual collection process, this information is not available in one place—and some of it is not available at all—making account reviews time consuming and less comprehensive.

ENDNOTE

1. Dun & Bradstreet, Credit Risk Monitor, Equifax, Experian, F&D Reports, Fair Isaac, and Trade Credit Reporter, to name a few.

13

Deduction Management

The problem of short payments or deductions is a particularly bothersome collection issue. It is not so much the dollars involved—although if enough of these usually small balances are left unresolved, they can add up surprisingly fast—but the time it takes to either collect the balance due or issue a credit memo. Deductions can easily consume the major portion of a collector's time and focus, hindering that person's attention to more important and substantial collection issues. In this respect, deductions reduce the opportunity to accelerate collections from otherwise unaffected receivables.

Deductions can be likened to debris that has cluttered a stream. There may not seem to be much of a problem until the debris begins to accumulate. Before you know it, the dead branches have formed a natural dam that soon becomes solidified with silt. The effects are flooding upstream and limited flow downriver. With deductions, an inflated, difficult-to-manage, accounts receivable develops (the flood) while collections end up substantially below normal (reduced flow).

Breaking up the dam has the benefit of restoring the stream to its normal flow, but that is not necessarily a permanent solution. The logjam might re-form to yet again dam up cash flow. Trying to remove the debris as quickly as possible from the river does not guarantee long-term success. That approach will be labor intensive, time consuming, and therefore expensive. The only permanent solution is to keep the debris from ever entering the collection stream in the first place. While that is a worthy first priority, it is a virtually impossible goal. The second important priority should be to develop a process to segregate deductions automatically so that they do not infect the remainder of the accounts receivable portfolio. Then, the system will not get backed up and dilute the value of precious collection resources.

While time is the great enemy, the costs resulting from deductions are still substantial. It is not uncommon for companies that sell to retailers to suffer from a deduction rate of 15 percent. In such a circumstance, a $10 million accounts receivable will contain $1.5 million in deductions. Of this amount, typically only 10 percent is collectable. The remaining 90 percent will eventually be written off, though it is more likely that some sort of credit is due the customer. That means $150,000 worth of small collectable balances are sitting on this receivable. Most companies, because of limited resources, will collect only 10 percent of that value, a yield of only $15,000. That is not a particularly significant sum of money, and it can be very difficult and time consuming to retrieve it.

Even worse is the time and effort spent clearing up the other 90 percent of the deductions. Studies have shown that collectors can spend up to 75 percent of their time working on deductions. That time is at the expense of more critical collection activities. The problem collectors face is that if they do not effectively manage the deduction issues under their control, these problems will multiply, with the potential for creating serious credit and collection situations.

Collectors are not the only employees affected by deductions. Salespeople who are brought into the deduction-resolution process can typically find themselves devoting 10 to 40 percent of their time to solving these problems.[1] Here, the opportunity costs can get substantial as time is taken away from selling, and lost sales do not contribute anything to the bottom line. Other functional areas that are touched by deductions can be similarly affected: customer service, shipping and receiving, or quality assurance, for example. In every instance, deduction resolution will detract from the function's core responsibilities, with deleterious effects on departmental and corporate performance.

Another characteristic of deductions is that their root causes are usually internal. This holds true for 75 to 80 percent of the deductions a company experiences. Sometimes this is intentional, as is the case with promotional deductions and advertising allowances. Such programs are designed to generate additional sales, and the deductions are expensed accordingly. This does not mean that such deductions do not need to be managed. In fact, there is an imperative to manage these types of deductions very competently; otherwise, the incentives they were intended to create will be dissipated. In this case, the opportunity cost of the mismanaged promotion and advertising translates to reduced market share and sales growth.

For many companies, however, most deductions are the result of unintended but preventable consequences. Such deductions represent a breakdown or weakness in the order processing/billing system. Overly complex pricing structures, poor shipping controls, or too many handoffs involving paper-based order processing documents, for example, have the potential for creating persistent, system-clogging deductions. The obvious solution is to eliminate deductions at their source. That requires first identifying the different types of deductions affecting accounts receivables and the collection effort, and that is where automated collection software can be of great benefit.

PROBLEM IDENTIFICATION

Identifying the primary causes of deductions is just the first step toward reducing the number of deduction issues that may clog accounts receivable. It is not very difficult. What takes a little more thought is a system for cataloging and then quantifying each type of deduction with a minimum of effort. This is necessary for several reasons.

First, a baseline analysis of the extent to which deductions have infiltrated an accounts receivable portfolio provides a benchmark for measuring improvements. Comparisons require a fixed standard. One must know the type and dollars involved with each deduction. From this data, it is then possible to quantify the number of each type of deduction that has occurred within a specified time frame or that remain unresolved as open accounts receivable details.

Second, a baseline analysis reveals the relative effect of each type of deduction. It is not always obvious which types of deductions are having the greatest economic impact on a company's accounts receivable and collection functions. For example, most of a company's deductions could be caused by a multi-tiered pricing mechanism, but the resolution of these issues is relatively quick and simple. At the same time, the number of deductions for advertising allowances could be considerably fewer, but the dollars involved and the time and effort necessary to reconcile these issues could be considerably greater than that required of the pricing issues, making advertising allowances a much more significant drag on productivity, not to mention expense. Accordingly, it would then make sense to address advertising allowances before pricing procedures. A well-constructed baseline analysis provides data for intelligently prioritizing the assault on the root causes of deductions.

Finally, a baseline analysis provides a yardstick for measuring the impact of changes in corporate policy. Companies are not static creatures, and they are periodically going to change the way they do things. In particular, sales departments have been known to try different tactics that may or may not affect the accounts receivable. Having completed a baseline analysis, it is much easier to identify and quantify the impact of policy changes or new programs as they relate to the creation of deductions. Without this knowledge, corporate decision makers can be grossly misled in their analysis of a particular program's success.

After identifying the different types of deductions that occur, the second step is to catalog each occurrence. This is best done by assigning a code to each type of deduction. Many companies will assign a numeric code, but the problem with this is the need to constantly look up the deduction type for each code number. Memorization is another option, but it opens the door for making mistakes. The best solution is alphabetic codes that do not require any translation. Exhibit 13.1 provides an example

Exhibit 13.1 **Sample Deduction Codes**

Numeric Code	Alphabetic Code	Deduction Type
01	Price	Pricing
02	Return	Returned goods
03	Short	Short shipments
04	Quality	Quality problem
05	Discount	Unearned discount
06	Freight	Unpaid freight
07	Ad	Advertising allowance
08	Promo	Promotional allowance
09	Misc	Miscellaneous

of how these reason codes might be assigned. This data then becomes a part of the accounts receivable database.

The third step involves analyzing this data. Deductions can now be analyzed by type, number, dollar amount, and age. Generating reports that include this information is by itself a powerful tool for eliminating the root causes of deductions. Without this information, it is difficult for credit and collections to convince other corporate functions of the seriousness of deductions. Being able to quantify the pervasiveness of a particular type of deduction goes a long way toward getting the key decision makers within an organization to take action. Without these people's involvement, it is virtually impossible to effect changes to a corporation's method of operations, and that is often what is necessary if deductions are to be minimized. (See Exhibit 13.2.)

Quantifying the different types of deductions serves to get the attention of all affected. It does not, however, resolve the underlying problem. That often requires the formation of teams, involving people from the different business units that either affect or are affected by the particular type of deduction in question. Using the data that has been collected, the team can then work to devise new business systems that will cause fewer customer payment deductions. For these teams to function effectively, they need the support and empowerment of upper management. After all, they may be trying to cut across a number of different departmental turfdoms, and that requires strong medicine.

PRESALE VERSUS POSTSALE ISSUES

Another factor in the deduction identification process is determining whether the short payment or deduction results from a presale or a postsale issue. Most presale issues are the result of

Exhibit 13.2   Automated Problem Tracking Provides
Multiple Benefits

One of the prime reasons Liener Health Products sought out an automated collection solution was to gain control of the payment deduction and chargeback process. It wanted to identify both the customers who were primarily responsible for issuing deductions and the types of deductions that recurred most often. Knowing that, Liener believed it could then institute the front-end controls to prevent deductions from recurring. To do that, it needed some sort of mechanism to track deductions and chargebacks.

With the automated collection system in place, Liener has found that not only does it have the information desired to make informed decisions in regard to deduction management, but it is also saving a great deal of time over its manual processes of compiling and sharing information about deductions. Previously, schedules for tracking advertising and pricing deductions had to be prepared manually before any information could be shared with other departments such as general accounting, sales, customer service, and order entry. With an automated system, as soon as problems appear, they are routed to the appropriate departments for handling, while the collectors retain the ability to keep track of these issues, both individually and collectively. What previously took a significant amount of collector time now takes only seconds.

In addition, the collective deduction information is indeed helping Liener identify and correct the root causes of its more serious deduction and chargeback issues. One check it has instituted is purchase order audits. It turns out that customer service was entering orders, often over the phone, but was never checking the confirming purchase orders. As a result, bottom-line pricing descrepancies are being discovered and resolved before orders are shipped. Besides saving processing time and reducing the number of deductions, automated problem tracking is also helping Liener maintain its sales margins.

system weaknesses, whereas postsale issues are often purposeful rather than accidental.

Advertising allowances fall into this second category. They are an anticipated cost of doing business that should be more than offset by the benefits of increased sales. The deduction is not caused by any activity that is a part of the presale process but rather as the result of the customer's fulfilling criteria stipulated by sales or marketing. For example, purchases exceeding a specified threshold might grant the customer the right to a credit for such and such an amount.

In contrast, deductions caused by pricing discrepancies are caused by something that occurs presale. Order-entry errors, shipping errors, billing errors, and so forth all fall into this category. When such deductions recur, they are usually indicative of some sort of a system weakness rather than just an accidental occurrence.

Whether a deduction issue is caused by presale or postsale circumstances will in large part determine how it is dealt with. On the one hand, presale issues require fixing. These are the deduction issues that should be eliminated, though that is often impossible. At the very least, then, the number of presale-induced deductions should be minimized to relieve the collection department of as much of the burden as possible.

Postsale deductions, on the other hand, need to be processed efficiently. In many cases, a large number of these deductions may indicate a favorable response by customers to a promotional program. As long as the cost of the deductions is exceeded by the marketing benefits, the primary concern is to process the deductions as quickly and efficiently as possible. This does not mean that the presale process need not be examined for this type of deduction. In fact, it is critical that any program intended to generate postsale deductions not contribute to inefficiencies when the time comes to process the deduction. That would only increase costs and mitigate the benefits of such a program. It also means that ample resources need to be made available for processing these intentionally created deductions, because a failure to process them quickly and efficiently will create very negative responses from customers.

It remains, that whether a deduction is caused pre- or postsale, the entire process leading up to the customer's short paying or otherwise taking a deduction must be entirely understood. Not only must the process be understood in terms of the work flow and the decisions that lead up to a deduction's being taken, but the costs associated with resolving the deduction—allowing it by issuing a credit, denying it and then collecting it, or writing it off as a bad debt—must be calculated.

PUTTING A COST ON DEDUCTIONS

Not fully understanding the extent and impact of deductions on corporate operations is a substantial hindrance to the effective management of deductions. Without this knowledge, the collection function has little ground for convincing other departments that deductions are a serious drain on their resources. Getting down to specifics and putting a cost on payment deductions provides collectors with the ammunition to systematically attack the problem.

Accumulating this intelligence requires a methodology for identifying, quantifying, and documenting the most costly types of payment deductions faced by a corporation. One hindrance is the perception that doing this is an enormous task. That need not be the case. For most companies, there are two or three categories of recurring deductions that are obviously major problems. In addition, there may be another half-dozen types of deductions that are significant though less pervasive. By analyzing the processes behind only the six to eight most common types of deduction, it is possible to calculate reasonable estimates as to the cost, and correspondingly the opportunities for improvement, for upwards of 90 percent of a company's deduction exposure.

To do this, the most common types of deductions need to be diagrammed; a computer spreadsheet is the easiest way to handle the data. As the key factors associated with each type of problem are entered into the spreadsheet, the resources being consumed by each deduction category become apparent and a summary of the overall collection environment is produced. From this information, resources can then be focused at the most opportune solutions.

These key factors can be identified by applying the questions from Exhibit 13.3 to each type of deduction. The idea is to identify problems that relate to the company's internal delivery and resolution systems. Neither cash flow nor delays caused by customers that collectors or deduction analysts cannot affect should be considered—only those issues that can be impacted. In this way, the diagram being created serves as a tool to identify the weakness in internal corporate systems.

Without diagramming this information, it is impossible to determine the actual impact of each type of problem versus another. A deduction problem that recurs regularly may involve only small dollars and is readily handled by a clerk, whereas a less frequent, though high-dollar, problem might absorb a considerable amount of a manager's time, and thus have a much greater effect on collections. Getting rid of lots of the small-dollar type of deductions is therefore less of a priority than reducing even a few of the high-dollar problems. These are the types of nuances that are revealed by diagramming deductions. Exhibit 13.4 provides an example of what these results may look like.

Once the problem has been thoroughly identified and system weaknesses exposed, working out solutions becomes much

Exhibit 13.3 **Twelve-Step Program for Identifying Customer Deduction Problems**

---

1. Who at your company, outside of your collections/deductions group, resolves this problem?
2. What information do they need to resolve this problem?
3. What do they do to resolve this problem? (i.e., What decisions do they make; what information and documentation do they provide?)
4. On average, how many minutes in working time should it take to resolve one deduction?
5. On average, how many days in elapsed time does it take to resolve one deduction?
6. How much of your collection time is being spent to resolve this specific type of customer problem?
7. What is the volume of transactions?
8. What is the dollar amount of accounts receivable involved in the specific problem being diagrammed?
9. Who in the collection/deduction group is primarily responsible for monitoring these types of problems?
10. How do your collectors check a deduction's status with the external department(s) involvement?
11. What percentage of these deductions are eventually collected?
12. What can your company do to resolve the source of this problem so that it never happens again?

---

more of a logical, systematic process. Though every corporate environment is different, different types of deductions retain common characteristics and therefore are susceptible to similar solutions. Exhibit 13.5 identifies many of these.

The primary weapon an individual or team will use to break down departmental barriers and address the core issues

Exhibit 13.4 **Deduction Diagram**

Question	Problem #1	Problem #2	Problem #3
1	Pricing discrepancies Customer service manager	Returned goods Receiving supervisors	Proof of delivery Traffic manager
2	Invoice Purchase order Customer sales contract	Return authorization Invoice and price adjustments Product numbers	Bill of lading Freight bill
3	Compare invoice and purchase order to customer sales contract Contact customer if differences	Inspect goods Contact Customer Service if different Return to proper inventory	Request purchase order delivery from common carrier
4	10 minutes	30 minutes	5 minutes
5	10 Days	30 days	5 days
6	30 minutes per transaction	20 minutes per transaction	10 minutes per transaction
7	75 invoices per month	60 invoices per month	25 invoices per month
8	$20,000 per month	$300,000 per month	$50,000 per month
9	Regional credit manager	Regional credit manager	Credit clerk
10	Weekly follow-up via e-mail	Meet monthly to review	Phone call after 10 days
11	15%	5%	95%
12	Simplify pricing and pre-audit all purchase orders prior to shipment and invoicing	Meet weekly rather than monthly to review Include product managers to help identify reasons for returns	Automatically request and then mail purchase order delivery to chronic offenders

Exhibit 13-4   *(Continued)*

Answer Table			
Coll./Ded. analyst time	37.5 hours per month	20 hours per month	4.17 hours per month
AT = ((#7) × (6))/60			
External dept. time	12.5 hours per month	30 hours per month	2.08 hours per month
ET = ((#7) × (4))/60			
Operational costs*	$1,250.00 per month	$1,250.00 per month	$156.25 per month
OC = $25 (AT + ET)			
Collected dollars	$3,000.00 per month	$15,000.00 per month	$47,500.00 per month
CD = (#8) × (11)			
Carrying (Fiscal) Cost	$6.58 per month	$98.63 per month	$52.05 per month
CC = ((#5) × CD)/365)8%			
Total cost month	$1,256.58 per month $208.30 per		$1348.63 per
TC = OC + CC			month

*$25 was chosen as a reasonable estimate of salaries plus benefits. Your figure will vary depending on the compensation of your personnel resolving deductions.

behind deductions is good intelligence. That can only be derived in sufficient detail and organization from a computerized database. Collection software provides such a database and tracks deduction-related data automatically. The collector does not need to depart from the routine when a deduction is encountered, because beneath the surface, the software is creating the intelligence that will guide management in formulating long-term solutions to these issues.

Exhibit 13.5   System Solutions to Deduction Problems

Cause	Solutions
Pricing disputes	Customers need to understand your price schedule. Keep pricing as simple as possible, and then make sure your pricing schedules are explained to your customer's decision makers.
Misinterpreted promotions	As with pricing, simplicity is key. Get input from trusted customers before distributing promotional material. Make sure they can understand your program from your literature.
Advertising allowances	Once you are sure your customers understand your program, you must be prepared to reconcile and process customer claims quickly and accurately. You do not want to give credit more than once.
Short shipments	These can be caused by sloppy handling, poor controls, or pilferage. Corrective steps are easier once the source is identified. Incentives for accuracy, better systems, and additional security should fix the problem.
Undocumented deductions	Insist that all deductions claims be documented. Responding immediately and following up aggressively should change the customer's behavior.
Unearned payment discounts	Document each instance provides a strong argument to present to the customer. Chronic offenders who won't change their ways should lose their discount terms.
Conflicts with terms or conditions	Make sure all accounts sign a credit agreement that stipulates terms and conditions. Once all parties know what the rules there are, should be no room for excuses.

Exhibit 13-5   (*Continued*)

Handling and penalty charges	These should be stipulated in the credit agreement. Again, it is important that everybody knows the rules.
Order entry, shipping, or billing process errors	Simplify the order fulfillment process by routing out excessive hand-offs, repetitive paperwork, the rekeying of data, and duplicated procedures. Preedit your customer's purchase orders before shipping.
Slowness issuing credit memos	Make timely issuance a performance criterion for the departments responsible for approving credits.
Returned merchandise	Streamline the process so that goods are quickly redisposed and a credit issued. The requirement that customers get authorization before returning goods can facilitate this process.
Duplicate deductions	Respond immediately with full documentation. Problem tracking helps identify each individual deduction.
Coupon redemption	This should be a part of your cash application process so that credits are issued immediately.

There are two levels on which automated collection software operates in terms of system-based solutions to deductions. The first is the identification and quantification of the different types of deductions. This information serves to help root out the internal causes underlying most deductions. The second is the ongoing problem tracking of individual deduction issues. This capability serves to facilitate the management of ongoing deduction issues.

PROBLEM TRACKING

Although this discussion has focused on deductions, it should be noted that tracking problems or disputed items has utility beyond the realm of deductions and short payments. Any number of problems can arise to prevent the payment of overdue items, often the whole payment and not just a part as with deductions. A customer may have a dispute with its supplier that precludes the customer from making payment. Usually, automated deduction management techniques are applicable to these types of payment problems as well. Problem-tracking capabilities, therefore, have broad application to all types of payment problems, although the primary use of these tools is for deduction management. (See Exhibit 13-6.)

Besides providing a mechanism for identifying problems, problem-tracking software can isolate the problem receivables from those that have not been affected. This allows two things. First, it allows collectors to exclude problem items from their routine collections. By doing this, the collector can be more productive, making the calls and other contacts that have the highest potential for bringing in the most money as soon as

Exhibit 13.6   **The Six Critical Functions Performed by Problem Tracking**

> 1. Separately identifies problems from other past due items
> 2. Identifies recurring deductions
> 3. Allows quantification of problem types
> 4. Enables prescribed strategies to be used to resolve problems
> 5. Tracks contacts with other internal functions
> 6. Speeds resolution

possible. This is because the collector will not be dealing with any known deduction issues or other time-consuming problems. This also facilitates the automatic exclusion of problem items from faxes so as not to frustrate or otherwise antagonize the customer.

Second, when it is appropriate for the collector to work on the deductions in his or her accounts receivable portfolio, they can be grouped together. Taking it a step further, the receivables to be worked can be grouped by common problem codes for more productive handling. In addition, each problem code can be assigned a resolution strategy to guide the collector and keep the resolution process moving along. Just as with the grouping of receivables by their stage in the collection process, grouping problems by type and stage in the resolution process allows the collector to work much more efficiently by focusing on a repetitive process rather than having to adapt his or her skills to a different collection scenario with each transaction.

Another advantage of the collector's working through problems in this way is that recurring problems become more apparent. It was one thing to quantify how many deductions are the result of shipping errors, for example. It is quite another thing for a collector to work through a queue of similar problems. In resolving similar problems en masse, much knowledge is gained in the process. The collector gains greater familiarity with the nature and, hopefully, causes of the problems when they are grouped by problem type in the work queue. Working on random problems, particularly deductions, does not have the same impact.

This effect also extends beyond the credit and collection department. If the collector is working on a group of problems that are of the same type and stage in the resolution process, then the other people in the company affected by this type of problem are forced to address these issues in batches, not individual occurrences. In this respect, the collector is aided in the tracking of internal communications by the problem-tracking software. Just as with past due customers, follow-up is critical to resolving problems in a timely manner. As the collectors communicate with their counterparts in other departments, all parties gain knowledge as they work through the problems, and the opportunity to discover permanent solutions to repetitive issues is enhanced.

PROBLEM RESOLUTION

In most companies, collectors serve as a sort of gatekeeper for the administration and resolution of deductions and other problems. Some companies delegate this gatekeeping responsibility to specialists, otherwise known as deduction analysts or administrators, whose function is essentially the same as a collector handling the problem. In either case, the people who are empowered to approve or deny the deductions, or otherwise resolve any problems, are staff members or managers of corporate functions other than in the finance area as is credit and collections.

This means that the key role of a collector or deduction specialist with regard to problems is to be a communicator. Having all the facts makes this task much easier, and that is exactly what problem-tracking software provides. Since problems need to be corrected at the source, which is usually internal, the collector or deduction specialist must be prepared to relay information back and forth between the customer and the decision maker. Documentation is usually the critical factor, so the collector or deduction specialist must be equipped to disseminate this information to both the internal and external parties to the matter at hand, and then be able to follow up with the decision makers until the problem is resolved. The automatic fax and e-mail capabilities of the problem-tracking software facilitate this task without creating additional paperwork.

Another gatekeeping role that is assisted by problem-tracking software is the ability to produce documentation sufficient to convince other departments of the seriousness of recurring-type problems. In conjunction with any baseline analysis that may have been conducted, collectors and deductions specialists can use this powerful tool for enlisting the support of other departments in rooting out the system weakness, policies, or procedures that cause most deductions. Documentation that shows costs and trends is hard to refute, even more so when people in other departments can see the impact deductions are having on their own performance. Change seldom occurs easily, and enlisting corporate-wide support is a critical element of the change process. That is more easily done when people admit there is a need for change and can then be shown the advantages of any new process or procedure. If other departments do not see a particular type of deduction problem as a serious matter, it is unlikely that they will agree to changes.

To be a problem solver, the collector or deduction specialist must be a communicator. Problem-tracking software therefore needs to enhance this task by serving as a communication tool. It does so by integrating the various information components—documentation, messaging, reporting, and follow-up—so the collector or deduction specialist can easily monitor and manage the entire process. That requires keeping all interested parties actively involved in the resolution of open deductions and other problems, essentially ensuring that the deduction issues keep moving along toward resolution. It also requires motivating the internal decision makers to take steps to reduce the number of unintended recurring-type deductions. In so doing, the overhead deductions created can be significantly reduced.

In a departmentalized setting, deductions are viewed by each internal business group as a problem in a box. No department sees the entire picture, and usually not even the same type of deductions. This situation does not facilitate system-wide fixes to prevent recurring deductions whose origins, effects, and resolutions are usually spread throughout the organization. An automated deduction management system thus becomes an extremely valuable communication tool that can facilitate real change in how deductions are managed.

REPORTING

Reporting is a key component of the problem-solving process. This is usually a weak point with manual collection systems even if receivables have been automated. The resultant inability to analyze the big picture makes it difficult to get a handle on the deduction situation. The difficulty in creating deduction reports from a manual system is twofold. First is a lack of information. Without reason codes linked to the accounts receivable database, nothing much can be learned except the total number and amount of deductions. Even if reason codes are available, that data is not tied into the collection process, making it difficult to measure the efforts and time frames encountered in resolving the deductions. In addition to the lack of information, manual reporting is extremely time consuming. Remember, deductions are a low-dollar, high-volume type of headache, so there are a lot of little, often very different items to count.

An automated collection system with a problem-tracking capacity is not encumbered by these restraints. Reports are easily generated, and it is a simple matter to view specific answers to specific problems. This is because the data can be sorted by any combination of problem type, product type, sales representative, or shipping point. This can help identify whether there is a correlation between any of the different types of deduction problems and these other identifiers.

If a company's pricing problems tend to originate from one or two salespeople, then corrective action can be taken. This scenario is indicative not of a system problem but of a staff issue such as training. By the same token, repeated problems at one shipping point over all others may also be a staff issue, but might also be a freight carrier problem or poor systems at that location. The reporting features of problem-tracking software should help define deduction issues in detail sufficient to suggest possible causes. Otherwise, anyone trying to analyze deductions will feel as though they are searching for a needle in a haystack. A good reporting system helps illuminate the target. (See Exhibit 13.7.)

Trends are also more observable from reports generated by an automated problem-tracking system. Being able to identify negative trends as early as possible allows for changes in tactics and the reallocation of resources to control the situation. Since the law of unintended consequences does not directly stipulate that deductions will necessarily increase when corporate changes affect the order fulfillment cycle, it is difficult to anticipate new trends. Deduction reports make this easier.

You cannot observe trends without an initial and secondary reference point. The data accumulated in between also makes it possible to project trends into the future. Being able to identify a trend early on, and then to be able to predict future deduction rates and cash flows, allows management to stay on top of the situation.

A good reporting system also allows the adaptation of auditing principles to deduction management. If over a period of time a particular customer's deductions are found to be legiti-

Exhibit 13.7   **Problem Balance by Category***

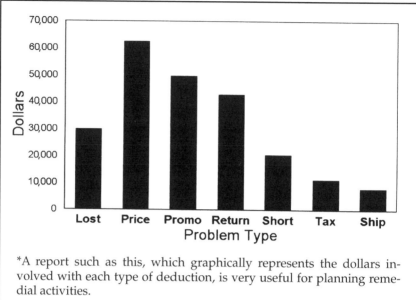

*A report such as this, which graphically represents the dollars involved with each type of deduction, is very useful for planning remedial activities.

mate, then it is reasonable to assume that future deductions will also be legitimate and to therefore accept them without further investigation. By the same token, if all pricing discrepancies within a particular sales rep's territory are ultimately approved, there is really no need to continue investigating such deductions, and instead a process should be established to automatically process the credit memos that will resolve these issues. Problem-tracking software makes these types of analysis possible. Then, only periodic audits need to be conducted to ensure that there is no slippage.

The same type of analysis can be done for small deductions. If most small deductions are legitimate, it is very likely that the expense of investigating all small deductions is greater than the potential collections, and companies are justified to automatically approve all deductions under a specified threshold. Incidentally, these items should be automatically processed at the time cash is being applied.

Reports are also a means of communicating how well other corporate departments are able to process transactions. Deduction systems track how long each transaction is held by a given problem owner prior to issuance of a credit or advice to the collectors that the matter should be collected. One example of a report that helps expedite the processing of deductions by other departments is listing the transactions that require action, aged by the date they were distributed to the external departments and grouped by the department responsible for resolving any problems. (See Exhibit 13.8.)

PROCESS IMPROVEMENT TO PREVENT PROBLEM RECURRENCE

As mentioned previously, the primary goal of deduction management is not processing more deductions faster, but rather correcting the causes of deductions in the first place (with the obvious exception being intentional promotional-type deductions). Without process improvement as the main objective, problem-tracking software merely helps the collector or deduction specialist do more work with only minimal productivity improvements. However, when problem-tracking software is used as a change management tool, a much higher operating efficiency is attained.

By using the reporting features of problem-tracking software to identify error-causing tasks and thereby involve the decision makers that effectively own the individual deduction issues, collectors and deduction specialists assume the role of change agents. To be effective change agents, they need to have an intimate understanding of the business

Exhibit 13.8 **Problem Status by Category (Detail) Report**

12/31/97

Cust. #	Customer Name	Invoice Date	Entered Date	Closed Date	Inv. #	Problem #	Open $	Closed $	Days Open
	Problem Category:	*Pricing Dispute*							
1091	Dianna Marketing	09/02/97	10/12/97	12/29/97	115065	159		$104.20	78
1825	Questron, Inc.	09/17/97	11/05/97		115973	165	$25,149.00		56
1096	Savant Solutions	08/21/97	11/06/97		114696	166	$7,384.20		55
1096	Savant Solutions	09/08/97	11/15/97	12/19/97	115616	181		$2,746.02	34
1096	Savant Solutions	09/29/97	12/02/97		116275	192	$2,247.38		29
1096	Savant Solutions	10/03/97	12/02/97		116587	193	$5,101.65		29
	Subtotals:	6 Items					$39,882.23	$2,850.22	$42,732.45
	Problem Category:	*Returned Goods*							
1232	Brevity Corp.	09/12/97	11/05/97	12/02/97	115596	163		$5,240.00	27
1232	Brevity Corp.	09/16/97	11/05/97		115612	164	$5,240.00		56
1564	Fidelity Armor	09/03/97	10/10/97	10/31/97	115099	155		$7,543.22	21
2154	Pacific Magtron	10/15/97	12/03/97		117465	195	$12,645.87		28
1786	S&D Distributing	08/15/97	11/23/97	12/31/97	114434	186		$2,415.76	38
1786	S&D Distributing	10/13/97	12/12/97		117209	201	$4,654.45		19
1096	Savant Solutions	09/29/97	12/02/97		116276	194	$3,005.99		29
	Subtotals:	7 Items					$25,546.31	$9,958.98	$35,505.29

processes that cause deductions and be able to work with all parties associated with these processes. In the end, deduction management is all about simplifying processes and quality improvement. This is where the collector's specialized knowledge can be transferred from process management to process improvement.

Reducing the hand-off of documents from one person to another and eliminating redundant data-entry tasks are good places to start. Hand-offs and data entry are prone to error, and they consume time unnecessarily. Process improvement teams charged with redesigning systems that will present fewer opportunities for deductions to be taken should keep this in mind. Simplicity is an asset.

Another important consideration comes down to knowing the customers and understanding their needs. If customers were getting everything they needed and they knew it, there would be no deductions, so in a sense deductions reflect breakdowns in customer support or the perception that there has been a breakdown in the delivery thereof. Customer input is therefore another essential input the process improvement team should consider.

In the final analysis, everyone benefits from systems that have been redesigned to minimize deductions. Customers are able to process payments more quickly. Their accounts payable personnel are no longer issuing as many debit memos or spending time trying to reconcile their accounts. Collectors get to spend more time focused on their core responsibility—accelerating collections—rather than resolving problems, which for the most part are individually insignificant. The same is true for other departments whose responsibilities are impacted by the order fulfillment and collection processes. Fewer deductions translate into greater productivity for all concerned.

SUMMARY

Deduction management requires a two-pronged strategy: eliminating as many deductions as possible and then managing those that remain as quickly and efficiently as possible. An automated collection system is almost indispensable to this task because of the large volume of small transactions involved. Unmanaged, deductions cause a serious drain on credit department resources, which has a very adverse affect on collections. By reducing the dilution in the value of accounts receivable caused by deductions, not only are collections accelerated but more dollars can be brought to the bottom line.

The problem-tracking capabilities of collection software provide the tools to identify the different types of deductions that are occurring and quantify the number and amount of each type of deduction by customer, sales territory, product class, and so forth. This information supports the task of raising the level of corporate awareness to the actual and hidden costs of deductions, and to thereby enlist support for process improvements that will reduce the opportunities for customers to take deductions.

Problem tracking also provides a mechanism so that collectors can manage their deduction load with only minimal interference to their core responsibility of accelerating collections. As such, problem tracking serves as a reference and communication tool, enabling the rapid dissemination of information to the various decision makers in the deduction-resolution process. By following programmed strategies, collectors can monitor the progress of deductions through the resolution process to ensure maximum recovery from those deductions that are not warranted and the timely adjustment of legitimate deductions off the accounts receivable so that other aspects of the credit and collection function are not adversely affected by the accumulation of deductions waiting for final dispensation. An automated collection system is therefore not complete unless it comprehensively addresses the issue of deductions.

ENDNOTE

1. John Metzger, "Customer Deductions: Hidden Profit Leaks," *Corporate Cash Flow*, March 1995.

14

Automated Cash Applications

The acquisition and application of remittances and the advice that goes along with them is an integral part of the collection process. For the most part, the depositing and posting of receipts has been a clerical function, often performed by accounts receivable clerks. This alone suggests that the cash application process is a prime candidate for automation. Over the past 30 or so years, progress has been made toward this end, but not in a comprehensive fashion.

Most notably, the advent of the bank lockbox has provided a platform for this sort of change. Banks have worked long and hard to add value to their lockbox services by adding features that promote an automated environment. In so doing, the banks have mostly worked with large corporations to implement various enhancements to the traditional lockbox, but the costs and economies of scale have hindered the widespread adoption of these innovations by small and mid-sized corporations.

One of the biggest hindrances has been the difficulty of writing software that merges data collected by the banks with corporate accounts receivable systems. In the first place, merging such data into accounting software that was not written with this eventuality in mind is a formidable project. For the most part, any corporation looking to do this would be required to create a custom program. As a result, each application essentially re-invented the wheel. The good news is that as time has passed, accounts receivable software packages have begun to address the issue of automated remittance processing.

A second hurdle involves the problem of how to handle exceptions. All the deduction issues discussed in Chapter 13 result in exceptions when applying remittance advice to accounts receivable. To automatically merge remittance data captured by the bank with a company's accounts receivable database requires that all exceptions be addressed. Posting less than entire deposits and working out the exceptions later causes problems, as does posting the exceptions without somehow identifying them. This is not an insurmountable programming task, but it is complex and therefore fairly time consuming and costly. It is not something an in-house corporate programming department can just whip together or a bank remittance processing group can comprehensively address.

The advent of personal computers (PCs) and client–server computing have opened up the opportunity for dedicated cash application software that acts as a bridge between a corporation's bank lockbox and its accounts receivable database. By preprocessing remittances in such a software package, the problems caused by exceptions are reduced. Remittance processing software also holds out the promise of fewer exceptions by increasing the hit rate—the number of remittances that can be automatically matched to the accounts receivable data without causing an exception. If an invoice is paid in full, the object is to have the remittance processing software handle the cash posting seamlessly without the need for human intervention.

These software advances are bringing the potential of automated remittance processing much closer to reality for many more corporations. Companies that have been able to automate remittance processing to fully integrate their accounts receivable are realizing tremendous productivity gains. Time previously spent applying cash can be redirected toward collection activities that generate better cash flow and therefore lower carrying costs. Just the fact that cash receipts are posted sooner speeds the collection process. In addition, by capturing deduction data up front when exceptions are being processed, the resolution of those issues is enhanced.

Because cash applications are at such a critical juncture in the collection process improvements, and for that matter deficiencies, are magnified during subsequent processes. Timely and accurate cash applications are critical to an efficient credit and collection operation, so it should be no surprise that automating remittance processing delivers significant dividends.

LOCKBOX SERVICES

The traditional lockbox was conceived to reduce mail float—the time it takes for mailed payments to reach their destination. Companies were taught to choose the location of their bank lockboxes based on studies that identified the shortest mail times in respect to the geographic distribution of customers. Thus, opening a lockbox helped reduce a company's collection cycle by roughly the same amount as mail float. Another criterion was how quickly the lockbox bank could clear the checks received. The incentive for reducing check float, or clearing times, is directly related to interest rates. Therefore, in the 1970s, when rates were high, lockboxes enjoyed a period of high growth and acceptance.

Once they became commonplace, and compounded by declining interest rates in the 1980s, banks sought to add new services to maintain the growth rates in their lockbox operations.

This has involved finding ways to collect and clear checks faster on the one hand, and improving the process by which remittance advice is delivered to customers on the other. Since the biggest payback in reducing float comes from opening a lockbox in the first place, subsequent improvements in collections or clearing remittances have been incremental at best. In contrast, improving the delivery of information does not do anything to reduce float, whether in mail time or in check clearing, but it does offer opportunities for companies to further reduce their collection cycles.

One of the innovations banks have devised is the lockbox network. Many companies that sell nationally have multiple lockboxes in different parts of the country to minimize mail float. This places funds in multiple accounts in multiple banks. As soon as checks clear and funds become available, most companies transfer these funds to a consolidation account before beginning the investment and disbursement processes. With a lockbox network, all the funds are deposited into one account, even though the remittances are received at multiple locations. As a result, costly transfers are unnecessary, and the remittance acquisition process is simplified.

Most of the other improvements and innovations in lockbox service have dealt with data handling. As lockbox volume increased, banks invested in automation to maintain or improve their level of service. Imaging systems allowed much more efficient processing of remittance advice by eliminating the need to pass paperwork from one clerk to another. Instead, by having keypunch operators view the images rather than the remittances, the banks were able to process many more deposits and, because of automated checks within the system, with much higher accuracy. This also made it more feasible for the bank lockbox operation to capture additional remittance data. One way this was used was to give companies same-day deposit details. Typically, a company would dial up the bank, using bank software, to get the total lockbox deposit for that day along with the payee name on the check, the check number, and the check amount for each item in the deposit.

While the deposit totals helped companies calculate their cash management needs, the remittance details provided little advantage. The details did allow credit departments to release orders on credit hold for which a payment had come in, but, as discussed in Chapter 6, many collectors noted these remittance details on their aged accounts receivable trial balances, thereby duplicating the efforts of the remittance processors a day or two later, after the paper remittance advice was received. However, this did prepare the way for the electronic transmission of remittance advice.

Bank lockbox operations were already capturing images of the checks received and any accompanying remittance advice. In addition, they were keypunching and electronically storing some of the remittance details, and could easily capture all remittance details to create a complete electronic record of every item deposited. At this point, it was only a small step to deliver remittance advice in either an electronic or an imaged format. Until phone lines are able to handle broader bandwiths, most imaged data is delivered on a CD-ROM. This is because an electronic image is memory intensive, and so transmitting imaged copies of all the paper documents received by the lockbox would take an inordinate amount of time, not to mention money to cover the communication costs. Electronic records, however, are easily and quickly transmitted and can then be merged with a company's accounts receivable database.

Receiving remittance advice in either an image or an electronic format holds a distinct advantage over the delivery of paper-based remittance advice. Most companies that get paper remittance documents receive a photocopy of the deposited check, originals of the other contents of the envelope, and, if the terms of sale include a discount, probably the original envelope via a next day courier service. For many individual payments, there is no need for all this information, unless there is some discrepancy in the application of the cash received to the outstanding accounts receivable balances.

Even when remittance data is delivered electronically, the paper advice is also forwarded so that any exceptions can be investigated. In this case, only the physical documents for the payments in question are handled by the cash applications clerk. With images delivered, usually by next day courier, on a CD-ROM there is no need for any paper documents. Of course, cost is always a factor, so companies that choose to have remittance documents delivered in an image format generally are dealing with a high volume of remittances passing through their lockbox.

ELECTRONIC DATA INTERCHANGE

At the same time technological advances were enabling banks to enhance their lockbox services, electronic data interchange (EDI) and electronic funds transfer (EFT) systems were being developed. The impetus behind the electronic exchange of information is straightforward: substituting a seamless sequence of electronic transactions that eliminate paperwork and associated document hand-offs will be manifestly more productive than traditional commercial transactions. One benefit of EDI is the speed at which transactions can be processed. Eliminating document hand-offs (in particular, the need for sign-offs) and not moving information at the speed of light is the primary contributing factors for using EDI. The key factor contributing to the productivity gains that come from implementing EDI is the elimination of repetitive keypunching. This does save time, but more importantly, it eliminates the chance for errors. Electronic Data Interchange, therefore, offers speed and accuracy to transaction processing.

These are key components for any enhancements to transaction processes. However, EDI did not gain acceptance as quickly as predicted. This is because early efforts at EDI required a series of complicated software interfaces. Adding to the design burden was the fact that each EDI partnership had its own idiosyncracies. Under these circumstances, the programming costs involved favored large trading partners. For this reason, EDI has been a top-down proposition, with the largest companies being the early adopters and then forcing compliance with their trading partners. Mid-sized companies, for the most part, reluctantly embraced EDI only when forced to by their larger trading partners.[1] As time went on, improved standards and advances in EDI software made implementation of EDI partnerships somewhat easier.

However, from a cash application standpoint, the problem of how to handle the exceptions without delaying the entire process remains. Deductions and other payment discrepancies are just as difficult to apply if transmitted through EDI as through any other electronic communication. In most instances, a labor-intensive solution is required to support the EDI transaction process, mitigating the benefits of adopting EDI. Overcoming this obstacle holds the promise of significant productivity gains.

PREPROCESSING SOFTWARE SOLUTIONS

The advent of client–server computing has provided a solution to the problem of applying electronic payment advice that includes deductions to a computerized accounts receivable. Preprocessing software has been developed that acts as a bridge between the bank lockbox or the transmitter of EDI remittance advice and the computerized accounts receivable. The client–server aspect comes into this because very often this preprocessing software is running on a personal computer networked with the host computer, on which the accounts receivable software resides.

As with collections, this type of remittance processing software draws information from the accounts receivable database so that information can be processed and adjusted apart from the corporation's accounting software system. The system integrity of the accounting software is guaranteed because processing is done in a segregated environment. Only when the remittance has been fully processed is that data transmitted back to the host-based accounts receivable software system, and then in a format that is wholly compatible with the accounts receivable software. That transmission in effect replaces the final step of the typical cash application process for most companies that must have their remittance advice keypunched in order to enter that information in their accounts receivable database.

The integrity issue is also served, because there is no need to rewrite portions of the host-based accounts receivable software package in order to accommodate electronic remittance advice. Any time modifications are made to an integrated software package, which is the case with most accounts receivable modules, there is the risk of unintended consequences. In addition, such modifications often face restrictions in their utility because of the parameters of the computing environment in which they are being written. This often makes the writing of substantial modifications a daunting task for overworked MIS departments.

It should be noted that with time, more and more accounts receivable software modules are including EDI and electronic lockbox transmission capabilities. Still, the critical factor for these systems is how to handle deductions. As a result, most of these systems choose to preprocess remittance advice before actually posting payments to the accounts receivable.

In a preprocessing system, the electronic remittance advice is matched against current accounts receivable details outside of the accounts receivable software module. This is done by copying all open accounts receivable details to a separate database that is part of the remittance processing software, usually kept on a networked PC. The electronic remittance advice is also transmitted to the remittance-processing software. Lockbox advice is usually transmitted in either an electronic Bank Administration Institute (BAI) or EDI format, which the remittance-processing software can easily recognize. (See Exhibit 14-1.)

At this point, following a set of prescribed algorithms, the remittance-processing software matches the remittance advice to the accounts receivable details. Ideally, invoice numbers indicated on the remittance advice will exactly match those in the

Exhibit 14.1 **Sample Reference Matching Schemes**

Remittance Advice Reference	Invoice Number	Type of Match
43789659	43789659	Exact match
4378965	43789659	Reference missing last digit. Customer system may only have the capacity for seven digits.
3789659	43789659	Reference missing first digit. See above.
X43789659	43789659	Customer has added a prefix, possibly to indicate receiving location for this order.
X437896	43789659	Customer has added a prefix and dropped last two digits.
2334-43789659X	43789659	Customer has added a prefix and suffix.

accounts receivable detail. If that is not the case, the software will take the reference numbers accompanying the remittance advice and try to find a match by more sophisticated methods (see Exhibit 14.1). These essentially involve trying to find a matching string of characters between the customer's reference numbers from its remittance advice and the original invoice number by dropping either or both leading and trailing digits. If account numbers and purchase order numbers are included in the customer's remittance details, that data is also used, in much the same way as invoice numbers, to come up with a confirmed match. The other variable for comparison is the amount of the invoice. If the software is able to find a probable invoice number match, and the amount being paid matches the original invoice amount, it assumes it has an exact match.

If the invoice amount does not match the amount being paid, the software creates an exception for manual review by the cash application clerk. Likewise, if a likely invoice number match is not found, an exception item is created. In some instances, the remittance-processing software will suggest a likely match or course of action for an exception item. In such a case, the cash applications clerk need only verify the suggested operations with a single keystroke. For example, many companies write off all small-dollar exceptions. A typical threshold might be $25. The remittance-processing software can easily identify these items, and present them as exception items for the cash application clerk's approval. A minority of exceptions will require more significant attention by the cash applications clerk.

Over time, customer payment idiosyncracies become more easily recognized through the use of remittance-processing software. With this knowledge, additional fine-tuning of the remittance matching algorithms is made possible, resulting in higher "hit" rates. The more exact matches the remittance processing software can find, the more productivity benefits it will provide. Another factor that can increase hit rates is payment promises recorded in an automated collection system. Prior knowledge that a customer is paying specific invoices or making partial payments can be used to enhance the matching routine.

As long as the system is not being used in a high-deduction environment and a good set of matching algorithms have been developed, exceptions can be kept below 10 percent, often well below 10 percent. That translates into a significant time savings for the cash application clerks. Because the exceptions are naturally the toughest items to apply, eliminating the necessity of applying more than 90 percent of the remittances translates into a reduction in the time spent applying cash by 50 to 75 percent. In a high-volume environment in which several clerks apply cash manually, automating remittance processing can free up some of these personnel for other credit and collection activities.

Typically, customer payment deductions will account for the largest number of exceptions. By beginning to address these issues during the cash-application process, the deduction-resolution process is initiated at the earliest possible moment and automated deduction handling is enabled. Remittance-processing software should allow the cash applications clerk to enter a reason code with the payment so that proper handling down the line is assured. In fact, sophisticated matching software can identify reason codes automatically. For example, by being able to calculate sales tax, an automated matching program can identify sales tax deductions. The same holds true for freight deductions, which can be captured if the software has the ability to review remittance advice by line item. By passing these reason codes on to the problem-tracking feature of the collection software, these deduction issues automatically fall into the prioritized work queues generated by the collection software. This includes matching the deduction issues with a corresponding collection or resolution strategy. The collectors not only get immediate visibility of new deductions, but they also are prompted to take action appropriate to resolving each individual issue as quickly as possible. In addition, using e-mail, the deduction codes can be forwarded automatically to problem owners that are outside the collection group.

Once every item in the remittance batch has been coded properly, the remittance details are sent in batch format to the accounts receivable software for application to the accounts receivable database. Since the remittance is already in balance as confirmed by the remittance-processing software, the accounts receivable database can be updated without further manual intervention. Therefore, most remittance details are passed along seamlessly and effortlessly from the bank lockbox operations center to the company's accounts receivable database.

As mentioned, this also holds true for EDI payments and, for that matter, any other type of automated funds transfer such as wire transfers (Fedwire or SWIFT) and automated clearing-house (ACH) transactions. In the case of EDI, the most important data package is the remittance advice that is sent in EDI 820 format. This protocol allows for the proper referencing of payments, and may even include deduction reason codes in addition to the other reference information. If electronic funds are sent simultaneously with the EDI 820 format data, so much the better, but it is the automatic application of the remittance advice that brings the greatest productivity savings. It is not uncommon for the EDI 820 format data to be sent when a physical check is processed. This allows the processing of this remittance data in advance of the receipt of funds. Then, when the check does arrive at the lockbox, the remittance-processing software is able to merge the remittance details with the lockbox deposit, and to therefore be able, without delay, to update the accounts receivable database with the deposit information.

As such, remittance-processing software provides a gateway for companies to acquire EDI capabilities. Without remittance-processing software, companies must commit extensive MIS resources to the EDI implementation process. In contrast, remittance-processing software has already built the necessary bridges so that the addition of EDI partners is a routine operator task rather than another programming project.

PAYMENT FORECASTING

As remittance-processing software is utilized, it accumulates payment data that can be translated into intelligence regarding customer payment habits. Once enough details have been recorded to create a baseline, this information can be used to provide fairly accurate forecasts of anticipated cash receipts. When this historical payment data is combined with information about promised payments from the automated collection system, even more accurate reports can be created.

This is done by having the system look at open items in order to project an expected payment date based on previous experience with each customer. Any payments noted in the collection system as promised can then be advanced or moved back, based on the customer's commitment and its track record in regard to keeping payment promises. The result is a more accurate cash forecasting report than it is possible to derive from the typical accounts receivable database. On a company-wide basis, this intelligence is crucial to maximizing the utility of corporate resources. Otherwise, when cash projections are suspect, investment alternatives often have to be delayed or opportunities missed.

In terms of collections, payment forecasting also provides insight into the effectiveness of recent collection activities. If the system is reporting that payments are expected to slow over the next 2 to 3 weeks, credit management should want to find out why. If this slowdown in any way correlates to either fewer contacts being made by collectors or a lack of customer payment commitments being obtained by the collectors, steps should be taken to get these activities back on track. Of course, slowing payments can be indicative of economic or industry-wide conditions such as seasonality. These may or may not require that management implement initiatives to address such issues.

Cash forecasting is also important on the individual customer level. Payment trends will dictate future collection strategies. For example, an account that is showing signs of slowing down can be assigned an accelerated collection strategy in an effort to reverse the trend. Payment forecasting is thus an important component when it comes to developing customer collection strategies and departmental collection initiatives.

SUMMARY

The accurate and timely posting of remittance advice is a critical factor in terms of the level of success a credit and collection department can achieve. If payments are not posted quickly, collectors must work with out-of-date information and waste time contacting customers for items that have already been paid. By the same token, if remittance details are not posted accurately, much time is wasted reconciling accounts instead of accelerating subsequent customer payments.

By automating the remittance-processing function, data-entry time is dramatically reduced. Commensurate with this is a very significant reduction in data-entry costs, which are labor intensive by nature. These benefits can be achieved by using remittance-processing software to electronically receive lockbox information, which is then preprocessed for final application to the company's accounts receivable database. By using algorithms that match remittance details to invoice numbers, this software greatly reduces the time required by cash-application clerks to process deposits. Remittance-processing software also provides a bridge so that EDI remittances and other types of electronic funds transfer can be integrated into a companies cash receipts processes.

While the cost savings can be very significant, the primary benefit from implementing an automated cash-application process is the redirection of often limited collection resources from posting customer payments to more vital collection activities. By spending less time on remittance processing, collection departments can devote more time to the collection process and, more specifically, to contacting customers for the payment of overdue balances. Automating the remittance process expands a company's overall collection capacity. In addition, automating remittance processing will increase productivity by providing detailed historical payment information that can be used to analyze and fine-tune the collection process.

ENDNOTE

1. In EDI parlance, trading partners are simply two companies that have an established buy–sell relationship. The more important the relationship, and the greater the number of transactions, the greater the incentive to look for EDI-based data transfer solutions.

15

Third-Party Collections in an Automated Environment

It has long been a common practice of commercial enterprises to send uncooperative and otherwise unproductive customers to a third party for additional collection efforts. This has usually involved hiring the services of a collection agency to pursue seriously past due balances. When the collection agency is unable to collect the debt through its own efforts, it may in turn, with the creditor's permission, turn the claim over to an attorney. A smaller number of creditors bypass the collection agencies to directly place collection claims with a collection attorney.

This is no longer the only type of third-party collections. About 1980, the deduction outsourcing industry was born to help overworked credit and collection departments cope with the burden of resolving payment deduction issues, which is typically a time- and resource-consuming process that has only an incremental monetary impact. The growth of this industry has paved the way for other aspects of the collection process to be outsourced, and in some cases the entire collection process. Adding fuel to this trend are corporate belt tightening and downsizing programs that leave credit and collection departments understaffed.

As a consequence, third-party collections are an integral component of the collection cycle. This being the case, automated collection processes need to account for the practice of placing specified segments of the accounts receivable portfolio with third-party collection services. In addition, an automated collection process should track the progress of these third-party efforts as well as their costs.

COLLECTION AGENCIES AND ATTORNEYS

"Placing an account for collection" has long been the final stage of most collection strategies. When every means for collecting an account in house has been exhausted, the option of turning over an overdue account to a collection agency or attorney provides a last hope for a satisfactory recovery. It should be noted that just the threat of placing an account for collection is a powerful payment motivator, so the final demand is deservedly the second-to-last collection stage. Placing collection claims, therefore, should be a final component of a well-conceived collection strategy. It is not to be done lightly, nor should turning accounts over to a collection agency or attorney be delayed, because with each passing day the chance of collection is diminished. When collection strategies are automated, overdue customers get more attention sooner, so those that turn out to be unproductive will tend to be placed for collection earlier than if they had been worked within a manual collection process. The early placement of claims has the benefit of then increasing the chance and amount of recovery by the collection agency or attorney.

With an automated collection process, the placed-for-collection stage of each collection strategies becomes the jumping-off point for tracking these activities. This stage serves to separate these receivables from those being actively pursued for collections in house. By excluding all receivables in the placed-for-collection stage from management reports such as the aging report, metrics are then not affected by receivables that have been placed for collection. This is especially important for companies that charge balances placed for collections to bad debt expense. In any event, it is important that third-party collection balances do not cloud the analysis of in-house receivables or by their presence distract or interfere with the collector's normal routine.

Using the same sort of mechanism to identify third-party collection accounts, reports can be generated that list only these customers. This is necessary for the monitoring of accounts placed with individual collection agencies or attorneys. Though these accounts are being actively pursued by a third party rather than by in-house collectors, it is still necessary to monitor the third party's efforts. There are three reasons for this. First, collection agents should be following the company's guidelines in the conduct of the collection efforts. Second, it is important that the agent shows continued progress through its own collection strategies toward a final resolution of the matter. Sometimes, collection claims can even get lost or neglected due to clerical errors. By monitoring progress, the company can find this out. Third, the effectiveness of the third-party collector should be evaluated to ensure maximum recovery.

With an automated system, the first two factors—adherence to guidelines and a progression through the collection process— are served by the recording of contact information between the creditor and the third party. The agency should be providing an agreed-upon level of service in terms of submitting progress reports (usually monthly[1]) and transmitting copies of any significant correspondence with the debtor. A listing of completed activities can be provided in a printed report or record format extracted from the automated collection system being used by the third party's operation. This information is imported if an electronic or magnetic format is provided, but otherwise can be entered manually in the automated system along with appropriate follow-up dates, ensuring that the monitoring will be pursued on a timely basis. As a result, anyone reviewing an account that has been placed for collection can immediately determine its status.

Third-party effectiveness is best measured by the ratio of net collections to claims placed. Less important than the fee an agency charges is the percentage of claims placed that they recover. Net collections is the amount the agency remits less any out-of-pocket expenses incurred. Most collection services work on a contingency fee basis, so they deduct their fee from any funds received from the debtor. A discount collection agency with a low fee will probably not collect as much as a full-service agency and therefore may show a lower net recovery across a portfolio of claims. By the same token, claims that are forwarded to an attorney or furthermore go to suit also tend to have lower net collections than those that do not. Because performance between agencies on the basis of net collections can vary greatly due to pricing and internal practices, an automated system for tracking these details is extremely useful in monitoring and optimizing third-party performance.

The other key factor that determines an agency's effectiveness is how quickly claims are collected and then remitted. There is no benefit in an agency that collects from a debtor and then delays remitting the recovery to the creditor. Besides factoring in the cost of money, agencies that take longer to collect are generally less effective and often have a lower net collection ratio. One reason for this may be an agency's policy to make a strong initial effort on claims and then recommend that those that do not respond be immediately forwarded to an attorney. As mentioned above, this increases collection costs and, especially if a lawsuit is pursued, takes a considerable amount of time. An agency that is able to collect a high percentage of claims in house will usually be more cost efficient than the agency that turns more claims over to attorneys. An automated collection system, because of its monitoring capabilities, aids considerably in the monitoring of third-party effectiveness.

However, easily and comprehensively evaluating collection agency and attorney effectiveness is not the only benefit an automated collection process brings to the third-party collection environment. Rapid communications with the outside agency and a comprehensive record of the company's previous collection efforts assist the third-party collector. Reliable information is more crucial to an outside collector than to a company employee who has the advantage of being closer to the source of the information. The data accumulated by an automated collection process thus greatly benefits the efforts of the collection agent, who can then pick up the collection process right where the company left off. Claim details can be quickly and easily faxed or e-mailed to the collection agent, helping to speed the process. Also, simply because a claim has been placed with a collection agency does not mean that there will be no further interaction regarding the debtor. The outside collectors may require clarifications, additional documentation, or further instructions, and the communication tools that come with an automated collection process greatly facilitate these interchanges. Being able to respond quickly and comprehensively helps to shorten the agency's collection cycle and increase the chance and amount of any recoveries.

OUTSOURCING COLLECTION ACTIVITIES

Many companies make the mistake of deciding to outsource a portion of their collection process on a purely tactical basis. Expediency is the driving force in these decisions. "We are understaffed and can't keep up with deductions, so let's outsource that function" is a typical line of reasoning. While such decisions usually produce at least a satisfactory result, they often miss opportunities to achieve even better rewards.

Outsourcing decisions are best made as part of a strategic initiative. Plugging in an outsourcer to fill a need will generally not be as effective as a comprehensive plan for maximizing collections that then uses outsourcing to complement, rather than merely supplement, internal resources. Once the strategy has been set, the tactical means of achieving the strategic initiative can be formulated. Also, it is much easier to adapt and change tactics under the umbrella of a strategic plan. Without that umbrella, every tactical change becomes an opportunity for dissenters to raise theoretical arguments that would have been answered at the strategy level.

In terms of outsourcing, one of the key objectives of the strategy level is to define core and noncore activities. For a collection department, this requires asking the question, "What activities and accounts is it absolutely necessary that we handle in-house?" By the same token, activities and accounts that do not need to be managed by the collection staff must be identified. Left between these extremes will be the accounts and activities that can be handled either way. When making these distinctions, it is also necessary to consider the skills and activities at which the collection staff is best. Essential tasks, primary customers, and predominant skills or areas of understanding define a collection department's core competencies. Core activities and competencies should be closely aligned with corporate philosophy and goals.

For example, if the company's philosophy is to hire the best, its collection staff may consist of experienced credit and collection professionals who are all capable of handling large accounts. If the company has a lot of small customers, the collectors' talents may be wasted making a great number of daily reminder calls on mostly small accounts with small overdue balances. In this situation, especially if the collection department is understaffed, it would make strategic sense to outsource collections beneath a specified threshold so that the collectors could concentrate their efforts on what they do best— manage the big, large-dollar accounts. However, a company with similar accounts whose philosophy is to dominate the market by being the low-price provider should invoke a different strategy.

Once the strategy elements have been settled, tactical considerations come into play. At this juncture, an automated collection system presents many more options than are possible with a manual process. One big difference is in the area of precision. With a manual system, it is not easy to define small groups of accounts that may require special attention or, for that matter, routine handling. The portfolio analysis tools that are part of an automated collection process make this a very easy task. In fact, a portfolio approach to accounts receivable management is necessary in order to derive maximum efficiency from an outsourcing program. In a manual collection environment, one is often faced with much more of an all-or-nothing equation.

Also, the strategies that drive the automated collection process can be easily adapted to include a "send-to-third-party" stage. With a manual collection system, this sequencing capability does not exist, so third parties tend to be brought in only at the very beginning or the very end of the collection cycle. With an automated system, there is considerably more flexibility in terms of who to outsource and when to do it.

This flexibility enables the employment of innovative outsourcing programs. For example, in a high-volume environment, one collection strategy involving a collection outsourcing provider might involve the following sequence:

1. Ten days before an invoice is due, a courtesy fax or letter is sent by the automated collection system to make sure there are no disputes or other problems that could delay payments.
2. If the invoice is still open 5 days after its due date, a third-party collection outsourcing firm begins a series of three low-intensity collection calls, one a week.
3. Invoices overdue more than 30 days are then brought back in house for the more intensive portion of the collection strategy.

This type of scenario will dramatically decrease the workload for the in-house collectors, allowing them to concentrate on the real problems. The results of the outsourcing firm's contacts would be entered in the system (ideally, this would be done by the outsourcing firm) so that the in-house collectors lose no continuity when the accounts come back in house. Manual collection systems are not suited to this type of integrated solution.

Both parties benefit when there is a high level of integration between the creditor and its receivables outsourcing partner. Real-time access to the creditor's information resources makes the outsourcing partner's job that much easier, as does the ability to communicate by e-mail with the creditor's internal problem owners. As a result, employees of the outsourcing firm are able to act much like actual employees, making their involvement all the more transparent to the customers. In fact, as more third-party outsourcing is done, the need to code and distribute problems throughout the organization becomes greater. That cannot be done easily in a manual or even an unintegrated environment. The bottom line with integration is: Everyone knows what everyone else is doing, so handing off both tasks or information is greatly facilitated, without administration becoming burdensome.

The possible outsourcing tactics that can be developed are virtually endless, especially in an integrated environment. Furthermore, with an automated collection process, they are all easy to monitor. Just as with the use of collection agencies and attorneys at the end of any collection strategy, outsourcing programs must be monitored. The same tools to measure net collections apply to outsourcing firms as they do to collection agencies. In the same way, the communication tools built into the automated collection process supplement the outsourcing process by keeping both creditor and outsourcing firm on the same page in terms of status and documentation. Closely integrated systems make it easier for the creditor to evaluate the performance of its outsourcing partner and better manage the relationship, because all pertinent data is resident in the automated collection system.

This is especially true if the outsourcing firm is provided dial-up or Internet access to the automated collection system. This makes it even easier for the outsourcing firm's employees to interact with customers on the company's behalf without revealing the fact that they are third-party collectors. The bottom line is that an automated collection system can help the outsourcing firm's collectors to become a valuable extension of the company's collection staff. (See Exhibit 15.1.)

Keep in mind that most collection and deduction outsourcing firms are technically astute in their specialty. They are able to competitively price their services because they have automated either the collection or the deduction process. They have already made an investment in training and software that allows them to be efficient service providers. After all, their core competency is solely in collections or deductions, and thus they are able to derive additional value from efficiently working with these processes.

Exhibit 15.1 **Sample Outsourcing Tactics**

- All deductions
- Deductions older than a specified age
- Specific types of deductions
- All collections
- Specific types of customers
- Invoices within a certain age range
- Invoices under a specified amount
- Any combination of the above

SUMMARY

The use of third parties, whether they be collection or deduction outsourcing firms, collection agencies, or attorneys, within the scope of the collection process can improve performance. Many companies with a manual collection process choose to outsource deductions or specific accounts or collection activities to compensate for staff shortages. In such a situation, the outsourcing firm is likely to significantly improve collections due to two factors: (1) The outsourcing firm has specialized skills in its area of practice, and (2) it has automated the collection or deduction processes it handles.

Companies that have automated collections will not gain as much advantage from such a purely tactical use of outsourcing. After all, in this situation, the outsourcing firm is not bringing superior technology to the table, just specialized skills. This does not mean that outsourcing has no use for companies that have automated the collection process. It does, however, require a different approach. Outsourcing best serves the collection function when it has a strategic place in the overall collection process, whether that process is manual or auto-mated. Tactics then follow from strategy.

A strategic approach to collection outsourcing requires an understanding of a company's own core competencies. Only then can the skills and technology of outsourcing firms be ob-jectively evaluated in terms of the collection process and a com-prehensive strategy developed that will maximize collection resources. Integrating an outsourcing firm with the collection process then becomes a nuts-and-bolts, tactical exercise.

The integration of outsourcing services is benefited by an automated collection process. For one thing, the integration process is easier when both the in-house and the outsourced systems can exchange data electronically, minimizing the ad-ministrative interface between the two parties. The collection strategies and portfolio management tools implicit to an auto-mated collection system also provide the intelligence needed for maximizing the economic decisions regarding which cus-tomers will be handed over to a third party and when. Doing this right increases collection productivity. Also, automation al-lows for more alternatives and innovation in terms of how the two parties are integrated. Outsourcing strategies can involve either a segment of the receivables portfolio or a portion of an account's assigned collection strategy, or even a combination of both. Last, monitoring the third-party relationship and perfor-mance is enhanced by an automated collection system.

All of this is possible because third-party involvement is assigned a separate stage in the client-specific collection strate-gies that drive the automated collection process. All third-party activities can be recorded and then reviewed just as easily as if collections was being handled by an employee. Those receiv-ables being worked by the third party can be easily separated from in-house accounts for monitoring purposes, so they do not hinder in-house collections. This benefit is maximized when the creditor's automated systems are integrated with those of its external partners. Driving these benefits is the wealth of information an automated system can provide for a third party. The other factor is enhanced communication capabilities. Outside collectors are much more effective when all the facts are available to them. With an automated system, there is no administrative or clerical burden in providing them with this information. Automated collection systems, especially in an integrated environment, enable outside collectors to work seamlessly with in-house collections.

ENDNOTE

1. With automation, the monthly (or in some cases quarterly) reports provided by collection agencies and attorneys, can now be made available on a weekly or a real-time basis. Many agencies have begun providing such status information via the Internet.

16

Automated Collections and the Internet

As with most business professions, the growth and increasing acceptance of Internet applications is having an effect on credit and collections. These are exciting times, because while one can see some of the places the Internet is going, no one can be certain where the Internet will end up. Although the opportunities are sometimes tantalizing, reality can present some daunting challenges. Therefore, when one talks of automating collections, the impact and opportunities presented by the Internet must be considered.

One label ascribed to the Internet is the "information highway." This view of the Internet as a medium for transmitting or receiving information from one place to another provides the promise of instantaneous communications between companies, their customers, and their third-party collection services. Such an automated communications network that has the capability of almost instantaneously relaying data between all interested parties has obvious applications for the automated collections environment.

E-MAIL CAPABILITIES

Throughout this book, the use of e-mail, which is essentially an Internet application, has been discussed. As more employees get access to the Internet, it is unthinkable that the use of e-mail in collection applications will not grow. In fact, most new releases of accounting software programs include e-mail utilities built into their accounts receivable, purchasing, and accounts payable modules. Transmitting purchase orders, invoices, and other documents related to the collection process will only get easier and faster. It does not matter whether this data is being exchanged internally or between a creditor and a customer, a creditor and its outsourced collectors or deduction analysts, or a third-party collection service and a debtor. In all these situations, e-mail allows collectors to complete their tasks more quickly. (See Exhibit 16.1.)

E-mail is particularly suited for receiving and answering queries between a creditor and a third-party service provider. While some outsourcing situations dictate that the third party's employees work on site, in most instances these virtual employees are at another location and therefore do not have direct access to the creditor's physical records. This can create many requests for additional information, especially a high-deduction or -dispute environment. E-mail allows the timely, efficient exchange of information without the negative impact of interruptions. In response to this situation, an automated collection system should exploit all the capabilities promised by e-mail.

VIRTUAL CREDIT COMMUNITIES

Likewise, the exchange of information between a creditor and its third-party collection providers can also be expected to increase. Collection agencies are already providing dial-up facilities so that their customers can check on the status of claims

Exhibit 16.1   **Mass Merchandisers Encourage E-Mail Use to Resolve Deductions**

When a company sells to multiple locations of the same account, there are simply more opportunities for deductions to arise. In retail, with some accounts having hundreds of locations, resolving deductions can be just as time consuming for a centralized payables function as it is for their vendor's collectors. As a result, many retailers are insisting that their vendors provide deduction details in a spreadsheet format. This enables payables and collections to deal with hundreds of deductions at a time. Updated information, questions, explanations, and so forth are simply referenced on the spreadsheet with the open deduction in question. The spreadsheets are then transmitted back and forth by e-mail, eliminating long phone calls and repetitive data-entry tasks. In effect, both buyer and vendor use the same report, which is updated as needed, to resolve deduction issues.

and access both debtor and agency performance data. These agencies are providing their customers with more performance data than ever before, and on a real-time basis to boot. In the past, one of the difficulties in monitoring agency performance and collection claim progress was the scarcity of information contained in the reports provided by the agency and the time it took the agency to prepare those reports—typically, about a month. In today's fast-paced business world, such monthly reports are mostly obsolete by the time they reach the creditor. That is not the case when this data is available on-line.

Another intriguing use of the Internet's communication capabilities is for the dissemination of data among members of an industry credit group. These associations traditionally meet monthly or quarterly to discuss problem customers. Fair trade practices limit their discussions to past credit and payment experiences, but they have proven to be a highly useful tool for collectors in terms of identifying and better managing high-risk accounts. These industry credit groups also create networking opportunities for their members to interact on a one-to-one basis, especially when problem situations arise between meetings. The Internet provides a viable platform for these forums, and, in fact, the first Internet Industry Credit Groups have been formed.

The primary benefit the Internet affords these groups is improved communications. The process of collecting payment experiences, compiling them, and then disseminating this data to all group members typically took weeks. Now, as soon as members submit their data, this information is available to the group. In fact, it is available for lookup at any time by any group member, whereas in the past reports were provided only in hard copy. Submitting payment experiences electronically speeds the process even further. Bits of news, usually derogatory events about their common customers, are transmitted almost instantaneously via e-mail once they have been posted to the group Internet site. Automated industry credit groups that utilize the Internet as a communication and database platform will be much more cost effective and powerful credit tools than their manual predecessors.

CREDIT MARKETPLACES

Another analogy applied to the Internet, and the World Wide Web in particular, is that of a virtual trade show. In a traditional trade show, exhibitors set up what they hope are attractive booths that will entice visitors to stop and browse. The exhibitors are fishing for prospects, and their bait is information. The visitors want to satisfy needs, and so must sort through all the information being thrown at them by the exhibitors in order to find the relevant goods and services that will satisfy those needs.

Websites on the Internet serve essentially the same function. They are, in effect, virtual trade show booths. Visitors to the World Wide Web are likewise shopping for information that will satisfy specific needs. Collectors are really no different than other shoppers in that they have unique needs. Not surprisingly, there are some exhibitors seeking to fulfill those needs. (See Exhibit 16.2.)

One thing collectors need to occasionally shop around for is third-party collection and deduction services. Collection agencies, outsourcing providers, deduction management firms, and attorney networks all have booths on the World Wide Web. While one might turn to the World Wide Web to find prospective collection agencies or outsourcing services, the use of these firms requires strong relational aspects, necessitating a comprehensive selection process. A company should know who its collection agency will be before it has any claims to place, on the assumption that, over time, it will place a significant number of claims. However, although domestic collection agencies are easy to come by without having to search the World Wide Web, foreign collection agencies are another story. For example, a company that is beginning to export in earnest to South America may want to search the Web for collection agencies in those countries where their customers are located. That type of information is not readily available anywhere else.

Collectors sometimes need to act quickly. A situation might call for an attorney's intervention, but a company in the Northeast is unlikely to have attorney contacts in the Southwest. In such a situation, an Internet Attorney Network can match a creditor with a qualified solicitor. Using the World Wide Web and e-mail, an attorney can be put on the case the same day. That sort of quick action can produce a powerful impact.

Yet another information resource springing up on the Web is access to bankruptcy proceedings. Besides tracking the

Exhibit 16.2 **Internet Sites of Interest to Collectors***

bankrupt.com	Internet Bankruptcy Library and Worldwide Troubled Company Resources—provides information and links to other resources related to bankruptcy.
www.acfe.org	Association of Certified Fraud Examiners—credit fraud is just one of the issues forensic accountants investigate.
www.adr.org	American Arbitration Association—when feasible, arbitration is a less costly alternative to lawsuits and an economical forum for dispute resolution.
www.anglefire.com/biz/ NCFC/index.html	National Check Fraud Center—this organization's database is tied into the banking network and law enforcement in the battle against bad checks.
www.collector.com	American Collectors Association—provides information about the collections profession and an extensive listing of links to agencies, lawyers, and other related services.
www.creditworthy.com	Credit Management Information & Support—seeks to be a virtual credit community and is the most extensive gateway to other credit and collection–related Internet sites.
www.getpaid.com	GETPAID Software—includes a demo of a fully integrated and automated collection system in addition to providing more information about automating collections.
www.law.cornell.edu	Legal Information Institute—a research project of Cornell University, this site provides extensive information resources concerning commercial law issues.
www.nacm.org	National Association of Credit Management—provides forums and information regarding credit and collections, plus links to some very interesting affiliate Internet sites.
www.repoman.com	REPOMAN, owned and operated by USAWEB Internet Advertising, is an international listing of collection agencies, products, and services, from skip tracing to software, all geared toward professional collectors.

*No listing of Internet sites can ever claim to be comprehensive, but these 10 sites cover all the major aspects of collections and also serve as excellent gateways to most, if not all, of the other credit and collection Internet sites in existence today.

progress of bankruptcy cases and verifying claims, collectors can expect to file claims through the Internet. Other public records are increasingly available on the Internet. For collectors in the construction industry, Internet access to bonding information and lien filings holds the promise of easing the administrative burden in their collection processes. One of the critical success factors for credit and collections is the convenient access to reliable information. The Internet and the World Wide Web help fulfill this need. (See Exhibit 16.3.)

Exhibit 16.3 **The Internet as a Platform for Collection Software**

One intriguing application of Internet technology to the collection process is as a software platform. Collection software on an Internet server provides access to any authorized user with a personal computer (PC) and a modem from anywhere in the world. Unlimited connectivity allows collectors to work from their office, their customer's office, a hotel room, or from home.

One such product is CollectNet® (www.collectnet.com). Instead of buying collection software, users access it through the Internet. It provides calling queues, reminders, automatic or manual account updates, and extensive reporting capabilities including individual collector statistics. Users enter their customers' accounts into the CollectNet® system, define their collection strategies, and then go to work. Also, because it resides on the Internet, CollectNet is able to provide a number of other services including letter printing and mailing, skip tracing, credit bureau reports, and bankruptcy reports.

Bundling services is another Internet trend that should ultimately benefit collectors. To add value to their products, service providers—whether a software company or collection agency—are finding that the Internet provides a mechanism for better meeting the diverse needs of the marketplace. The key is the ability of the Internet to serve as a sort of universal platform and interface.

SUMMARY

Above all else, the Internet serves as a platform for compiling and disseminating information. Physical location is no longer important as long as the Internet can be accessed. With Internet access, the technology already exists for collectors to function as efficiently on the road or at home as they would in the office, and with more tools at their disposal than they ever had before. Of course, companies willing to invest in dial-up capabilities and the supporting data-processing technologies have been able to so equip their collectors for some time now without any reliance on the Internet. The difference the Internet makes is that these capabilities, plus the bonus of access to much more information, are now available to nearly everybody for a relatively small investment.

In addition, the Internet holds promise as a communication tool and interface between companies and third-party collection service providers. E-mail and the World Wide Web are making it easier for collectors to gather and exchange critical information with third parties. When used properly, these tools take more time out of the collection process, speeding collections. They also enhance the collector's access to timely and reliable data, a critical success factor for the collection process.

17

Final Thoughts

The idea that computers would provide a means for automating collections has been around since the first accounts receivable software package was written. Of course, that resulted only in a manual collection process that was dependent on a computerized accounts receivable system. Although the clerical burden of processing receivables manually was partially solved, in some ways the collection process was made more complicated. Incremental improvements were made, often in house, but these did not address the weaknesses in the interface between manual collections and computerized receivables.

The earliest efforts to automate collections dealt in the area of contact management. The idea of keeping notes on the computer system, and linking them with the computerized accounts receivable database was tried by many companies. The advent of personal computer (PC)-based contact management software opened up this option to many more companies. The problem with most of these off-the-shelf programs was that they were written with primarily a sales function in mind, and so were not structured to address the complexities of the collection process. That such programs could provide some benefits to the collection process was a step in the right direction, but hardly a solution. The better programs were at best a partial solution. Others simply created another layer of clerical, low-productivity tasks that further complicated the collection process.

With the development of fully integrated collection software products based on a single database, an expanded contact management function, and a full range of communication tools, users began achieving impressive productivity gains. Clearly, what had been needed was not an automated contact management solution but collection software to drive an automated and redesigned collection process. However, a funny thing happened with the companies that implemented this software. They found that as they worked the software and implemented all its capabilities, they were impacting the customer support process as much as collections. The effects of collection software were not limited to shortening the collection cycle or even just the collection department. Business processes that impacted credit and collections were also affected, particularly those related to managing customer relationships.

Collection software was not impacting customer relationships in a vacuum. The idea of "getting close to the customer" and the concept of "total quality" created an environment receptive to the input provided by automated collection systems. Collection software proved very efficient at identifying and quantifying the business processes that were causing problems. With this intelligence, the collection function is able to work with other business units to develop solutions to these problems, particularly recurring issues, which are usually a symptom of system weaknesses.

Collection software also becomes a repository for customer-specific intelligence. Every customer is unique, but this fact was overlooked by the first business computer software packages, which were focused on transaction processing. Under this mindset, efficiency of operations was achieved by standardizing the treatment of all customers. However, "total quality" and "getting close to the customer" run counter to standardization, and collection software serves to bridge the gap.

Tied in with this has been a recognition that credit, collections, and customer service all fulfill a very close relationship in the order-to-cash process. Re-engineering initiatives and the use of customer support teams have contributed to this awareness. One goal of these programs has been to provide customers with a single point of contact for all their order processing needs. Accordingly, collection software has provided a platform that helps support that goal. An automated collection system also provides the mechanism for sharing customer intelligence throughout the organization through reporting, notification, and customer lookup. With an automated collection system, customer service, order entry, sales, and credit and collections can all work from the same page, so to speak.

As more corporations automate the collection process, it stands to reason that more attention will be directed toward the integration or interface of additional customer support functions with collection software. The Internet will certainly play a role in how this is accomplished. As a consequence, data will flow seamlessly between customer, customer support staff, and any other problem owner connected with the process. In effect, communities of interest will develop on the customer–vendor level, with everyone involved highly knowledgeable of his or her neighbor's functions, policies, situations, and characteristics. In this environment, both payment and collections become subservient to the ongoing customer–vendor relationship.

These trends also bode well for credit and collection professionals. Those who are willing to upgrade their skills and accept expanded responsibilities are being given the opportunity of managing a larger part, if not all, of the order-to-cash process. More and more credit veterans are having credit and collections dropped from their titles as they assume the role of customer financial service managers. Without process re-engineering and automation, this would be a daunting, if not impossible, undertaking. In companies that have automated the collection process, the assimulation of customer support functions by credit and collections has instead occurred in the natural course of events. Of course, there is another side to the equation. Taking a narrow view of collections tends to pigeonhole the function and its practitioners. When collections is confined to a functional silo, there are fewer opportunities for personal growth, and it is more difficult to increase the contribution of credit and collections to corporate growth and profitability.

IMPLEMENTING AN AUTOMATED COLLECTION SYSTEM

Significantly improving collections without automating a redesigned collection process is simply not practical. Aside from throwing a wealth of human resources at the problem, there is really no way to upgrade a competently managed collection function without automating. This puts those companies that do not automate their collection process at a competitive disadvantage.

Cash is king, and if a company allows its competitors to collect cash faster, then that company will be fighting an uphill battle on several fronts. First, the company that does not automate collections will be paying additional carrying costs on funds tied up in their accounts receivable as opposed to those companies that automate. Second, the company that automates is more likely to be paid by any cash-strapped customers at the expense of its nonautomated competitors. Last, companies are able to use the intelligence created by their automated collection system to improve other business processes and enrich customer satisfaction—chores that a manual collection process does not accomplish.

If automating collections is clearly advantageous over collecting with a manual process, then the question of cost must be answered. The tangible costs of purchasing and implementing collection software, as well as the hard dollar benefits, are easily enough calculated. In contrast, the physical time and effort to install collection software is not so easily quantified. However, the good news is that automating collections does not have to be a long, drawn-out, difficult process.

For one thing, it is not necessary for every company that wants to automate collections to re-engineer the collection process. A good collection software package will have already done that. For most, if not all, companies, there is no need to reinvent the wheel and design a proprietary collection process.

In addition, installing collection software is not the same as installing or upgrading accounting software. With the latter, there is usually a period of running parallel, during which both the old and new systems function in tandem until there is an assurance that the results from the new system are identical to those of the old. With collection automation software, this is not necessary because the software does not affect financial record keeping.

Also, because collection automation software draws information from the accounts receivable database but does not send any data back, customization is minimal. The only programming necessary is to create the accounts-receivable-to-collection software interface. In many instances, companies running off-the-shelf accounting packages will find that an interface has already been created for their accounting software, making this task even easier.

As a result, many companies that have chosen to automate collections are able to complete the project in only a month or two. Programming the interface can usually be accomplished in a couple of weeks. Configuring the software and setting collection and strategies takes some thought but can be done in short order. Loading data into the collection system can be the biggest task, depending on the number of customers to be monitored, because automated collection systems will utilize multiple addresses, contacts, fax numbers, and phone numbers. Accounts receivable software databases handle much less customer contact data, so the amount of information that can be directly downloaded into the collections software can be quite limited. Fortunately, entering this information into the system is a straightforward data-entry project. That leaves training the collectors to use the collection software, but that too is a short project, as has been discussed earlier.

Once the decision has been made to automate the collection process and collection software selected, it is not unreasonable to expect a return on this investment by the next fiscal quarter. Time and time again, automated collection systems have begun yielding dividends almost from day one, with significant results acheived within the first 4 to 6 weeks. For many companies, deciding what to do takes longer than that. The decision to automate collections should not be taken lightly, but in the final analysis, it is the key to dramatically improving collections.

Index

Index

Credit and collection departments:
  challenges facing, 70
  goals of, 29–30
  operating as functional silos,
    27–29
  relationship to sales, 27–28,
    31–33
  resource problems, 71–73
  traditional role of, 29
Credit clerks, automation effects
    on, 18
Credit manager evaluation, 30
Credit marketplaces, Internet,
    310–313
Credit memos, slowness issuing,
    265
Credit policy effects, 29–30
Credit Research Foundation, 82
Crisis management, 73
Customers:
  acquisition process and, 31–33
  characteristics of
    collector preparation and, 41
    sample types, 217
    setting priorities and, 213–214
    setting strategies and, 215–217
  collection software effects,
    316–318
  credit and sales input and, 33
  inquiries by, 154–155
  payment deductions and, see
    Adjustment volume;
    Deduction management
  preparatory information
    regarding, 40
  relationship management,
    89–90
  satisfaction
    automation effects and,
      154–156
    re-engineering issues and,
      64–66

Customer service:
  automation effects, 10
  collector's role in, 34
  as customer advocates, 34
  customer service calls, 155,
    156
  interfacing with, 226–228
  issues database, 153

D

Daily work list, automating,
    146–148
Database integration, 46–47
Data-entry operators, 18
Data formats, collections focused,
    205
Data screens, customer, 169
Days sales outstanding, 53–55
Deduction administrators, 268
Deduction analysts, 268
Deduction management, 251–277
  areas affected by, 252–253
  automation effects on, 85, 257,
    270
  causes of deductions, 253
  corporate practices and, 84
  cost impact of deductions,
    82–83, 252, 259–265
  diagraming of deductions,
    262–263
  follow-ups and, 84–85
  presale vs. postsale issues in,
    256–259
  problem identification and,
    254–256
  problem resolution and, 268–270
  problem tracking and, 266–268
  process improvement and,
    273–275
  repetition and recurrence and,
    85–86
  report analysis and, 270–273

Returned merchandise, 265
  deductions and, 262–263
Risk:
  classification, 239–240
  evaluating and payment history,
    141

S

Sales:
  credit and collections
    relationship to, 27–28, 31–33
  strategy interface with,
    226–228
Sales weighted days outstanding,
  158
Scheduling, automating, 131–132
Scripts, automating, 176–178
Semi-automated tools, in manual
  collection process, 96–97
Short shipments, 264
Simple notes organizers, 196–199
Slow payments, 66
Small accounts, overlooking,
  80–81
Small-balance strategy, 227
Software:
  accounting
    collection system
      requirements and,
      203–206
    enhancements and, 199, 201
    upgrades or major changes to,
      203–206
  cash applications and, 280–281
    preprocessing, 285–291
      deductions and, 286
      electronic data interchange
        capabilities, 290–291
      exception handling,
        288–289
      hit rates and, 288–289
      modifications of, 286

reference matching
  schemes, 287–288
  remittance, 286
collection
  customer service problems
    and, 10
  external data storage and,
    238–239
  installation time, 319–320
  management reluctance to
    implement, 9–10
  portfolio management and,
    236
  requirements of, 205–206
  running parallel and, 319
  staff savings and, 10
problem-tracking, *see* Problem-
  tracking software
using multiple, 8
Staffing constraints, 87–89
Staff shortages, 61
Stages of collection, 224–225
Standardization, account
  handling, 139
Statements, inefficiency of, 195
Step, collection, groupings,
  168–169
Step, collection, recommendations,
  166
Strategies, collection, 209–230
  aggressiveness of, 211
  in automated environment, 215
  contact methods and, 223
  by customer, 152
  customer collection types and,
    215–217
  customizing automated systems
    and, 172–173
  development of, 139–142
  elements of, 219–226
  sales and customer service
    interface and, 226–228